STUDIES IN CHURCH HISTORY
VOL. VI

Edited by

Matthew Spinka   Robert Hastings Nichols

PREACHING IN THE
FIRST HALF CENTURY
OF NEW ENGLAND HISTORY

PREACHING IN THE
FIRST HALF CENTURY
OF NEW ENGLAND HISTORY

By BABETTE MAY LEVY

NEW YORK / RUSSELL & RUSSELL

PREFACE

This study concerns itself primarily with the Puritan preaching of New England's first fifty years of settlement. During this period English-bred ministers were in control of the village pulpits, but in the 1650's and 1660's the first Harvard graduates began to take the places made vacant by the deaths of the first pastors. I have not included men who reached their preaching-prime in the last decades of the century. They should be judged with the next, purely American-bred generation. On the other hand, in dealing with earlier men, I have not hesitated to cite an occasional sermon delivered in the 1670's, if it seemed to be typical of a man's previous preaching; my theory in so doing has been that the thought and style of a mature minister would hardly suffer essential changes in a few years.

No one library has a complete collection of these early sermons. Hence, ever since Dr. Ralph L. Rusk of Columbia University suggested to me in 1929 that this field had possibilities for scholarly investigation, I have made use of the library of the Union Theological Seminary, which, with the McAlpin Collection, is particularly rich in English printings of books originally written in America; of the New York Public Library, which has a growing collection of seventeenth-century *Americana;* and of the Boston Public Library, which with the Prince Collection as a nucleus, owns many important items. Some material is also to be found in the possession of Harvard College in Cambridge, the Boston Athenaeum and the Massachusetts Historical Society in Boston, the American Antiquarian Society in Worcester, the Essex Institute in Salem, the John Carter Brown Library in Providence, Yale University Library in New Haven, The Watkinson Library and the Connecticut Historical Society in Hartford, and the Theological Seminary Library in Princeton. To the librarians of all these institutions I am very much indebted for their co-operation.

Dr. William W. Rockwell, Librarian Emeritus of Union

v

Theological Seminary, has long been an inspiration to me because of his scholarship, which he so generously shares with all. During the years that I worked upon this subject I called upon his knowledge many times, and his reading of my manuscript has been of incalculable benefit to me. I am very thankful to Dr. William Haller of Columbia University for his critical suggestions, to which he could bring the results of his long and intensive study of Puritan thought. I am also grateful to Dr. Oscar James Campbell of Columbia University for his valuable advice on a number of occasions. Dr. Mary E. Lyman, formerly lecturer on the Bible at Union Theological Seminary and now dean of Sweet Briar College, was kind enough to read and criticize the first chapters; Dr. Robert Hastings Nichols of Union Theological Seminary read my manuscript and gave me his opinion on several important points. For a good many years I have had the habit of calling upon the classical and Biblical learning of Miss Madge McLain of Hunter College, once my instructor in Latin, now my colleague, but still my teacher in more ways than I can name. To all these kind scholars I owe much and I have the deepest sense of obligation to them, as I have to the American Society of Church History for the generous award of the biennial Brewer Prize. And no list of my debts would be complete without mentioning the faithful assistance and never failing encouragement that I have received from my mother.

BABETTE MAY LEVY.

Hunter College,
March 1, 1944.

CONTENTS

CHAPTER I

THE BACKGROUND AND PREPARATION
OF THE PREACHERS

Puritan faith and Puritan life were closely bound together, and nowhere is this union better expressed than in the sermon literature of the period. Nor did the Puritan separate faith from reason; on the contrary, he devoted all his intellectual powers to a proper interpretation and fulfillment of God's will for man. The sermon was the Puritan minister's attempt through reason to encourage faith as it affected this life and the next. His intellectual honesty, as well as his ultimate dependence upon faith, may be seen in the final admission, openly voiced, that there were some impenetrable mysteries: reason told that men were vilely sinful, and faith told that some are elected to salvation, but the basis of the choice remained beyond all human comprehension. Nevertheless, despite his acknowledged inability to explain the great mysteries of faith and salvation, he believed that all lesser matters could be clarified by a proper interpretation of the Bible and by the logical application to life of the wisdom thereby gained.

Puritanism in Massachusetts and Connecticut was at first practically unhampered in its development. True, only one type of Puritanism flourished and the whole colonization experiment was on a limited scale, but it had to waste its energy neither in resisting persecution and combatting prejudice, nor in contending with schism within its own ranks. Politically, too, New England Puritanism was at a great advantage. English Puritans, confronted with an established government, always faced the dilemma of having to compromise with their own ideals of the perfect commonwealth or of having to oppose a government which was protected by tradition and their own avowed respect for authority. American Puritans were able to form their own theocracy as they would have it, according to their interpretation of the Bible; to them fell the different task of operating and conserving what they had so carefully constructed —a way of being ruled in which church and lay authorities closely co-operated, final authority being vested in the ministers as the most skilled interpreters of Holy Writ.[1]

In another way, too, Puritan sermon literature is peculiarly revealing. Every minister was pledged by his own creed to use a plain style, easily understood by all. To make doubly certain that every man in his audience understood him, a preacher resorted to simple, concrete illustrations of each point. Because he scorned strained allegorical exempla as smacking of popery and because he avoided elaborate conceits as portraying a deplorable worldliness, he used for this purpose similitudes, usually taken from everyday existence. Naturally, some of these comparisons were standard rhetorical equipment, a direct inheritance from medieval preaching.[2] Not given to much observation of nature, the minister was still a little apt to confine his examples from nature to soaring eagles, swelling toads, amazing cockatrices, and gymnastic adders that were able to stop their ears upon demand—fabulous creations that were a direct survival of the old bestiaries. And just as in medieval sermons the priest had attacked man's sins of pride and avarice with homely thrusts at family and community life, so the Puritan preacher was apt to look about him and cite the erring ways of merchants with their dishonest weights, of poor housekeepers, of recalcitrant children. Still seeking telling illustrations for somewhat intangible spiritual ailments and panaceas, he, like his predecessors, talked of physical illnesses and their cures; still aware of the contrasting dramas of man's daily struggle for a living and of his occasional journeyings forth by land and sea, the preacher made good use of his congregation's knowledge of ordinary life. He instinctively took good care that the sinners he mentioned, their illnesses and cures, their trades and travelings, would seem wholly contemporary, part of the common experience of all; even the historical characters mentioned had to be easily recognized. In so adapting his teaching to his followers, the New England preacher was simply doing what he had heard done many times in England by other Puritan preachers. Many of his illustrations could even be the very ones he himself had

1 Perry Miller, *Orthodoxy in Massachusetts* (Cambridge: Harvard University Press, 1933), 34.
2 G. R. Owst, *Literature and Pulpit in Medieval England* (Cambridge, 1933), Chapters IV, V, VI, VII.

used at "home" or would have used if his preaching career there had not been cut short, but occasionally some bit of early American life crept into a discourse to add interest for later generations of American readers.

There is one other advantage in studying New England's pulpit literature. If we consider the sermons only, and avoid the innumerable eristic books of the period—the endless disputes about Arminianism, Antinomianism, Antipaedobaptism, Familism, and the many other schisms of the Puritan movement—we shall also avoid confusing our picture of the average seventeenth-century settler. For even if the period's general interest in religion is recognized, the fact remains that only an extremely limited number of men (for the most part, only the ministers) were so trained that they were able to follow the more abstruse points of theological controversy. Again, if we study the sermons only, we shall also escape many of the long and—to the layman—tedious disputes over such points of church polity as the question of Separation and the Presbyterian-Congregational controversy. The wrangling ministers themselves (and undoubtedly their congregations even more frequently) had moments when they realized that such questions were relatively unimportant, except as they bore upon the greater problems of the survival of the colonies and the salvation of the colonists. The very fact of a sermon's being published during New England's first lean years shows that its preacher had been somewhat successful in his labors and that his discourse had been deemed of value to the community. Then, as now, in order to have his preaching meet with even outward success, any minister had to stay more or less on the level of his audience; his rendering of doctrine and his means of presenting his argument had to appeal to the great majority's reason and sensibility. If we also keep in mind that the whole population of the town was obliged to attend church' we may believe that a consideration of the pulpit oratory to which every settler and his family listened will reveal much about the average Puritan mind.

The sermons are many and long—and far more interest-

3 Herbert L. Osgood, *The American Colonies in the Seventeenth Century* (New York: The Columbia University Press, 1930), I, 216.

ing than the average modern reader, frightened by the very
word "sermon," might suppose.   The seventeenth century was,
of course, a time of general interest in pulpit oratory, and consequently of high standards for the art.   We must also remember that the ministers who came to New England ranked with
the best in England, at least in the Puritan party.   The Reverend Charles Chauncy, later to be president of Harvard College,
was long remembered as an outstanding scholar at Cambridge,
where he took three degrees, including that of Bachelor of
Divinity, and served for several years as the Greek Lecturer
at Trinity; he also enjoyed some celebrity for his Hebrew scholarship and for his ability to write Greek and Latin verse.[4]   The
Reverend John Cotton had three Cambridge degrees, and he was
closely connected with Emmanuel College, where he became fellow, dean, head-lecturer, and catechist; later, during his years
as vicar of St. Botolph's in Boston, Lincolnshire, his no small
reputation as a preacher and theologian increased; the Master
of Emmanuel, the Reverend John Preston, honored him by sending him divinity students to complete their studies.   Some measure of Cotton's position in Puritan circles may be seen in the
fact that he was included in Samuel Clarke's *A Collection of the
Lives of Ten Eminent Divines* (1662), a volume of the lives
of the most noted nonconformists of the sixteen thirties and
forties.[5]   The Reverend Thomas Hooker, who was to become
the democratic founder of Hartford, also had a distinguished
career at Emmanuel as scholar, fellow, and dean; then as Curate
of Esher, Surrey, and lecturer at Chelmsford he became widely
known as a preacher and as a writer on the psychology of conversion.[6]   The Reverend Thomas Shepard, later the influential
preacher of the Cambridge, Massachusetts, church, had a less
distinguished career at Emmanuel, but he soon became known
as such an extraordinarily effective evangelistic preacher that
Bishop Laud took pains to confront him with evidence of his
nonconformity and to silence him twice.[7]   The Reverend John

---

4 Samuel Eliot Morison, *The Founding of Harvard College* (Cambridge, 1935),
   90-91.

5 *Ibid.*, 101-102, 373; William Haller, *The Rise of Puritanism* (New York:
   Columbia University Press, 1938), 69-70, 106.

6 Morison, *The Founding of Harvard College*, 100-101, 382.

7 Samuel Eliot Morison, *Builders of the Bay Colony* (Cambridge: The Riverside Press, n.d. [1930]), 109.

Davenport, later to be the conservative leader of the New Haven church, was a well-known London preacher and a worker, with other prominent nonconformist leaders, on projects dear to Puritan aspirations. With Richard Sibbes, Thomas Goodwin, and Thomas Ball, he had helped edit Dr. John Preston's sermons. Again with Sibbes and with William Gouge and other famous men of the party, he had labored to establish a way of raising funds to promote spiritual preaching.[8]

These emigrating ministers, and others only in a lesser degree, had established reputations as Puritan scholars and preachers; they came to the New World because they were, for the most part, the younger men of the Congregational faction of the Puritan party. True, a very few men of Presbyterian leanings also decided to take this step. But most of the emigrants were men who felt themselves doubly out of favor while the Presbyterians were in control of the Puritan party. As nonconformists of Congregational beliefs, they were open to attack from Anglican bishops without even the limited protection of their own party leaders.[9] The decision of whether to stay in England anyway or to risk the less known perils of America was not a matter of courage, as either course promised its difficulties. Older men were more likely to persuade themselves that their duty lay in fighting for their principles at home; younger men—or those with a spark of adventure still very much alive—were able to convince themselves that they could lead lives of greater service in the new settlements.

The present study is concerned with the preaching of these English-bred ministers, with the pulpit literature of New England's first fifty years. Colonial prose, perhaps because it has the one dominant theme of religion running through it, has been too often judged as a whole. Forgetting how quickly the New World, with its many advantages and limitations, changed men, we ignore the mutations in thought that started from the very beginning of the settlement of the colonies. Consequently, the more fanatic and—to the modern reader—more amusing pulpiteers at the end of the century have been taken as representative of the whole period. A careful reading of the ser-

8 Haller, *The Rise of Puritanism*, 67.
9 For the position of Congregationalists, see Miller's *Orthodoxy in Massachusetts*, 73-101.

mons reveals that this generalization simply is not true; the later Mathers and the Willards, loyally as they worshipped their forefathers, were far removed in spirit from the first preachers, born and educated in England. Cotton Mather tells us that there came to this country before 1640 no fewer than seventy-seven ministers who had been preaching in England.[10] In this number he does not include the stray Baptists, Episcopalians, and irregular Congregationalists who had somewhat unhappy careers in New England; the seventy-seven were the regularly settled pastors and teachers of the rapidly developing towns of Massachusetts and Connecticut.[11]

While only a fraction of the preaching of relatively few of these men survived its occasion, a great many sermons and volumes of sermons were printed. The men who were prominent in England had a tendency to keep their position of importance, perhaps because they had churches in the larger towns. A great many discourses by three of these men—John Cotton of Boston, Thomas Hooker of Hartford, and Thomas Shepard of Cambridge—were published during their lifetimes and shortly after their deaths and so may be followed over long periods of time. Orthodox John Davenport of New Haven also left a generous amount of his oratory. Richard Mather of Dorchester and Charles Chauncy of Plymouth and Scituate, later president of Harvard College, are represented by a number of sermons. And some of the less famous preachers had a little of their pulpit work published: included in this group are such men as John Allen of Dedham, Edward Bulkeley of Marshfield and Concord, Peter Bulkeley of Concord, Thomas Cobbett of Lynn and Ipswich, Elder Robert Cushman of Plymouth, William Hooke of Taunton and New Haven, John Norton of Ipswich and Boston, Samuel Whiting of Lynn, and John Wilson of Charlestown and Boston. Occasionally sermons in manuscript

10 Cotton Mather, *Magnalia Christi Americana* (London, 1702), Book III, 2-3.

11 At first each New England church had a pastor and a teacher. As John Cotton explained, "The Office of a Pastor, is to attend by Exhortation, and therein to Dispense a word of Wisdom. The teacher is to attend unto Doctrine, and therein to attend to a word of knowledge. *Eph.* 4:11. *Rom.* 12:7, 8. *Ezek.* 3:18, 19. *Heb.* 13:15." The teacher usually preached one of the two Sunday sermons and sometimes alternated with the pastor in giving weekly lectures. The difference between pastor and teacher soon broke down, and the colonists discovered they could manage more economically with only one minister in each town.

survived the hazards of time, and one such discourse by John Wheelwright, a fast-day sermon of 1637, has since been printed because of modern interest in its author's stormy career. In addition to these mature men, many of whom came with their own followers from their English pastorates, fourteen others came, as boys and young men, with their education incomplete and with no practice in the ministry save what they later attained in New England. Of this number, four—Samuel Arnold of Marshfield, James Fitch of Saybrook and Norwich, John Higginson of Saybrook, Guilford and Salem, and Thomas Thacher of Weymouth and Boston—had their sermons published.

Gradually these English-born preachers were replaced in the next generation by Harvard men and by a second, smaller influx of men from England after the Restoration. The influence of the latter group was relatively slight, and of the ministers who came to New England in the 1660's, only two, John Oxenbridge of Boston and Thomas Walley of Barnstable, have had their sermons survive. As the first settlers had planned in promptly establishing a college, it was the Harvard graduate who replaced the pioneer minister. Samuel Danforth of Braintree and Roxbury, Leonard Hoare of Harvard, Samuel Hooker of Farmington, William Hubbard of Ipswich, Eleazer Mather of Northampton, Jonathan Mitchell of Cambridge, Urian Oakes of Cambridge and Harvard, Joseph Rowlandson of Lancaster and Wethersfield, Thomas Shepard of Charlestown, Samuel Torrey of Weymouth, and William Stoughton, an "unsettled" minister with no one church, were all Harvard men preaching in the 1650's and 1660's—and now and then preparing their sermons for the press. In fact, as more of the work was done at Cambridge and Boston instead of distant London, and as printing in this country became more convenient and satisfactory, later generations published with increasing frequency, until the prolificacy of such men as the Mathers, Increase and his son Cotton, and of Samuel Willard, became a source of amazement and amusement to subsequent critics.

These later divines were quick to acknowledge the superiority of their predecessors in New England's pulpits, but this evaluation in many cases must have been based on memory and oral tradition, for many of the first ministers never had their sermons published. Most of those that have been preserved in print were the work of those leaders whom their fellow Puritans of the Bay Colony, of Connecticut, and of New Haven highly respected as brilliant, intellectual conservatives in matters of religion; consequently, the thousands of closely printed pages which give us the pulpit oratory of John Cotton, of Thomas Shepard, and of Thomas Hooker tend to obscure the fact that we know little of the actual preaching of a number of other ministers probably equally able. We should like to have a few samples of Roger Williams' "prophesying" at Salem and Plymouth; or of his sermons during his many years in Rhode Island, where he apparently preached frequently. Even those last missionary discourses which Williams himself prepared for the press, but could not publish for lack of money, have disappeared.[12] And what did that other and less successful visionary, gentle, generous John Eliot say to his own congregation during the nearly sixty years he was teacher of the church at Roxbury? We know surprisingly much of his missionary methods and of his preaching to the Indians in their own language. But we also know that he did not let his love for his poor friends and his eagerness to learn their tongue interfere with his duties to his own parishioners.[13] And Nathaniel Ward, who showed his intellectual keenness as the chief collaborator in the Bay Colony's famous Body of Liberties of 1641, and his wit as the "Simple Cobler of Aggavvam,"[14] left us no product of his three years of regular preaching in the Ipswich pulpit or of the many other years (before his return to England) during which he probably "exercised" occasionally. Even the New England preaching of energetic, public-spirited Hugh Peter is known to us only through notices in Winthrop's *Journal,* although a few examples of his preaching in England have survived.

Unrepresented, then, in any study of New England's early sermon literature are many of the great eccentrics, the original

12 Romeo Elton, *Life of Roger Williams* (New York: G. P. Putnam, 1852), 135-136; James Ernst, *Roger Williams New England Firebrand* (New York: The Macmillan Co., 1932), 520.

13 Letter to Winslow, July 8, 1649, quoted in Convers Francis' *Life of John Eliot, the Apostle to the Indians* (New York: Harper & Brothers, 1844), 218.

14 *The Simple Cobbler of Aggavvam in America* (London: Printed by John Dever and Robert Ibbitson for Stephen Bowtell, 1647).

thinkers of their period, and we cannot help suspecting that their sermons may have been more interesting than many that have been preserved in print. The sermons of these preachers would aid us in knowing what emphasis they put upon their doctrines, what they thought their congregations had to be taught, and what common basis of knowledge and belief the minister and his church stood upon; on the other hand, we know, from their other publications, what these leaders thought and most probably preached. But what of the other worthy ministers who never published their ideas and who remain little more than names to us? These were the unrenowned, faithful men, often serving in smaller parishes; their sermons may have been as good as any preserved, for preaching genius does not always find its way into print. We think first of John Harvard, the London-bred boy who gained immortality by giving his library of sermons and theological treatises to the newly proposed college and who had had the privilege of sitting under the great Lancelot Andrewes. There are many others. For example, Jonathan Burr preached so well that Thomas Hooker, no mean preacher himself, said, "Surely this man won't be long out of Heaven, for he preaches as if he were there already."[15] Then there was John Sherman, who fed his church "with the fattest Marrow of Divinity," using "a natural, and not affected Loftiness of Stile; which with an easie Fluency bespangled his Discourses with such glittering Figures of Oratory, as caused his ablest Hearers, to call him a Second Isaiah, the Honey dripping, and Golden-mouthed Preacher."[16] The preaching of these ministers and of many more survives only in terse notices of their sermons in their contemporaries' diaries and in the pages of almost steady eulogy in Mather's *Magnalia*.

With what background to aid them did these first English-born ministers, Mather's noble "one Seven more than Seven decades of Persons,"[17] inaugurate the village churches of New England? The lives of a few are known in some detail: Thomas Shepard and his career, for instance, can be clearly traced in his friendly letters, his autobiography, his daily meditations and intimate diary—all of which, as well as twenty-odd less personal

15 Mather, *Magnalia*, Book III, 81.
16 *Ibid.*, 164.
17 *Ibid.*, 3.

publications, are still available. But other preachers left little self-revelatory material behind them, and their lives can be known only in outline and in meager detail. But from the lives of all these men considered together, a pattern evolves—a pattern which permitted much variation, variation we must remember, lest we create too much of a stereotype for very human beings. The typical emigrating minister had been born into a middle-class family—frequently poor, as Thomas Shepard's and Richard Mather's were, occasionally well-to-do, as Henry Whitfield's and Peter Bulkeley's were. Sometimes the father was of the professional class—John Cotton was the son of a lawyer, and a number óf men were the sons of ministers.[18] Usually the childhood of the minister-to-be was spent in a small town or hamlet; but John Harvard and probably John Davenport were among the city-bred. Some happy chance of birth or of a good schoolmaster gave the young boy the right training for one of the universities,[19] where he most likely spent seven years,[20] proceeding first to the bachelor's and then to the master's degree. Emmanuel College, Cambridge, was the choice of many Puritan families—John Harvard, Thomas Hooker, Thomas Shepard, Samuel Stone, Peter Prudden, John Cotton, and Samuel Whiting were all from Emmanuel; on the other hand, so many other colleges sent their sons to New England that it would be hard to prove that Emmanuel's influence was really dominant.[21] Very

18 Peter Bulkeley, Samuel Eaton, Thomas Parker, Nathaniel Rogers, Zechariah Symmes, Thomas Thacher, Nathaniel Ward, and John Wilson were of this number.

19 A very few men, including Jonathan Burr, Thomas Gilbert, and Samuel Arnold, did not attend a university.

20 Richard Mather, by way of exception, spent only a few months at Brasenose.

21 Among the ministers were graduates of Trinity, Jesus, Christ's, Corpus Christi, Clare, Pembroke, Queens', Sidney, Sussex, Caius, King's Magdalene, Peterhouse, Benet, St. Catherine's and St. John's of the Cambridge colleges; perhaps twenty men, including Thomas Cobbett and John Davenport, came from Oxford; New College, St. Mary Hall, New Inn Hall, Jesus, Trinity, All Souls, Balliol, Christ Church, Exeter, Magdalen College, Magdalene Hall, Oriel, Pembroke, Queens, St. Edmund Hall, St. John's, and Brasenose were represented. A few men, often from financial reasons (as many of them had to depend upon scholarships), shifted colleges during their university career —Francis Higginson was a student at Jesus and St. John's, Peter Hobart at Queens' and Magdalene, and John Wilson at Emmanuel and King's; John Oxenbridge attended both Oxford and Cambridge; George Burdett went from Dublin to Cambridge; and Thomas Parker, who could boast of the most varied academic career of all the university alumni, went from Dublin to Oxford to Leyden to Franeker, where he finally took his degree. (For Parker, vide Samuel Eliot Morison's "The Education of Thomas Parker, of Newbury" in *Publications*, Colonial Society of Massachusetts, XXVIII, 261-267.)

occasionally, a young man, though he was destined eventually for the ministry, had the educational advantage of spending a few years at the Inns of Court, as Henry Whitfield did; or of studying medicine, as Thomas Thacher and Giles Firmin did; or of travelling, as Nathaniel Ward did.

At some time during his youth the minister-to-be went through a period of mental anguish. Some preacher, some book awakened him from his casual life of study and pleasure, and, after a time of despair and of realization of his unworthiness, he felt that he was saved and that he had a definite call to be of service as a preacher of the Gospel. Therefore, after receiving his degrees and being ordained, he began his preaching in English churches, usually in ones with a decidedly Puritan bent. He might have a lectureship[22] such as Samuel Stone held at Towcester and Thomas Shepard at Earles-Colne; or be attached to one of the richer Puritan families, the way Samuel Whiting was chaplain to the families of Sir Nicholas Bacon and of Sir Roger Townsend, and the way John Norton served Sir William Masham's house; or even have a regular church and parish under a lenient bishop—William Hooke was vicar of Axmouth in Devonshire and John Cotton was rector of St. Botolph's in Boston, Lincolnshire. But sometime during these English years, perhaps after a few, perhaps after as many as Cotton's twenty and Peter Bulkeley's twenty-one, the Puritan minister's refusal to abide by the rules of the Established Church came to the attention of the church authorities, for the latter were steadily growing more rigorous in their discipline, especially after Archbishop Laud came into power. Abruptly, harshly silenced, the dissenter, who, perhaps, now had a wife and growing family for whom he had to provide some physical necessities even while he led (or sent) them firmly to heaven, was forced to recon-

22 During the early seventeenth century a number of lectureships were established in various parishes in England; in other words, a special, additional preacher was appointed to preach on Sundays at times other than the regular services and usually on weekdays as well. The lecturer, whose expenses were paid by the congregation or by part of the congregation or by some interested man of wealth, might very well make his influence felt in a number of neighboring parishes. This method of reform from within the church progressed for some years, but from 1629 on Laud was able to hamper the work of the lectureships and by the mid 1630's decrees had been passed to end them. This suppression failed to destroy Puritanism, as Laud had hoped, but only served to accelerate the split between the different parties of the church. *Cf.* Haller, *The Rise of Puritanism*, 52-53, 230.

struct his life. Sometimes he came to New England directly
from his English persecutors; sometimes there was a prelimin-
ary flight to Holland, where, as an English Puritan, and especially as a Congregationalist,[23] he found but limited opportunity
to lead a useful life of church service. Hampered in his natural
desire for an active pastorate by the combined intrigue of the
Presbyterian faction of the Puritan party, which was well represented in the Low Countries, and by the archbishop's agents,
he soon found the prospect of joining his fellow-Congregation-
alists in Massachusetts more promising than continuing to live
in a foreign country; his less impatient fellow-exiles lingered on
the Continent until after 1640 and then were able to return to
England. But among the prominent Puritans who sojourned for
a few years in Holland and then sailed for the colonies were
Davenport, Hooker, and Peter.

Once a minister had arrived in New England, he quickly
received a call from some church; he might be known to his
future parishioners only by reputation, or he might have
preached to many of them in old England. Settled in a village
church and at last safe from persecution though he might be,
not every minister was to have the satisfaction of a long and
undisturbed preaching career; a few, like Joseph Avery, John
Harvard, and Samuel Skelton, died young; others, like Giles
Firmin and Hugh Peter, returned to England; a very small
minority, like Stephen Batchelor and John Wheelwright, led
stormy lives, always in difficulties with their churches or with
the authorities. But the average man had a long New England
blossoming; most of the first ministers had fifteen years or more
of service in one or two New England towns, and some occupied their pulpits for remarkable spans—John Allen was at
Dedham for thirty-four years, Thomas Carter at Woburn for
forty-two years, John Warham at Dorchester and Windsor for
forty years, Thomas Harford at Norwalk for forty years, and
John Eliot at Roxbury for fifty-eight years. True, there were
difficulties. Living conditions were hard; sickness and death

23   Miller, *Orthodoxy in Massachusetts*, 106-107; for an interesting and detailed
     account of Congregationalism in Holland, see Raymond Phineas Stearns'
     *Congregationalism in the Dutch Netherlands; the Rise and Fall of the English
     Congregational classis, 1621-1635* (Chicago: The American Society of Church
     History, 1940).

were prevalent—children and wives were quick to die; the Indians were a constant and cruel menace; people at home, in old England—especially their fellow-nonconformists, the Presbyterians—were apt to misjudge their more daring brothers across the ocean. Nevertheless, if a minister wanted to serve God and God's elect, he had his opportunities. Church polity could be formulated; the magistrates could be influenced and shown most clearly God's will; a college and schools could be created —and all these were but means to an end, the salvation of those earnest men and women who had crossed the ocean, given up much and risked all material things for the sake of their souls.

That his time in the pulpit should be put to the best possible use was, above all, the essential duty of every minister. There was no doubt in any one's mind of the "efficacy of the Word preached." As Thomas Hooker said:

> Every sermon a man heareth, he is thereby nearer either to heaven or hell, either he is made better or worse by it.[24]

Accordingly, a New England minister did not spare his pulpit efforts. He preached for an hour or two once or twice and sometimes three times a week—that is, always once or twice on Sundays, often at a week-day lecture, and occasionally on days of fasting, of thanksgiving, and of election. His sermon-content was based directly on the Bible, for Scripture was the final and infallible authority by which every man was to govern his life. All matters of daily existence, ranging from a person's haircut to his choice of a ruler, could be established definitely by consulting God's Word. More important, by the Bible, and by the Bible only, could a man hope for the assurance of that everlasting salvation which makes mundane affairs seem trivial. Consequently, the doctrine for each and every sermon was taken directly from the Bible, and all proof rested in the Bible. No opinion on any matter—theological, moral, political, pragmatic—had any value unless it could be supported by definite Biblical references; in fact, to listen to ideas for which the speaker did not sincerely believe he had Scripture sanction, was to sin.

24 Thomas Hooker, "Wilful Hardnesse: or the Means of Grace Abused," in *The Saints Dignitie* (London, 1651), 234.

The inerrancy of the Bible as the canon of revealed truth was never questioned, but neither was the human fallibility of fallen man. Every minister could and did try to protect himself and his congregation from the weakness of his own frail human intellect in dealing with possibly ambiguous Biblical passages. No greater mistake could be made than to think that any Puritan preacher was willing to approach the problem of interpreting the Scriptures unaided except by his own ability and whatever inspiration the Lord might give him. On the contrary, the most thorough preparation was believed imperative. Before entering the pulpit, a preacher prayed for divine guidance, but he also had spent the preceding days in painstaking preparation. True, in making himself familiar with other men's interpretations of doctrine, he was getting aid from other minds that also suffered from their human limitations; but he could consult authorities who, despite these limitations, were gifted in a particular field of knowledge, according to the judgment of many. Then, too, he could consult men whose opinions on other doctrinal or exegetical matters he shared and so approved; apparently correct in many points, such kindred thinkers might well be right on another question, or, at least, their opinions were to be considered with respect—a viewpoint that led the ministers to do a good deal of reading in commentaries and tracts by slightly earlier and contemporary Puritans.

The Reverend Charles Chauncy, at the beginning of his career as president of Harvard College, voiced the general Puritan viewpoint on the value of education.[25] A few English zealots were claiming that a minister should concentrate his studying on the Bible and so not waste his time and brain-power on secular learning. Chauncy was quick to grant that learning certainly was not necessary for salvation. This was a point on which the Reverend Thomas Hooker had been reassuring his Hartford congregation for years, reiterating that the meanest saint knew more of God's love and promises than the most unregenerate doctors.[26] With scant courtesy to his beloved fol-

---

25 Charles Chauncy, *God's Mercy, Shewed to His People in Giving Them a Faithful Ministry and Schooles of Learning for the Continual Supplyes Thereof* (Cambridge, Mass., 1655), 54-57.
26 Hooker, *A Comment Upon Christ's Last Prayer* . . . (London, 1656), 404.

lowers, the Hartford pastor had illustrated this comforting theory that neither learning nor mind was essential for grace:

As suppose one dull blocke, and a quicke wit, are both set to one trade, yet
if the dullard had an expert master, and learn unto him the skill of the
trade, and the quicke spirit was with a master that could not teach him his
trade; wee see that the dull blocke is more wise in this trade than the other:
so it is here, they have the Lord for their master.[27]

Chauncy was even willing to accede to the idea that an education might not always be indispensable to a minister's perform-
ing his duties ably. But such arguments were beside the point:
in the name of expediency, he asked, what could be more ad-
vantageous to a preacher than a thorough training and some
scholarship?

The study of the arts and languages—and by "arts" Chauncy meant, as the context shows, physics, philosophy, ethics, political science, history, logic, and rhetoric—really conduced to
theological pursuits in the sense that each of these subjects
assisted in understanding Scripture. For example, secular historians, even heathen chroniclers, often support Scripture accounts; and truth is truth, no matter where found, and comes
from the God of truth. Again, a knowledge of physical science
might help one to comprehend the somewhat elliptic accounts
of events to be found here and there in both Testaments. Wording the argument another way, Chauncy also pointed out that
the Bible is really composed of natural philosophy together with
moral and political precepts, and some chronology—all being
frequently expressed through the medium of rhetorical tropes.
Any minister, accordingly, had a first and primary need of as
much knowledge as possible of the learned tongues in order to
be certain of the exact meaning of every Scripture word as it
had been originally written. In translations not only were such
precise shades of meaning lost, but also the connotations that
the original words carried with them were abandoned or perverted. Secondly, logic was invaluable if the minister was to
know when Scripture was being wrested out of its true sense
and when it was being truly applied to a problem. And thirdly,
without a thorough training in rhetoric a minister might fail
to understand the frequent tropes used throughout the Bible.

27 Hooker, *The Soules Effectual Calling to Christ* (London, 1637), 109.

While there were plenty of clear passages in the Old and New Testaments which gave the doctrines concerning faith and behavior leading to salvation, the meaning of other passages was admittedly cryptic. The hidden sense could be disclosed by comparison with clear passages, by a realization of the circumstances under which the obscure remark had been made, by the use of the rules of logic, and by a familiarity with the common ways of speaking in the past and in different lands; in other words, a good knowledge of logic, history, and linguistics would be most helpful. But a good many of the apparent difficulties in interpretation disappeared if a minister knew his rhetoric sufficiently well to distinguish the various tropes employed and to know the liberties of expression such figures allowed. Anthropopathia, metonymy, synecdoche, prolepsis, enallage, pleonasm, and irony were among the devices which accounted for the trouble uneducated men had in realizing that there were no contradictions possible in the Word of God.

Every preacher's duty, then, was to prepare his sermon as well as he could and to bring to his aid as much learning as he could possess himself of. But it was equally the preacher's duty to conceal the help he had received from other scholars. Any ostentatious display of learning was considered decidedly out-of-place; in fact, proper names other than Biblical ones seem to have slipped in almost against a preacher's will. How well and how deliberately a minister managed to screen the preparation that went into the making of a sermon may be seen by a comparison of Thomas Shepard's ordinary preaching to his congregation with some of this preaching rewritten and prepared for the benefit of young Harvard students.[28] The Cambridge pastor's church listeners rarely had a secular reference come between them and the Bible; the young ministers-to-be at the college were given many such references to consult. This policy of not naming sources of information and of illustrative story was adopted in no spirit of self-exaltation; on the contrary, credit was to go to the Divine Spirit as it manifested itself both in the Bible and in the inspiration of the deliverer of the sermon in explication of the Bible. To name authorities for various points made in the development of a thesis might cause

28 *Theses Sabbaticae* (London, 1649).

the attention of some members of the congregation to deviate from the central thought of the discourse, which would be lost in the endeavor to recall some stray point of controversy or biography.   Furthermore, the frequent use of similitudes or anecdotes that named characters and places might prove distracting in much the same way.   To justify himself further in his attitude of seeming to preach directly from Scripture, aided by no man's reasoning powers except his own, a Puritan minister had only to turn to the instructions of the Reverend William Perkins, an English writer whose voluminous theological works were ranked by seventeenth-century Puritans with those of Calvin and Luther.   Perkins' *The Arte of Prophecying,* the manual that every nonconforming preacher studied, is definite in its warning to young clergymen against disclosing their informational sources:

Humane wisdome must be concealed, whether it be in the matter of the sermon, or in the setting forth of the words; because the preaching of the word is the *Testimony of God, and the profession of the knowledge of Christ,* and not of humane skill; and againe, because the hearers ought not to ascribe their faith to the gifts of men, but to the power of God's word.[29]

To aid him in such special preparation as he found necessary for each sermon, practically every New England minister brought the education that the universities of the day provided and encouraged.   As an Oxford or Cambridge Master of Arts, he knew, besides English, three other languages,—Latin, Greek, and Hebrew.   During the four years that he had been a candidate for the Bachelor of Arts degree, he had had a thorough training in logic, philosophy, Latin and Greek classics, and Latin composition.   Then during the three years that he had studied for his next degree he had learned Hebrew and had laid the foundation of his knowledge of theology, a study which he would continue for the rest of his life.   And his academic career had been planned to develop his forensic powers, since the final test of his scholastic ability would still, as in medieval days, take the form of disputation.[30]

29 William Perkins, *The Art of Prophecying.   Or, A Treatise Concerning the Sacred and Onely True Manner and Methode of Preaching.   First written in Latine by Mr. William Perkins: and now faithfully translated into English . . . by Thomas Tuke.   In The Workes* (London, 1613), 670.
30 Morison, *The Founding of Harvard College,* 67-78.

Most of this general education was put to good use in his preaching, although his reading in the classics was not very obviously helpful. As a matter of fact, the average minister in his preaching referred to his classical reading only rarely and briefly —and then for terse quotations or but sketchily outlined historical anecdotes. Nevertheless, most Puritans believed that the reading of heathen writers could be well justified. There was a decided feeling that these great writers of the past often expressed deep-seated moral sentiments that every man, except the hopelessly depraved, could recognize as true and right; therefore, heathen poets and prose writers could be read and cited in support of moral points, if not of ethical or religious ones. Occasionally, too, these early writers, especially the historians, would be found to accord with Scripture in fact or prophecy. Perkins, for instance, urges every minister to note the consent in part of Homer and Plato (especially in the *Timaeus* dialogue) to the Genesis creation story; for the life and significance of Christ, he lists Josephus, Lactantius, Cicero, Virgil, Suetonius, and Tacitus; and for corroboration of various lesser Biblical tales and incidents, he mentions Pliny, Macrobius, Josephus, Eusebius, Plutarch, Alexander Cornelius, Berosus, and "the Poets."[31]

Like other clerics of the period, the Puritan preacher was trained in the methods of scholastic dialectic; as a Protestant he was vitally interested in logic, for he believed that by its aid he could deduce the truth from the Bible. At his university, especially if he was a Cambridge man, he had become familiar not only with the Aristotelian school of thought but with the newer Ramist one as well. Ramists considered themselves as far removed in their theories from Aristotelians, and not as merely shifting the emphasis of Aristotelian dialectic rather than contravening it. As a Puritan, the future New Englander found himself in sympathy with the general Ramist viewpoint,[32] which put much value upon the individual's ability to think for himself; and especially as Congregationalist, he approved of the application of this way of thinking to church polity, for the

31 Perkins, *The Arte of Prophecying*, 650.
32 For a detailed account of Ramus's influence on New England thought, see Perry Miller's *The New England Mind* (New York: The Macmillan Company, 1939), 116-153.

French logician was known to have favored allowing the power to choose their pastors and to pronounce censures to rest in individual congregations, rather than in a ministerial classis. More specifically, too, Ramist logic had its influence on Puritan thought and rhetoric. Ramus's simplified approach to a problem, with the emphasis always upon dichotomies, encouraged any Puritan follower to see his world as composed of opposites: deeds were either good or bad, depending upon their doer's state of grace; men were either saved or damned, depending upon their Creator's unfathomable will. The continued approval of arguing from general theories to singular cases—a method of procedure which Ramist logic did nothing to combat—also limited Puritan thinking in many ways, prohibiting any scientific approach to a problem; and the Ramist advocacy of arguing from the familiar or known to the strange or unknown encouraged a preacher to make his points by homely illustrations, the truth of which no one could question, and then apply to spiritual matters the obvious principle involved in physical or material cases. Even more definite Ramist influences may be seen in Puritan sermon methodology. The wording of texts was analyzed or "opened"; the results were combined, by the Ramist method of genesis, to form the doctrine. Every statement was followed by its reasons or proofs—a direct method of procedure relying much upon axiomatic truth rather than upon syllogistic reasoning. Then again, the Ramist idea was that the theory or art involved in solving a difficulty mattered less than the use or purpose to which one put the conclusion arrived at; a reflection of this utilitarian way of thinking may be seen in the long "uses" and "applications" of the doctrine with which each sermon came to an end.

Naturally, a Puritan minister's scholarly interests lay fundamentally in Christian philosophy and theology. To studying in these fields he had devoted himself while preparing for his life work, and he continued to read in them throughout his career, spending long days closeted with his books. The works of many of the church fathers must have been well known; Perkins, in fact, notes that any man expecting to preach satisfactorily would have to be familiar with Origen, Melito, Athanasius, Cyril, Cyprian, Hilary, Jerome, Epiphanius, John of Damascus, and Gregory Nazianzen. In the sermons themselves there are references by name to a good many of these men as well as to Justin Martyr, Chrysostom, Tertullian, and Ambrose. No one of these writers is named in the sermons more than very occasionally, although to call a man "Chrysostom" is a common compliment in adulatory prefaces to volumes of collected sermons. Naturally, Augustine, to whom much of what has been loosely called Calvinism can be traced, is referred to with some frequency.

Considering the Puritan's respect for what he regarded as the early, uncorrupted church, his interest in patristic literature is intelligible. The frequent references—and not always condemnatory ones—to scholastic and Jesuit scholars are more surprising, as the ministers, almost without exception, were in the habit of keeping their choicest opprobrium for Catholicism in general, with Jesuitism as the recipient of any extra objurgation that they might be able to recall. The reason for the seeming inconsistency is twofold: Puritan preachers, confident of the truth of their own beliefs, did not hesitate to read controversial literature; and they respected learning wherever they found it. They did not refuse to read their opponents' opinions nor did they scorn all of a man's thought because he had, in their judgment, wandered from the truth on some points. Consequently, definite references to Aquinas and Bellarmine are to be found in the sermons—Aquinas as the most representative exponent of the schoolmen and Bellarmine as a writer on Catholic and Protestant differences, especially on the vital difference between living under a doctrine of works and living under a doctrine of faith. Occasionally, too, there is evidence that other scholastic philosophers and clerics were not unknown. Duns Scotus, Ambrosius Catharinus, Suarez, Vasques, Smissing, Driedo, and Cornelius a Lapide are named. Especially noted for their scholarship were the two Jesuits, Pagninus and Caussin—Pagninus for his skill in the learned languages and hence for his commentaries on the Psalms and other parts of the Old Testament, Caussin for his moral reflections and for his Greek thesaurus. Bernard, the twelfth-century ascetic whose writings were praised by Calvin and Luther, is named and quoted now and then, as is his contemporary, Hugo of Saint Victor, the mystic who protested against over-indulgence in allegorical interpretation of Scripture. It is difficult to determine how often the ministers turned directly to these medieval writers; probably a good many of these Catholics and their ideas were better known through reformulations such as Alsted's *Encyclopaedia Scientiarum Omnium,* Keckermann's *Operum Omnium Quae Extant* and other similar, but less extensive, surveys of knowledge. These reference books contained in summary the conclusions which practically every thinker in every field had held; for instance, Alsted's volumes, with which New England scholars were very familiar, had brief surveys of the works of over five hundred earlier scholars.[33]

To the great minds of the Reformation the Puritans owed their interpretation of fundamental religious doctrines. But to their knowledge of the thought of such early leaders as Calvin, Luther, Beza, and Melanchthon, the ministers added their reading of the followers of these men, the scholars and polemic writers of the late sixteenth and seventeenth centuries. Since the prolific works of the latter were the books being constantly consulted as each sermon was being prepared—often as a direct source of information concerning some definite point—the ministers, if they are to be judged by the citations and quotations scattered through their preaching, perused an amazing number of controversial and exegetical books written by men of their own and their fathers' generations. Therefore, the sermons of early New England strongly suggest that their preachers had received their beliefs diluted through the minds of practically contemporary English Puritans and continental Calvinists. Nevertheless, while the citing of these authorities is obviously indicative of a type of specific reading-preparation that a minister made, care must be taken in judging the general intellectual background by these references. Cotton was a lifelong student of Calvin. No day passed that the Boston preacher did not "sweeten" his mind with a little of his favorite author; yet in Cotton's works Calvin's name does not appear often. As a rule, books of general influence apparently were less likely to be named than ones that could be used in connection with a definite Bible text or tenet of faith. This natural limitation is

33 Miller, *The New England Mind,* 102-103.

to be seen also in the lack of references to books that were not exegetical or did not bear directly upon the religious controversies of the day. So Erasmus, whose humanistic teaching had a decided effect upon Puritanism,[34] and whose *Colloquies* were much used by young students,[35] is referred to but once or twice in all this pulpit literature. Ramus and Talon, who applied Ramus's principles to rhetoric, do not seem to be mentioned at all, though the influence of Ramist logic was admittedly very great and their books were in the Harvard library.[36]

Although some well-studied books may not be cited in the sermons with any frequency, there is no doubt about the conclusions to be drawn from the references that have slipped into these discourses. Numerous continental scholars of current renown were consulted, among them Aretius, Junius, Rivetus, Vermigli, Zanchius, and Voetius—to name but a few of the many. A great many writers on controversial subjects were known. Many of these were, of course, ardent Puritans and Congregationalists; some, however, were of different opinions concerning important questions of immediate interest to all, and while these adversaries were held up to scorn, they were at least read. In the latter category were such men as William Dell, Tobias Crisp, John Cameron, and John Ball—all writers who did not share New England's beliefs on such points as the value of education, the evil of Antinomianism, the salvation of only a limited group of believers, and the advantages of Congregational church polity. But above all, the New Englanders read and re-read the numerous publications of the more prominent Puritan leaders. They knew the writings of the first preachers, Thomas Cartwright, Richard Greenham, and Richard Rogers; they reverenced the work of such men as Lawrence Chaderton, Arthur Hildersham, and John Dod, who came to be known as the patriarchs of the spiritual brotherhood of Puritan preachers; they respected the dicta of Paul Baynes, Richard Sibbes, William Gouge, Robert Parker, William Perkins, John Preston, Thomas Goodwin, and William Ames, all prominent men of

34 Morison, *The Founding of Harvard College*, 51-52, 54; *Harvard College in the Seventeenth Century* (Cambridge, 1936), 165-166.

35 Morison, *The Founding of Harvard College*, 68; *Harvard College in the Seventeenth Century*, 178.

36 Morison, *The Founding of Harvard College*, 265.

their own generation.[37] These were the dominant spirits of the English Puritan movement; more than that, they were the intimate friends of many of the emigrant ministers. Bonds may be easily traced between preachers who chose to stay in England and those who preferred to settle in New England. For example, Cotton had had his ideas colored by Hildersham, Dod, and Sibbes; in turn, he had, before he left England, converted Goodwin and Preston; and he was always a close friend of Preston and Baynes. Davenport, who also had come under the sway of Dod, was a particular friend of Sibbes and had left the impress of his way of thinking upon William Kiffin, another prominent Puritan writer. Similar connections for a number of the ministers can be established;[38] as young men, often while at Cambridge, they had been converted by the older preachers; later, the future New Englanders had become the fellow-laborers and friends of prominent nonconformists of the next generation. What was more natural than for the exiles to read diligently, avidly, the numerous publications of their former instructors, companions, and disciples?

As all these English Puritans were experienced ministers, many of their works offered good examples of preaching skill as well as doctrinal and controversial material. But when a Puritan wished more specific advice concerning his pulpit duties, he had at hand a number of instructional books. One of them, Richard Bernard's *The Faithful Shepheard*,[39] was a popular treatise on ministerial duties, with special emphasis on the proper method and style to be used in sermon-construction. Bernard was useful authority, beginning as he did with the problem of the choice of a text and including in his discussion the use of similitudes; but the most frequently quoted of these manual writers was William Perkins, the author of a great many treatises much admired by his Puritan contemporaries. His influential *The Arte of Prophecying*[40] gives a complete course of

---

37 Haller, *The Rise of Puritanism*, 49-82.
38 Miller, *Orthodoxy in Massachusetts*, 105, 121-123; Haller, *The Rise of Puritanism*, 79.
39 Published 1607, 1609; enlarged edition 1621; for the importance of Bernard, see Haller, *The Rise of Puritanism*, 137.
40 Published in *The Workes*, 1613, 1616; for the importance of Perkins, see W. Fraser Mitchell, *English Pulpit Oratory from Andrewes to Tillotson* . . . (London, 1932), 116-120.

reading which a conscientious preacher would want to follow; even more valuable is the consideration of the plain, dignified style which every Puritan preacher should seek to develop. While Perkins gives much good advice about avoiding Latin and Greek phrases and learned allusion, lest the audience be distracted, his main contribution is his insistence that the intellectual level of the average listener be always kept in mind.

Aided by the common background which they shared with their congregations, by their knowledge of their own religious experiences, by their distinguished scholarship and their diligent reading of current books on what were the important topics of the day, by their years of successful pulpit work, these ministers who had decided that their duty lay in the New World had good reason to be hopeful of rendering a good account of themselves. Even more important than these obvious advantages was their spirit of dedication and determination. If ever there were men who were certain that they were right and who had the full strength of their convictions, these men were the Puritan ministers of New England.

II

THE DOCTRINE AS IT WAS PREACHED

A serious misconception concerning the early New England pulpit has persisted since the beginning of scholarly interest in American literature. According to the traditional idea, these early preachers devoted most of their energy to describing the torments of hell; in other words, they attempted to frighten their parishioners into heaven. Even as important a scholar as Moses Coit Tyler[1] stresses the descriptions of hell-fire that these ministers supposedly loved to dwell upon. Though Vernon Louis Parrington, a more modern student of American thought, does not fall into this error, he has much to say about the Calvinism of most of the ministers, in contrast to the Lutheranism that was evident in the spirit of a few; and by this antithesis he suggests that most of the preachers neglected to put forward the hope of the New Testament in order to spend their pulpit time in emphasizing the law of the Old Testament and the stern principles of an authoritarian system of determinism which sent most of humanity to an everlasting damnation.[2] And the editors of modern collections of early American literature[3] are apt to choose damnation passages to show the sternness of these early writers in contrast to modern urbanity and liberalism. But considered in relation to the mass of sermon literature produced in New England between 1620 and 1670, such horrific descriptions of the fate of the unelect are infrequent, at least in the printed sermons.

Undoubtedly, the ministers both knew and practised the preaching method which all their venerated authorities, starting with Augustine, had advocated. This theory had been worded with emphatic lucidity by Luther:

For not one word of God only, but both should be preached; new and old things should be brought out of the treasury, as well the voice of the law,

1 Moses Coit Tyler, *A History of American Literature* (New York: G. P. Putnam's Sons, 1878), I, 200, 209-210.
2 Vernon Louis Parrington, *The Colonial Mind* 1620-1800 (New York: Harcourt, Brace & Co., 1927), 11, 14-15.
3 *Cf. Colonial Prose and Poetry*, edited by William P. Trent and Benjamin W. Wells (New York: Thomas Y. Crowell & Co., 1901), I, 225-226, 241-244, 249.

as the word of grace.   The voice of the law should be brought forward,
that men may be terrified and brought to a knowledge of their sins, and
thence be converted to penitence and to a better manner of life.   But we
must not stop here; that would be to wound only and not to bind up, to
strike and not to heal, to kill and not to make alive, to bring down to hell
and not to bring back, to humble and not to exalt.   Therefore the word of
grace, and of the promised remission of sin, must also be preached, in order
to teach and set up faith; since, without that word, contrition, penitence,
and all other duties, are performed and taught in vain . . .   For repentance
comes from the law of God, but faith or grace from the promises of God.[4]

In other words, "legal" preaching, which stressed the law of the
Old Testament, was to be followed by gospel preaching, which
stressed the hope of the New Testament.   Accordingly, Thomas
Shepard wrote that when he started his preaching career he
dwelt on the misery of man, the glory of Christ's redemption of
man, and by what means and in what manner man should walk
with the Lord.[5]   Later, it is true, he urged that all preach humiliation that men may develop a sense of wrath and misery to
come;[6] but he shows his own spirit better when he speaks of "the
infinite unknown sweetness, and mercy, and presence of God."[7]
Charles Chauncy, too, evidently followed much the same method
as Shepard.   The eminent president of Harvard wrote this sound
advice to a young man just starting his career:

Preach much about the misery of the state of nature, the preparatives to
conversion; the nature of conversion, or effectual calling; the necessity of
union and communion with Christ; the nature of saving and justifying
faith, and the fruits thereof—love and good works, and sanctification.[8]

Chauncy was a great man in his day and held an influential position, but his fame as a godly instructor could not touch that of
the much-read and revered William Perkins.   The latter started
his preaching manual, *The Arte of Prophecying,* with the statement:

Preaching of the word is Prophecying in the name and roome of Christ,
wherby men are called to the state of Grace, and conserved in it. 2 Cor. 5-19.[9]

4   Martin Luther, *First Principles of the Reformation or The Ninety-five Theses
    and the Three Primary Works of Dr. Martin Luther Translated into English.*
    Edited with theological and historical introductions by Henry Wace, D.D., and
    C. A. Buchheim, Ph.D. (London: John Murray, 1883), 124.
5   *The Autobiography of Thomas Shepard,* with additional notes of his life and
    character, by Nehemiah Adams . . . (Boston, 1832), 32.
6   Shepard, Letter to Giles Firmin in *The Real Christian* (London, 1670).
7   Shepard, *A Treatise of Ineffectual Hearing the Word* (London: Printed by
    T. R. and E. M. for J. Rothwell, 1652), 189.
8   A letter, dated December 20, 1665, quoted in Mather's *Magnalia,* Book III, 138.
9   *The Arte of Prophecying,* 646.

And the learned author ends with "the summe of the summe": "Preaching Christ by Christ to the praise of Christ."[10]

Such, then, was the theory: after man was duly humiliated by a knowledge of his natural, fallen estate, he should then be encouraged by much preaching about Christ and the Covenant through which he saved man. Certainly such was also the practice, if we judge by Cotton Mather's statements of what was being preached in the first years in contrast to his own time. Mather writes, for example, of the Reverend Peter Bulkeley, teacher of the Concord church:

At Concord he preached over the Illustrious Truths, about the Person, the Natures, the Offices of Christ. (What would he have said, if he had lived unto this Evil Day, when 'tis counted good Advice for a Minister of the Gospel, Not to preach much on the Person of Christ?) . . ."[11]

Quite as definite as this is Mather's description of the preaching of John Eliot, who was able to do double service as missionary to the Indians and as teacher of the church at Roxbury. Here the comment is on his regular weekly church duties:

As 'twas noted of Dr. Bodly, that whatever Subject he were upon, in the Application still his Use of it would be, *to drive Men unto the Lord Jesus Christ;* in like manner, the Lord Jesus Christ was the Loadstone which gave a touch to all the Sermons of our *Eliot;* a Glorious, Precious, Lovely *Christ,* was the Point of Heaven which they still verged unto."[12]

Because Eliot was known for his tireless habit of making regular visits to the neighboring towns of Boston, Charlestown, Dorchester, and Cambridge to hear the weekly lectures of his fellow-ministers, his own testimony is even more interesting. Mather reports him as frequently saying

O blessed be God, that we have Christ so much and so well preached in poor New-England!"[13]

The surviving volumes of sermons tell us what part of Christology the ministers deemed of greatest value to their congregations. The dual nature of Jesus Christ was "strong meat,"[14] not milk for babes; nevertheless, this part of the doctrine was not neglected. Christ was revered as the God-man,

10 Ibid., 673.
11 Mather, *Magnalia*, Book III, 97.
12 *Ibid.*, 185-186.
13 *Ibid.*, 186.
14 Perkins, *The Arte of Prophecying*, 666.

who by his two natures is the perfect intermediary between God
and man.   For man, out of great and unmerited love, Christ
performs three offices, prophetical, priestly, and kingly: that is,
he interprets God's wishes, redeems man, and rules the church
of the redeemed or elect.   Or, to put Christ's services less prosaically, we can quote John Cotton's ecstatic words:

In regard of his Priestly office hee [Christ] is pure as silver, to cleanse our
impurity, and to abide the fire: In regard of His Propheticall office hee is
precious as gold, to enrich our poverty: In regard of his Royall and Kingly
office he is glorious as purple, and cloathed with it, to advance our basenesse;
His heart, or middest, is even paved with love of us: His heart is an hearth
(for so the word signifieth) whereon the fire of his love towards us burneth
continually; let us then love the Lord Jesus againe, and receive the seeds
and fruits of his grace, and then shall we see his heart flaming with love
to us: and then whatsoever befals, bloudshed, warre, captivity,&c. all come
from love; his whole heart is paved with love.[15]

Apparently there was very little emphasis upon the birth
or the earlier earthly career of Jesus.   Christmas was looked
upon as a papist holiday, and John Davenport, the New Haven
pastor, argued at some length that the Messiah must have been
born in September.[16]   Davenport also shared Grotius's opinion
as to the importance of the miracles as manifestation of Christ's
glory and of the truth of the Gospel; prototypes of the Savior
were another subject of interest to the New Haven minister.
But commonly only the last period of Christ's earthly life, the
period of greatest sacrifice and suffering, came in for much attention.   Again and again the faithful were reminded of the
marvelous truth that Jesus Christ, out of love,[17] had been willing
to appear as man, and a humble man at that, not a ruler, not a
king.   Despite the fact that the ministers, again on guard against
papist ways, carefully avoided mentioning the Lenten holy days
and Easter, they found that the tenets of their faith led them

15   John Cotton, *A Brief Exposition of the Whole Book of Canticles*, . . . (London,
      1642), 97.
16   The theory of a September birth came from Scaliger. *Cf.* Petro Allix, *Diatriba
      de Anno & Mense Natali Jesu Christi In Qva Omnia Qvae Ex Historia Ervi
      Possunt Ad Hujus Argumenti Dilucidationen Facientia, Accurate Discuti-
      unter; Et Praecipui Veterum Ac Neotericorum Errores Huc Pertinentes
      Refelluntur* (London: Impensis Davidis Mortier, 1722).   For a historical
      summary of the observance of Christmas, see Katherine Lambert Richards,
      How Christmas Came to the Sunday-Schools (New York: Dodd, Mead and
      Company, 1934), 1-108.
17   John Davenport, *The Knowledge of Christ* . . . (London: Printed for L.
      Chapman, 1653).

to tell fairly often the moving tale of the Redeemer's passion and death, by which man had been ransomed from some of the penalties of Adam's fall. At least one minister, the Reverend Richard Mather of Dorchester, then stressed the idea that Jesus Christ's sufferings were caused by the sins of God's people, not by the wrong-doing of the wicked.[18] But careful explanation was always made that Christ's agony was primarily mental, not physical. To think otherwise was an insult to his name, because any man who was not extraordinarily pusillanimous could and would bear any pain and death willingly and without complaint, if it were for his religion. What Christ had borne, for man's sake, was God's wrath, which no ordinary man had ever endured on earth. So intense had been the agony of his soul at the idea of his Father's anger that he had cried out thrice that the cup might pass from him and had sweated blood; but still, as a final torture for his soul in his assumption of man's position, although he really had God's love and favor, he had given himself up to a sense of the loss of that love and had cried out that most pathetic of all lamentations: "My God, my God, why hast thou forsaken me?"[19] Indeed, so great was the mental suffering involved that the Savior died from it, rather than from his bodily injuries, although these may have hastened the end.[20]

From this worship of Christ—and not a few of the sermons consist largely of paeans of praise and of exhortations to love him—interest naturally was wont to shift to the more egocentric problem of personal salvation. Christ as intermediary had secured for man the Covenant of Grace, vastly superior to the earlier Covenant of Works. This idea of a contract or agreement between God and man was of particular interest to the Puritan, as it seemed to him to offer a plausible and definite explanation of the puzzle of man's position in relation to his Creator's will. Long series of lectures, especially in the period following close upon the Anne Hutchinson difficulties, were de-

18 Richard Mather, *The Summe of Certain Sermons upon Genes. 15.6* . . . (Cambridge: Samuel Green, 1652), 43-44.
19 Thomas Hooker, "The Gift of Gifts: or, The End why Christ Gave Himself," in *The Saints Dignitie, and dutie* (London: Printed by C. D. for Francis Eglesfield, 1651), 12-15.
20 John Cotton, *The Covenant of Grace* (London: Printed by M. S. for Francis Eglesfield and John Allen, 1655), 157-158.

voted to a comparison of the two covenants. This interest was a natural outcome of this threatened schism in the churches, as Mrs. Hutchinson had accused the Reverend John Wilson and most of the other ministers of being under a Covenant of Works. The charge was vehemently denied, but it aroused a great deal of discussion concerning the two contracts between God and man. The Reverend Peter Bulkeley of Concord, for example, could find a number of points of similarity in the old and the new covenants: both had one Author; the two parties, God and man; the same end, the glory of God; not to mention other points of likeness. But he really shows his power of analysis when he finds at least fifteen points of dissimilarity, some of which border rather closely on each other. But, in general, under the old Covenant, dependence was on man; under the new, it is on God. Man formerly lost his hope of salvation by one sin, now his sins are forgiven; in other words, the possible had been substituted for the impossible (for fallen man could not hope to be sinless), peace for suspense. Perhaps Bulkeley's thirteenth point is the most interesting: The Covenant of Works was revealed by the light of nature—anyone could understand that man ought to do good; but the Covenant of Grace needed for its comprehension the supernatural light of the Bible, and therefore was the superior covenant. While Bulkeley's *The Gospel Covenant*[21] became something of a classic as a discussion of Pauline doctrine concerning the distinction between the law and the gospel, similar lengthy comparisons of the two covenants are to be found in the sermon series of Cotton, Hooker, Mather, and Shepard.[22] But in all these discussions the basic difference between the two covenants resolved itself into one of works versus faith. Under the old covenant, your works were judged, and cost you your

21 London: Printed by M. S. for Benjamin Allen, 1646. Enlarged and corrected edition London, 1651.

22 Among other sermons on the subject are John Cotton's *The Covenant of Gods free Grace Most Sweetly unfolded* . . . (London: Printed for Matthew Simmons, 1645) and the *Covenant of Grace* (London: Printed by M. S. for Francis Eglesfield and John Allen, 1655), Thomas Hooker's "Grace Magnified" in *The Saints Dignitie and Dutie* (London: C. D. for Francis Egelsfield, 1651), Richard Mather's *The Summe of Certain Sermons upon Genes. 15.6* (Cambridge: Samuel Green, 1652), and Thomas Shepard's *The Saints Iewell* (London, 1642). Earlier influential discussions by English Puritans include John Downame's *The Christian Warfare* (1604) and John Preston's *The New Covenant, or the Saints Portion* (1629); William Perkins, William Ames, and Richard Sibbes had also developed this covenant concept in their various works. See Miller, *The New England Mind*, 502-504.

salvation; under the new, only your faith mattered, and yet you behaved yourself, or endeavored to, because with that faith you had entered into a kind of superior, voluntary contract with your Creator.[23]

While the replacing of the old covenant by the new was an incomparable and totally unmerited blessing, salvation was still far from easy. Although God would have no man perish, faith had to come first from Christ; otherwise man was helpless. Man could make preparation by seeing that his heart was utterly humble and contrite, that he depended solely on God and not on himself. Then might come a great change. And with this justification or absolution from sin,[24] would come reconciliation or peace with God, adoption or the privileges of sonship, and sanctification or the turning from sin to God. The last great benefit only began in this world, of course, and must be completed after death, but even the beginnings of it went far beyond that inward peace and that carefulness not to sin that characterized spiritual life in general. For man would find that his new oneness with God was, paradoxically, a source of joy and grief at once, of joy and fear, even of joy in affliction; he would be patient with other men's weaknesses—but only patient, not forbearing; meekness would be his typical mien, but he would be strictness itself in adhering to the truth; modesty and magnanimity could at the same time be his; he would be diligent in worldly affairs, do his daily task well and expeditiously, and at the same time, in a truer sense, he would be dead to the world and to worldly interests; above all, the new saint could and did love not only his brethren but also his enemies.[25]

But what if this "ingrafting," this union did not take place? Some of the ministers argued that proper unconditional submission to the will of God meant that man must gracefully ac-

23 For a detailed study of the Covenant of Grace and its importance in New England, see Miller, "The Marrow of Puritan Divinity," *Publications of the Colonial Society of Massachusetts*, XXXII, 247-300, and *The New England Mind*, 365-397. For the effect of the Covenant upon political theory and upon church polity, see *The New England Mind*, 398-431 and 432-462.

24 Richard Mather's *The Summe of Certain Sermons upon Genes. 15.6* dwells upon this point at length. So does a good part of Charles Chauncy's *The Plain Doctrin of the Justification of a Sinner* . . . (London: Printed by R. I. for Adoniram Byfield, 1659).

25 John Cotton, *Christ the Fountaine of Life* . . . (London: Robert Ibbitson, 1651), 92 *et seq.*

cept damnation, if God so decreed for his greater glory."[26] On the other hand, man should never despair: he must be always hopeful, mindful of God's great unmerited kindness in saving some. It was freely admitted that here was a point of the divine plan no human mind could satisfactorily explain. The question of election, the question who was chosen and why, remained a mystery into which man should not ferret. And acceptance of God's will in the matter should come not from filial love, as Luther had argued,[27] but from the recognition of justice. After all, man deserved damning. Adam, who had had freedom of will, had fallen, and with him mankind. True, man had not chosen Adam as his representative; but God had, and surely God by his nature loved man more than man could love man. If this explanation did not fully satisfy everyone, here was another question to be answered in heaven.[28] At any rate, because of the very nature of the Deity, no one could question God's justice in punishing man with sin, both innate and actual, and with death, both bodily and spiritual. If man were to be saved, it was through God's grace or mercy, as the Hebrew word for "grace" suggested; man had entirely forfeited any rights he had ever had.

The only uncertain point was God's intention about the fate of infants and children and irresponsible people. Extremists believed that the only sure sign of election was faith with its fruits, and that, therefore, no one could be certain of the fate of any infant. Since God certainly had his elect among the babies too, some children would be saved; but no bereaved parent could be positive that his child was of the elect. Apparently the Reverend Michael Wigglesworth of Malden, who assigned all but the elect babes to "the easiest room in Hell,"[29] was of this opinion. But most of the earlier men were broader souls who wished to interpret the Bible in all charity. Quite frankly they said that this, too, was a questionable point of doctrine, but, knowing the infinite love of God, they hoped for the

26 Thomas Hooker, *The Soules Effectvall Calling to Christ*, 212.
27 Martin Luther, *Vorlesung über dem Römerbrief* (edited by J. Fisher, 1908), II, 155.
28 Thomas Hooker, *The Covenant of Grace opened* ... , 24. Also Thomas Shepard, *The Sincere Convert* (London, 1640).
29 Michael Wigglesworth, *The Day of Doom: or, a Poetical Description of the Great and Last Judgment*, 1662, Stanzas CLXVI-CLXXXI.

best.   Believing parents who entered into the Covenant, entered for their children also, as shown by *Deuteronomy* 29:10; on this account, while parents were not able to communicate grace to their children, God does give these children a relative holiness or spiritual privilege.[30]   Although Cotton believed that children were capable of grace as soon as of reason, or perhaps a bit earlier, he also stressed the importance of the behavior of the parents:

Peter Martyr saith, If they die when they are Infants, they are certainly saved. I cannot say it so fully, nor have I any thing against it: this I can say, that they are *holy* for so saith the Scripture, and therefore they are in the *Covenant* generally; sometimes *Parents* may *cut off* the free passage of their *Covenant* from their seed: though God give them one child and another, they are not greatly sensible what need the poor Infant standeth in of a *Covenant* of grace; they do not *believe for* their children, nor *humble themselves* in respect of them; and then no wonder if the child miscarry through the unbelief of his Parents.[31]

The children of the godly, then, had a good chance of salvation and should be baptized promptly, although the seal did not give grace, as the ignorant might believe, but was merely the sign that the child had this first grace.[32]

But the non-elect were justly damned because of their innate sin.   Such a rare and lofty thinker as Charles Chauncy saw that hell, in its essence, was not so much a place of torture as the withdrawal of God's love. For God's favor in hell would make a heaven for any man.[33]   As Chauncy saw the divine plan, there plainly was need of some place for man to pay his debt or his penalty for sin, and that place was named hell.   But this philosophical view of damnation did not satisfy the other preach-

---

30   Thomas Hooker, *The Covenant of Grace opened* . . . , 35-40; John Cotton, *New Covenant, Or a Treatise, unfolding the order and manner of the giving and receiving of the Covenant to The Elect* . . . (London, 1654), 229-230.   The question of the Half-Way Covenant, which was much discussed a little later, did not arise until after the period under discussion.

31   John Cotton, *New Covenant*, 229-230.   Pietro Martire Vermigli (1500-1562) was commonly referred to as "Peter Martyr."

32   Thomas Hooker, *The Covenant of Grace opened* . . . , 15-24.   Luther stressed the general necessity of baptism for the infants to be saved; Calvin and Beza affirmed that children of believers, baptised or unbaptised, "are rightly holy from their mother's womb by the inheritance of the promise" and enjoy eternal salvation.   (Benjamin B. Warfield, *Two Studies in the History of Doctrine*. New York: The Christian Literature Company, 1897.)

33   Charles Chauncy, *The Plain Doctrin of the Justification of a Sinner in the Sight of God* . . . (London: Printed by R. I. for Adoniram Byfield, 1659), 56.   Cf. Augustine. *De Civitate Dei*, XIX, 27 *et seq*.

ers; nor were many of them content, as the Reverend Leonard Hoare was, to accept the concept, based directly on *Revelation,* of the double death of the ungodly:

Its a dark passage into the bottomless pit: they are led through the prison of the grave to the place of execution. Death temporal ushers in death eternal.[34]

For most of the ministers, however, hell was a definite place of punishment, a bottomless pit, a stinking lake, an unquenchable fire, where millions of damned creatures dolefully shrieked from their torments. Such descriptions are few, but the vehement, almost hysterical tone of the hell-fire passages in which ministers occasionally indulged may be seen in a particularly unpleasant attack that the Reverend Samuel Danforth of Roxbury made upon the "wanton and lascivious persons" before him:

Hasten you after your lecherous Kindred into the stinking Lake; sit down with your Brethren and Sisters in the depths of hell. As you have partaken with them in their sordid Pleasures, partake with them also in their Plagues and Torments. Let thy lustful Body be everlasting Fuel for the unquenchable fire: Let thy lascivious Soul be eternal Food for the never-dying Worm. Let Indignation and Wrath, Tribulation and Anguish be thy portion world without end. Hell from beneath is moved to meet thee, and is ready to entertain thee.[35]

But the elect could die joyously. At best, earthly existence was a painful struggle; if a man had a strong body, he spent his life fighting against his lusts; if he had a weak body, fighting against his ills.[36] But all sorrow was but preparation for future bliss. According to the orthodox view, at death the soul would go to heaven, there to await the final trumpet call, when it would be reunited with the body for perfect delight. Some men, however, had gone back in their belief to the millenarianism of such early commentators as Lactantius, Justin Martyr, and Irenaeus, whose interpretation of *Revelation* was in the spirit of Jewish apocalyptic literalism. These New England chiliasts therefore

34 Leonard Hoare, *The Sting of Death and Death Unstung* (Boston, 1680), 11.
35 Samuel Danforth, *The Cry of Sodom Enquired Into:* ... (Cambridge: Marmaduke Johnson, 1674), 14-15.
36 John Norton, *Three Choice and Profitable Sermons* (Cambridge: Printed by S. G. and M. I. for Hezekiah Usher, 1664), 26. The second sermon is devoted to the idea of joyful dying. Leonard Hoare's *The Sting of Death and Death Unstung* shows at length the difference between the fearful death of the wicked and the hopeful death of the saints.

had to wait until the millenium, Christ's earthly reign, and the Second Judgment had taken place; then they could enjoy the full pleasures of complete sanctification and beatitude for all eternity.[37] But this heaven of heavens to which the faithful were destined was well worth waiting for. With curious consistency, no minister ever referred just to "heaven," but always to the "third Heaven" or to "the Heaven of Heavens." Apparently, the standard phrase "third Heaven" came from Paul's solitary use of the expression in 2 *Corinthians* 12:2, but there are a number of Biblical references to the "heaven of heavens" (*Deuteronomy* 10:14, 1 *Kings* 8:27, *Psalms* 148:4, 2 *Chronicles* 2:6, 6:18). This idea of three or more heavens is more fully developed in the apocalyptic book, *The Testaments cf the Twelve Patriarchs*[38] (*Levi* 2:7-3), which is now classified as Old Testament apocrypha. The scholastics, moreover, taught that there were three heavens—the first one, the visible firmament that all can see; the second, spiritual in nature, for it is the abode of the saints and angels; the third, intellectual, for there the blessed would enjoy the immediate vision of God.[39] But Hooker explained simply to his congregation that there were three heavens—

Heaven where the birds are, the Heaven where the starres are, and the highest heaven.[40]

The last has never been defiled, even by the fallen angels, because it is the chamber of God.

The earlier ministers were content to feed their flocks with a general idea of this third heaven as a place of unimaginable and eternal spiritual felicitation, of perfect freedom from evil, and consequently from sorrow, and of perfect enjoyment of all good. A rewarding understanding of God's mysteries would come with the final beatitude of seeing the Creator, whose goodness had hitherto been known only indirectly by his works. But by the 1670's, heaven had been in the saints' thoughts for so

37 John Davenport of New Haven was one of the most prominent chiliasts.
38 Translated from the editor's Greek text and edited . . . by R. H. Charles (London: Adam and Charles Black, 1908), 27-36.
39 K. R. Hagenbach, *A Text-Book of the History of Doctrines.* The Edinburgh Translation of C. W. Buch, Revised with large Additions . . . by Henry B. Smith, D.D., (New York: Sheldon & Co., 1864), II, 130.
40 Thomas Hooker, *A Briefe Exposition of the Lords Prayer*: . . . (London: Printed by Moses Bell for Benjamine Allen, 1645), 9.

long that it had become curiously concrete and regimented, and nearer to the Catholic conception of a systematized beatific state. Even as the sermonizers had plotted hell, they diagrammed heaven. In William Hubbard's bliss there were many Pauline ranks: "cherubims as well as Seraphims, Arch-Angels as well as Angels, Thrones and Dominions, as well as Principalities and Powers"[41] with the spirits of just men made perfect as in a middle rank. And even in this "middle ranke" there will be distinctions: not every one shall have such a crown as Paul's, Jonathan Mitchell wisely remarked.[42] How shall the blessed, risen in perfect body and soul, spend their time in this third heaven? Partly in telling their experiences on earth, partly in listening to sermons. Nothing could be more pleasant than hearing of

the Lords admirable variegate Dispensations; the embroidered work of Providence, when the whole piece shall be made up and finished, the curious needle-work thereof (the Coat of many Colours that God hath made for his Church, and for all his Beloved ones in the varieties of his dealings with them.)[43]

Incidentally, all the saints will be on friendly terms, Paul and Barnabas, Hooper and Ridley, Luther and Zwingli, at last fully reconciled with each other in the truth.[44] And what was more probable than that Jesus Christ himself, the incomparable preacher, would there expound the Scriptures, lay open the depths of the book of God and of the mysteries of divinity?[45]

The Creator of man and of heaven and hell and, somewhat incidentally, of this world, was an Augustinian God of infinite love. As Samuel Whiting, with a typical seventeenth-century burst of italics, wrote:

41 William Hubbard, *The Happiness of a People*, 9. Hubbard here was elaborating upon *Colossians* 1:16; he may also have had in mind *Ephesians* 1:21.
42 Jonathan Mitchell, *A Discourse of the Glory* . . . (London: Printed for Nathanial Ponder, 1677), 81. The theory that there are degrees of felicity in heaven is based on *John* 14:2; and had been discussed in some detail by Gregory of Nazianzen (*Orationes* XXVII, XIV, XIX) and by Augustine (*De Civitate Dei*, XXII).
43 Mitchell, *A Discourse of the Glory* . . . , 50.
44 *Ibid.*, p. 15. This idea of all the saints' knowing each other and rejoicing in sweet fellowship was stressed in Bolton's current tract on heaven (*Mr. Bolton's Last and Learned Worke of the Foure last things, Death, Iudgement, Hell, and Heaven* . . . London, 1632, 1635, 1639). The Reverend Robert Bolton was much respected by the Puritans, and he is often referred to as an authority on eschatological problems. Gregory of Nazianzen and Anselm are quoted by Bolton in corroboration of this particular point; he might also have referred his readers to Origen and Augustine.
45 Mitchell, *A Discourse of the Glory*, 28.

It's *great,* and *large,* it's a *Sun,* a *Sea*: and the Sun is not so full of *light,* nor the *Sea* of *Water,* as he is of *Love.*[46]

Considered from a less ecstatic point of view, God was a powerful being who had created men so that he might have spectators for his glorious works. But abstract discussions of the nature of God were rarely indulged in. He was, theoretically, an eternal, independent essence, or being, or spirit, infinite, all-understanding, loving, omnipotent, constant, truth-demanding, and faithful. As the Trinity is only one pure essence, all three Persons are co-equal and co-eternal. God's wisdom is the unseen harmony of all things, the "perfect platform" in his mind.[47] He wills himself directly according to the greatest good, governing and ordering all things so that Satan and his instruments, in seeking to cross the revealed will of God, really fulfill his secret will, to their own confusion.[48]

But this was only the God of direct definition. Although an honest effort was made not to reduce God to man's shallow comprehension of him, the ministers really created for their followers a far more finite Deity. The most common metaphor in the sermons is that of God or Christ as a King and King of Kings, to whom one owes implicit obedience, for whose reception one makes elaborate preparation, and whose very kindness to his unworthy people is royal condescension. This Creator is not only an arbitrary and supreme Ruler, who may seek to cure his people of their evil ways by sending them remedial, healthful suffering; when wearied, he is also likely to avenge his injured Majesty. Thomas Hooker could cry out in warning to England:

I will tell you we are a burthen to God, he cannot beare us, he will think his paines well over when he hath destroyed us.[49]

And the men of New England should bear no "secret grudge against any word or truth of God," for

if you doe, the Lord in stead of directing you, will delude you; and in stead

46 Samuel Whiting, *Abraham's Humble Intercession for Sodom* . . . (Cambridge, 1666), 74.
47 Thomas Shepard, *The First Principles of the Oracles of God* (London, 1648), 5.
48 John Davenport, *The Saints Anchor-hold, in all Storms and Tempests* . . . (London: Printed by W.L. for George Hurleck, 1661), 97.
49 Thomas Hooker, *The Danger of Desertion* (London: Printed by G. M. for George Edwards, 1641), 18.

of informing you, will besot you, and give you over to blind minds, and hard hearts.[50]

Repeatedly, the congregations were warned that God would leave them because of their declination from the rigid virtue of the first settlers; the frequent deaths among these first comers—who, in the normal course of events, were dying in the mid years of the century—were taken as signs that, as other men pack their plate before moving to a new place, God was taking his "Props and Pillars" before leaving New England's shores.[51]

This liberal employment of anthropomorphism and of anthropopathism obviously had its basis in Biblical usage. The ministers fully recognized that the God of the Bible had been given very human characteristics by transcribers and by translators. There were even things spoken of God which carry with them the appearance of evil, as in *Nehemiah* 9:37 or *Isaiah* 19:14; of course, the meaning in each case was that these events had happened with his operative or working permission. Again, certain lines in the Bible raised the question of God's will and his power. For example, the Reverend Urian Oakes, a distinguished scholar and president of Harvard, got into some difficulty while expatiating upon *Deuteronomy* 32:29. If God had wished the Israelites to be wise, as he said he did, why had he not willed accordingly, giving them wisdom? Oakes carefully explained that God is here speaking after the way of man; if the Deity had really willed that the Israelites should become wise, wisdom would have been conferred upon them.

But we must say, *cum toto theologorum Choro* (as judicious *Ames* speaks) that God in such forms of speech, that he may commodiously treat with man, both *induere se homine,* put on Man (as it were) or vest himself in the condition and properties of man, and propose his counsels to us in such a way wherein we may best apprehend them, and they may be most familiarized to us. . . . The great God in this *querimonicus* form of speaking resembles himself to a Father.[52]

This explanation of Biblical phraseology may or may not have

50 Thomas Hooker, *The Soules Effectuall Calling to Christ,* 56.

51 Eleazar Mather, *A Serious Exhortation* (Cambridge: Printed by S. G. and M. J. 1671), 8. The Reverend Eleazar Mather (1637-1661) was a son of Richard Mather.

52 Urian Oakes, *New England Pleaded With* . . . (Cambridge: Samuel Green, 1673), 6.

been completely clear to that general audience gathered to hear
the election sermon of 1673. But we can see that the ministers
realized that all descriptions of God and his dealings with man
were apt to result in anthropomorphic and anthropopathic expressions. The question remains whether the average man,
constantly hearing and reading this terminology, thought of God
more frequently as a benevolent First Cause than as a somewhat irate Father and King, who should not be offended too
often, lest he desert his family and people.

III

SUCCESS: THE PURITAN HIGH ROAD TO DAMNATION

Oddly enough, the very success of the church frightened the saints. From the beginning they could see that, spiritually, prosperity was more difficult to bear than adversity. And, considered from any material point of view, the church did thrive. For years, until 1665, no sect was able to found a permanent communion within the boundaries of the Bay, Plymouth, Connecticut, and New Haven colonies. All disturbers of the peace, all adverse critics, were silenced, apparently convinced of their errors and openly penitent; or they were driven back to England; or they were banished outside the limits of these colonies, frequently to New Hampshire or Rhode Island. Even the Quakers, gluttons for punishment though they might be, could not establish themselves for some years after their coming in 1656.

Week after week, all but the extremely wicked and profane (who were willing openly to break the law) were supposed to gather in the town church to hear at least two sermons on the Lord's day. No respectable family thought of staying away. Unless a man was willing to be branded as abnormally sinful, to be an outcast from society, he made an effort to go to church regularly on Sundays and to see that all the family and servants went there. The normal, lawful, and regular thing to do was to attend both the morning and afternoon Sabbath services; many also heard Thursday lectures, delivered either by their own teacher or minister or by some neighboring pastor whose church was within walking distance. Thus practically everyone listened to the preaching and conformed generally to the rules and customs of the church. Then, too, every man attending, from the most spiritual to the most mundane, hoped fervently to become a member of the church, to share in all the sacraments. Some sign that God had selected him to be saved would mean that he was of the elect: after death he was destined to bask in the Eternal Presence for all eternity; in the

meantime, earthly honors would come. For if a man could tes-
tify that he had had a definite religious experience which led
him to believe that he was one of God's chosen sons, then he
could have a vote in church affairs and take an active part in
the management of the colony.[1]

1

Instead of being gratified by the flourishing condition of
the churches, the ministers were reduced to a state of gloomy
apprehensiveness. This was true, first, because the very ascen-
dancy of the church tended to produce hypocrisy. The most
dangerous of all sins was always recognized to be that form of
"self-hypocrisy," of self-deceit, which permitted a man to be
dishonest with himself about the state of his soul—in other
words, to persuade himself that he had received the first signs
of saving grace. But the saints also had enough common sense
to realize that the outward pressure of their system might very
well lead to another and more palpable kind of hypocrisy. A
man need not conceal his individual sins; for these he would
be forgiven if he were indeed of the elect and if he made retri-
bution for his evil-doing. But a man might in the larger sense
play the hypocrite by claiming fellowship with the saints. Incidentally, nothing annoyed the ministers more than the charge
made in their own day, and repeatedly ever since, that the Puritans thought themselves free from sin. On the contrary, the
whole Calvinist doctrine taught them that man was innately
evil and that no complete sanctification could take place this
side of heaven. Inasmuch as all men, even the elect but much
more obviously the unelect, were sinful, what was more natural
than that the churches were harboring many imposters?

There were many of these "cursed Hypocrites" who lived
in the church, but had the form of godliness only. Even while

1 All freemen had to be church members, although not all church members
were freemen. In Massachusetts and New Haven only freemen could vote
for the governor, magistrates, and deputies; non-freemen who had taken the
oath of fidelity were given the right to vote in town affairs. In Connecticut,
too, all were to submit in larger affairs to the rule of the saints, but the
local franchise was given to the people, with the exception of women, servants, and apprentices and those convicted of scandalous crimes. Charles
M. Andrews, *The Colonial Period of American History* (New Haven: Yale
University Press, 1934), II, 104-107; Miller, *Orthodoxy in Massachusetts*, 243-
245.

the ministers had little hope that much could be done to make these erring souls see the truth, a good deal of harsh language was devoted to analyzing the various types of dissemblers in any congregation. There were the "wrangling hypocrites," to whom it was useless to reveal their duty, for, as Hooker sadly pointed out,

they will search farre and neere to make it no duty, they will rake the Divels skull, and invent some new shift to prove that it is not needfull to be done.[2]

Almost as annoying were the "whining hypocrites," who daily abused the Gospel and daily bemoaned their sin—"ever complaining, but never amending." Of the opposite sort were the "presumptuous hypocrites," content to rest upon their presumed faith and "make a drudge of Christ" instead of striving to be worthy of their Maker. All Familists might be so classified.[3] But even worse were the "vaineglorious hypocrites." They were willing to pray, to fast, to listen to sermons, to behave correctly in great matters and small—but always for their own sake, not for Christ's. Papists were of this number, but so were many New Englanders that had a chance to know better.

All these conscious hypocrites might, for what they could thereby gain, pretend to virtues they did not possess and so tear down the reputation of the churches. But far worse was the problem of the "self-hypocrites," men who deluded themselves into the belief that they were of the elect. The Reverend Thomas Shepard of Cambridge was especially concerned with the plight of those who allowed their desire for salvation to convince them that they could be certain of it.[4] While they were falsely thinking that they were of God's elect, their very over-

2 Thomas Hooker, "Spiritual Love and Joy," in *The Soules Implantation* (London: R. Young, 1637), 219-220.

3 Mrs. Anne Hutchinson and other Antinomian rebels against the church were accused of approaching Familism in their religious beliefs. *Vide Infra*, 50-51.

4 This fear was so frequently apparent in Shepard's preaching that the author of *Good News from New England* (London, 1648), in his list of the various varieties of preaching to be heard in the New World, identifies Shepard by this theme:
"One Sheppard he makes restlesse pains that none
 Themselves delude with happy state as one
Belov'd of God in Christ, and therefore makes
 Clear evidence from Gods word, whom he takes
And wholly bent to save his flock from tearing,
 With watchful eye 'way sheepslaying wolves is scaring."

confidence would betray them to the devil. Sermon after serman was devoted to this vital point: nothing could be more essential than that every man sincerely question himself and his
own honesty if he deemed that he need no longer pray for the
first signs of saving faith.

2

The prospering of the church might, then, lead many to
ride along with the tide, to assume a virtue they had not; but
the success of the church was also felt to have a detrimental
effect on many whose good intentions were not to be questioned.
Insincerity was not the only evil attendant upon success; New
England's sins, upon examination, proved to be many and yet
basically one. Paradoxically, even as many of the ministers
were fearing that the glory of the saints would lead to hypocrisy in lesser and less fortunate souls, these same preachers
were complaining that this glory was being rapidly diminished.
In want and misery, men turned to God as their only hope; in
prosperity and plenty, the same men, over-confident, begin to
feel that this success is the result of their own efforts and ability.
As St. Augustine had argued, Adam had fallen through pride
which had turned him from a humble man to an over-confident
one who put his faith in himself rather than in his Creator.
Still looking through St. Augustine's eyes, the ministers discovered that all man's forms of baseness had their source in this
pride or self-love, which was really a turning away from God.
Then, too, when adverse circumstances are alleviated, men cease
to think that spiritual values are all-important and that earthly
delights and pains are but transient and paltry. With renewed
interest in physical life comes indulgence of the body's desire
for pleasure. This pampering of self, any Puritan would say,
is but a short step to actual evil-doing.

Most of the earlier ministers believed that the key to the
good life is faith, not a rigid standard of behavior. Intellec-
tualists rather than moralists, they had either little heart for
or little need of describing in any detail the wayward paths that
men might follow. Thus, though there are fairly frequent
complaints that congregations seemed heavy and earth-bound
in spirit, only occasionally are adultery and drunkenness spe-

cifically attacked.[5] The emphasis, moreover, was not on the sin
or on the sinner, but on the offense to God. So Shepard always
stressed the idea that it is far worse to err in spirit or deed on
the Lord's Sabbath than on any week-day.[6] And Hooker gravely told his congregation that the smaller the amount involved
or the satisfaction gained, the greater the sin. Far worse to
cheat a housewife or child out of a few pence in change than to
engage in a large, nefarious scheme. Was it not more degrad-
ing to man and more insulting to God to break the sacred Covenant between God and man for a small temptation?[7] Following
the same line of reasoning, Hooker argued also that lukewarm-
ness in religion was baser than profaneness.

Such was the spirit of the first few years, but very soon
the cry went up, rising into a crescendo in the 1650's, 1660's,
and 1670's, that many were falling away, some even falling scan-
dalously. Each pastor seemed to fear sincerely that his flock
might fall into some particular pitfalls that he believed to be
most common. Always the older generation, either that of the
minister or of his father, was being put to shame by the vile
conduct of their sons. Formerly, good men had grown in this
land "by clusters." But the rising generation, as Richard Mather painfully and pathetically noted in 1657, had much ado to
avoid the common sins of adultery, fornication, lasciviousness,
drunkenness, profaneness, swearing, and scoffing at godliness.[8]
"God sifted a whole Nation that he might send choice grain into
this Wilderness,"[9] said the Reverend William Stoughton in an
effective and much quoted metaphor. But he went on to say
that a rapid and sad metamorphosis had taken place on New
England's shores. The rising generation was guilty, among other things, of worldliness, whoredoms, fornications, revellings,

5 *Cf.* Thomas Hooker's "A Godly and Profitable Serman, Of Gods Eternitie
   and Mans Humanitie. Or, The Stirring of the Lord with Sinners" (London,
   1639). In *Three Sermons* . . . (London: Printed by M. P. for John Stafford,
   1638).
6 Thomas Shepard, *Theses Sabbaticae Or, the Doctrine of the Sabbath* . . .
   (London: Printed by T. R. and E. M. for J. Rothwell, 1649), Part IV, 31-50.
7 Thomas Hooker, *The Application of Redemption. The Ninth and Tenth Books*
   . . . (London, 1656), 168-174.
8 Richard Mather, *A Farewel-Exhortation to the Church and People of Dorchester in New-England* . . . (Cambridge: Samuel Green, 1657), 14.
9 William Stoughton, *New Englands True Interests* . . . (Cambridge: S. G.
   and M. J., 1670), 19.

drunkenness, rudeness, degeneracy from good Christian manners, formality, and profaneness. In general, men were "sermon-proof and Ordinance-proof," always "itching after new
things and ways" and gradually drawing loose from the Yoke
of God.[10] In much the same way, the Reverend Samuel Torrey, of Weymouth, in 1674 contrasted the first spiritual prosperity and flourishing state of the churches with the later domi-
nance of the spirit of profaneness, of sensuality, of gainsaying
and rebellion, of libertinism, of carnality, formality, hypocrisy
and spiritual idolatry.[11]

Some ministers were not content to catalogue New England's faults, but saw them primarily as manifestations of the
fundamental weakness of a people who were no longer putting
their reliance on God and his particular servants, the clergy.
The Reverend Samuel Whiting, for instance, has the ordinary
list of the forms this wickedness took: he observed such evil
ways as excess in eating and drinking, fornication, unnatural un-
cleanness, abundance of idleness, neglect of the poor and needy,
and conversation about worldly matters. But the underlying
and chief sin that led to all the others was pride.[12] But some
men were not satisfied with this general Augustinian answer.
One gentler soul, the Reverend Thomas Walley of Barnstable,
described New Englanders as sick with various diseases which
included a lethargy (making them insensible of sin) and a burning fever (leading to contention in towns and churches); and,
dreadful to consider, nearly all men seemed possessed by the
Evil Spirit, so that oppression, cruelty, covetousness, error, de-
lusion, pride, and disobedience were rampant. As a sick person takes no comfort from society, refuses nourishing food,
loses his beauty, and soon dies, New England was suffering and
nearing its end—or so Walley reasoned.[13] Although Urian
Oakes also joined in this general complaint of the prevalent
profaneness, turbulent heresies, blasphemies, injustice and dis-

10. *Ibid.*, 19-20.
11   Samuel Torrey, *An Exhortation unto reformation* . . . (Cambridge: Marmaduke Johnson, 1674), 8-10.
12   Whiting, *Abraham's Humble Intercession for Sodom* . . . , 45-48; *cf.* Augustine,
De Civitate Dei, XIV. 13:
13   Thomas Walley, *Balm in Gilead to Heal Sions Wounds: Or, A Treatise wherein
there is a clear Discovery of the most Prevailing Sicknesses of New England*
. . . (Cambridge: S. G., 1669), 5-14.

orders of the times, he thought the worst part of the degeneracy took the form of "a great Disaffection to the ministers of Christ."[14] This same root of the evil had been pointed out as early as 1655 by Charles Chauncy, who thought New England needed sharp reproof for not being more grateful to the ministry; he noted, too, that this abuse of the faithful pastors was accompanied by a general contempt of God's Word and ordinances, by a growing habit of listening to lying books and pamphlets that were being brought into the country, by a spirit of covetousness in many, and by the accompanying oppression of the poor, who could scarcely buy any commodity but for silver.[15]

Despite these grim accusations, the picture so far, in a sense, is not entirely discouraging. The ministers seem sincere and seem to be standing on high moral ground. While their language is harsh and plain, based as it often is on Biblical phraseology, they appear to be speaking only to arouse their congregations to avoid sin and to be charitable to the poor. But a closer examination of the sermons of the 1670's suggests a gradual debasement in the ministers themselves, which may or may not be a reflection of change in the community. The emphasis was more and more upon the dire results of God's displeasure with his people if they were not good. A "be good in order to avoid punishment" theme ran more and more prominently through all pleas for righteousness; and the fear grew that the penalty of wrongdoing would have to be paid on earth by all New England, not by individuals in hell. The lowered idealism of the preacher (and presumably of his congregation) is apparent in the Reverend Samuel Hooker's characteristic appeal:

O how would a soaking shower of righteousness settle our shaking times, repair our losses and restore the years which the Caterpillars, the Sword, and the Mildew have taken from us.[16]

And Samuel Hooker was far from being alone in his utilitari-

---

14 Urian Oakes, *The Unconquerable, All-Conquering & more-then-Conquering Souldier: Or, the successful Warre which a Believer Wageth with the Enemies of his Soul* . . . (Cambridge: Samuel Green, 1674), 33.
15 Charles Chauncy, *Gods Mercy, Shewed to His People in Giving Them a Faithful Ministry* . . . (Cambridge: Samuel Green, 1655), 19-20.
16 Samuel Hooker, *Righteousness Rained from Heaven* . . . (Cambridge: Samuel Green, 1677), 13. This passage is based on *Amos* 4:9-10. A similar example of the primitive theology of Israel is to be found in II *Samuel* 21:1-14, in which passage famine is regarded as the punishment of sin.

anism. In practically the same language Samuel Danforth
pleads with his listeners to reform so that the calamities of recent years would cease." Even more indicative of a change in
taste, if not of morals, are Danforth's lengthy analyses and
definitions in another of his sermons of all types of sin,[18] for the
reader cannot avoid the suspicion that all this bleak evil is being mouthed with enjoyment. Then, too, not content with dwelling on the various forms sin was taking or could take in the
once virtuous colonies, the ministers were quick to adduce other
evidence that God was threatening to desert his erring people.
Repeatedly the congregations were warned that there were undeniable signs that God was about to leave them. The death of
each man of prominence, especially of each minister, was given
a double significance: the demise of an able leader was not only
the strongest sort of suggestion of God's wrath upon evil-doing,
but it also indicated that God was taking his own to safety before letting his full anger descend on his erring people.

3

The gravest menace to the spiritual well-being of the saints
came, moreover, in a third way from the success of the church.
Religious concord had been one of the dearest aspirations of the
emigrants from factious England to this hoped-for Eden of
New England, and all were sadly disappointed to see their dream
vanish almost upon their landing. Persecution had brought
these colonists together, for common misfortune ties close bonds.
But, as the Puritans well knew, the experience of the world has
been that, if the danger be removed, many will follow their
own paths again, gradually wandering away from their former companions. If you threaten a man's right to do something, to believe some doctrine, to practise some way of life,
that man will devote all his energies to the pursuit of the for-
bidden. He will do at any cost what he wants to do and what
he believes right; furthermore, he will do his best to convert
his neighbors to his point of view. Once the pressure of persecution is taken away, a man will relax his efforts; given freely

17 Samuel Danforth, *A Brief Recognition of New Englands Errand into the
Wilderness* . . . (Cambridge S. G. and M. S., 1671), 10-20.
18 Danforth, *The Cry of Sodom Enquired Into: Upon Occasion of the Arraignment and Condemnation of Benjamin Goad* . . . .

what he wants, after a while he may not bother to avail himself of his opportunity. The Puritans had good reason to fear that the forced unity of their first years in the wilderness would rapidly crumble to pieces. Unless a concerted effort was made, not only would one church differ from another, but the members of any one church would also be in constant disharmony. Even more appalling was the thought that soon men would not care, that gradually the Satanic acceptance of tolerance would be wide-spread.

Although the first ministers—Cotton, Hooker, Shepard—spoke in hearty terms against the whole idea of toleration,[19] they saw the somewhat embarrassing position that such a stand put them in. It seemed as if the persecuted had but waited their opportunity to become the persecutor. Naturally, these New England Puritans also saw and were quick to point out the opposite side of the picture. First of all, they thought they had found (or rather, rediscovered) the essential Truth, which had been established in America. Why then allow anyone to wander from that rule? True, the first Protestant reformers had broken off from an established church which believed itself to be the only true church. But this parallelism was only specious, according to the Puritans, since their church was founded directly on God's revealed Word and the practices of the Roman church could not be authenticated by the Bible. It was also true that the New Englanders and their fellow-nonconformists at home were in disagreement with the controlling party in the Church of England, a party which also believed itself to be justified in persecuting those in disagreement with its practices. The Puritans, however, did not see themselves as disrupting the church, but as eventually restoring it to its pristine purity.

In spite of the fact that the preachers by this logic could justify their refusal to permit any sects to form communions in New England, one difficulty still remained: even the most sincere men, ardently believing that the individual's life and the church's organization should be based solely on Biblical teaching, might very well differ on the interpretation of certain passages. It was fully recognized that any man, even a minister,

19 If Roger Williams' sermons had been printed, they might offer an interesting and contrasting viewpoint on this subject.

might be mistaken in the sense of God's word, for the human mind is weak and the understanding frail. Only heretics, Papists, Familists, Anabaptists, and the like held to their beliefs against all counsel. The essential point to be remembered constantly was that a man should take cognizance only of such contrary views as had their origin in the Bible. Thomas Hooker says:

When a man is persuaded, that the opinion, or course he takes up is such, as God himselfe hath been pleased to make known unto him out of his Word: he is to receive nothing against this, but meerly out of the Word: let nothing unsettle our judgement in a plain and revealed truth, but onely hold to that: As I have been settled by the truth, so if ever I change my opinion, the truth is that which shall reform me; all the counsell I take up, and all the opinions I hold, shall be such as the Word of God shall reveal to mee.[20]

From the general tenor of the early sermons, it is plain that the ministers hoped that these impediments to complete conformity and accord would be transitory. Every one thought that each difficulty, if approached with humility and faith, could be resolved and finally done away with. It took some years for the preachers to acknowledge that men's judgments might continue to differ even after the most painstaking attempts had been made to agree upon the true meaning of knotty Scripture passages. A "boundless Toleration" remained intolerable: men could not be permitted to promulgate error concerning fundamental points; no one could openly deny Christ or the Word of God or the doctrine of Eternal Election.[21] "God never appointed a Sanctuary for Satan, nor a City of Refuge for presumptuous offenders."[22] Soon, however, contemporary with the change of feeling in England after the Restoration, "a well-bounded Toleration" was found to be desirable in all Christian communities; of course, neither blasphemy nor idolatry was to be allowed. On the other hand, if a man agreed with the general thought in larger things and did not attempt to infringe upon

20 Thomas Hooker, "Wisdomes Attendants: or the Voice of Christ to be obeyed . . ." in *The Saints Dignitie and Dutie* . . . (London: G. D. for Francis Eglesfield, 1651), 132.
21 Samuel Arnold, *David Serving his Generation, or A Discourse Wherein is shewed that, the great Care and Endeavor of every Christian ought to be, that he may be Serviceable unto God and to the present generation* . . . (Cambridge: Samuel Green, 1674), 16.
22 Hubbard, *The Happiness of a People in the Wisdome of their Rulers Directing And in the Obedience of their Brethren* . . . 39.

the just liberties of others, he might be allowed to differ in lesser things. Although man ought to contend for these lesser truths, truth never gained ground by a violent opposition to smaller errors.[23] This seems to be a fairly liberal policy, but it is noticeable that no essay was made to define just what were the permissible variations from the pattern set by the majority, and there was a decided feeling that the colonies, from their weakness, could not in self-defense permit the freedom that stronger states could safely sanction.[24]

4

While the church, ably aided as it was by civil authorities, kept firm control of the situation, it was not untroubled by an increasing number of men and women who wished to wander unpardonably far from its tenets. The Puritans' difficulties with the Quakers in the late 1650's and early 1660's have been much discussed, but as a matter of fact the determined martyrs of the Society of Friends were far from being the first or the only faction to disturb New England fellowship. Roger Williams was accused, among all his other errors, of being one of a sect who denied the validity of infant baptism. In a few more years Baptist influences were seen to be growing stronger and breaking out occasionally—once with the Reverend Obadiah Holmes as a spectacular martyr, again with prominent Henry Dunster, president of Harvard College, charged with Antipaedobaptism. However dangerous this Anabaptism might be felt to be to the continued welfare of the church, it was not anti-Calvinistic in its essence, and the ministers consequently did not fear this schism as much as they dreaded two other types of wrong-thinking, both of which they felt banished reason from religion. If a sinner put too much stress on faith, too little on reasoned obedience to the law, he was guilty of Antinomianism. Anne Hutchinson, John Wheelwright, Samuel Gorton, the Quakers were all accused of being under the influence of Antinomian thought; indeed, according to Thomas Shepard, the Antinomianism of Mrs. Hutchinson and her brother-in-law, the

23 Walley, *Balm in Gilead To Heal Sions Wounds* . . . , 15. Hubbard makes the same point in *The Happiness of a People*, 31, 40-41.
24 Hubbard, *The Happiness of a People*, 38-39; Stoughton, *New Englands True Interests*, 35.

Reverend John Wheelwright, came dangerously near the even more detested heresy of Familism. As Familists, the unfortunate pair would have been guilty of over-emphasizing love at the expense of doctrinal faith, and of accepting spiritual rather than literal interpretations of Biblical texts. A little later, a more persistent disturber of the peace, Samuel Gorton, was also charged with Familism.

But there was always the threat of the second type of wrong-thinking: if the sinner put his stress on works rather than on faith, a way of thinking which would lead him to believe in conditional election, not absolute predestination, then he had fallen into Arminianism. This heresy did not break out sporadically and spectacularly, as did Antinomianism. Nevertheless, Arminianism was felt to be the greatest danger of all, as it was a step toward Romanism. And most of the ministers, especially the first English-bred ones, would interrupt their own diatribes against Antinomianism for bitter denunciations of "Papist" thought and methods. For example, Thomas Shepard devoted his Thursday lecture-sermons for four years, 1636-40, to an elaboration of the parable of the Ten Virgins. The complete series had as its purpose Shepard's wholehearted endeavor to keep his parishioners from straying into Antinomianism or Arminianism. Now the interesting point is that, although the series was given during the years of great contention and controversy which followed Mrs. Hutchinson's Antinomian outbreak, Shepard reserves his most bitter and constant attack for "Papist" thought. Not only does he complain of "the dust raised" by popish interpreters of the parable, but he also tells his listeners that it was Rome's curse to be made "an habitation of devils" and that Jesuit attempts were constantly being made to bring all the world under "the hellish bondage and blind obedience of the See of Rome." Repeatedly he objurgates the "popish pack" "whose inventions smell above ground here" and whose plan it is to conquer religion by subtlety, that is, by causing dissension."[25]

As Arminianism always seemed to strict Calvinists dangerously close to Catholicism, Shepard was not the only minister

25 Thomas Shepard, *The Parable of the Ten Virgins* (London, 1660), *passim.*

to insert into his sermons denunciations of Romanism. Most of the early ministers kept this inbred habit,[26] undoubtedly a survival of their English days, for the next generation of preachers realized that the immediate danger of corruption by Rome was slight. But to the clergy educated in England the danger was real, perhaps because they were more aware of the complicated political and religious home situation with all its possibilities for plots and sub-plots. John Wheelwright, for example, at the time of the Antinomian difficulties preached a famous sermon for which he was censored because it was inflammatory in tone, rather than conciliatory. While he may have been directing his criticism toward those members of the community who were tending toward Arminianism, some of his most stinging remarks were kept for the Antichrist at Rome.[27] With similar virulence, Thomas Hooker uses the Gunpowder Plot as justification for a tirade against popish malice and methods;[28] elsewhere he speaks caustically of the papist "dreame" of purgatory as a money-making scheme.[29] But it is the Jesuits who arouse him to one of his most scathing denunciations:

The Brain of the Jesuits is the Womb that bore it, and their Forgery gave it its first being; a Brat of their Brain, a Conceit which they have Forged and anvilled out of the Froth of their own imagination. . . .[30]

Most of the ministers contented themselves with these sporadic accusations against particular Catholic doctrines and actions, but John Cotton, not content with this general practice, devoted at least two courses of week-day sermons to a very thorough arraignment of Romanism. In his discussion of his texts, from the thirteenth and sixteenth chapters of *Revelation,* while ostensibly using Luther's continuous-historical interpre-

---

26 Although the Puritans seem to have been particularly virulent in their anti-Catholicism, early Protestants of all denominations shared a general policy of contemptuous abuse of the "Antichrist" of Rome. *Cf.* Sister Mary Augustina (Ray), B.V.M., *American Opinion of Roman Catholicism in the Eighteenth Century* (New York: Columbia University Press, 1936), Chapter I, "The English Tradition to 1688," and 100-105 (for early American Baptist and Quaker condemnations of popery).

27 *John Wheelwright, His Writings, including his Fast-Day Sermon, 1637 . . .* (Boston: Printed for the Prince Society, 1876), 170, 175, *et alii.* (There was no contemporary printing of this sermon, which survived in two manuscripts.)

28 Thomas Hooker, *Foure learned and Godly Treatises* (London, 1638), 119 *et seq.*

29 Thomas Hooker, *The Unbeleevers preparing for Christ* (London, 1638), 164.

30 Thomas Hooker, *The Application of Redemption* (London, 1657), 415-416.

tation which embraces the important conditions and movements
in the history of the church and world from the writer's age to
the end of time, he was perhaps most interested in his own times
and those immediately preceding. Like all Protestant writers
of his day, he read into both chapters antipapal warnings. The
first beast (*Revelation* 13:1) is the Roman Catholic visible
church, the second beast (*Revelation* 13:11) is the pope in both
his spiritual and temporal dealings, and the dragon (*Revelation*
13:4) is Satan.[31] An ironical discussion of the great powers
which the devil gave the pope affords Cotton the opportunity to
criticize the Catholics on a great many widely divergent points:
their acceptance of the Apocrypha, their monastic practices,
their sale of indulgences, their interference in temporal matters to cause disloyalty, and their pretension to the power to
get people into heaven and out of purgatory and to ease the
torments of hell.[32] With similar energy the preacher expounds
the seven "vials of wrath" of the sixteenth chapter of *Revelation*
to be directed against Catholics in general (the earth), the
Catholic church (the sea), the priests (rivers and fountains),
the Emperor of Austria and the Pope (the sun), the episcopate,
the church, and government of England (the throne of the
beast), the corruption of Rome and of Turkey (the Euphrates),
and the "ignorant smoke of Rome" (the air).[33] In all this vitu-
peration Cotton shows that he had read Brightman's lengthy
explanation of *Revelation*[34] and had got not a little of his strained
allegory from it; but the New Englander is far more daring in
his attack on the English church and government. He is also
more fanatical, again and again allowing his zeal to conquer his
humanity and reason; for example, he argues in complete seri-
ousness that all Catholics should be immediately put to death as
they sin in the light of their own conscience.[35] His habit of

31 John Cotton, *An Exposition Upon The Thirteenth Chapter of the Revelation*
(London: Printed by M. S. for Lovewel Chapman, 1655), 1-23.
32 *Ibid.*, 23-24.
33 John Cotton, *The Powring Out of The Seven Vials: Or An Exposition, Of
The 16. Chapter of the Revelation, with an Application of it to our Times* . . .
(London: Printed for R. S., 1642).
34 Thomas Brightman, *A Revelation of the Revelation that is. The Revelation
of St. John opened clearely with a logicall Resolution and Exposition* (Amsterdam, 1615). A second edition was published the following year. Cotton
refers a number of times to "Holy Brightman."
35 Cotton, *The Powring Out of The Seven Vials*, 16-17.

opprobrious reiteration when other arguments failed him may be briefly seen in this typical passage:

> And yet is not this a great word and a great blasphemy, for the mother of Harlots to hold forth her selfe as the only immaculate Spouse of Christ upon the face of the Earth? Is not this a grand word for a common Harlot, the mother of Harlots, the lewdest Harlot that ever the earth bore, for her to arrogate this stile as the only Church of Christ?[66]

From all these fears—of hypocrisy, of carnal sinning, of toleration, of Catholicism—which motivated so much of the preaching, we can judge that a good part of the frequently discussed Puritan gloominess of spirit was not caused by constant or immediate dread of hell-fire. The Puritan was going to fight the good fight vigorously until the end; the elect were safe, and their grief was not for themselves. But an amazingly short time after the settling of their hoped-for Utopia in the New World, the ministers were well agreed that the original spirit of New England was rapidly deteriorating and that this general decadence was clearly manifested in her carnal and spiritual sins, the most detested of which was the growing spirit of tolerance. What, of course, they could not see was that one preconceived and fixed idea was warping their judgment; in fact, these fears were merely forms of this one idea. If ever men faced backward, these ministers did—the best had been, nothing in the present or future could equal the past. This was the accepted belief of most conservative people of the time, and the idea was simply more emphasized in men who devoted themselves to reading the Bible. Man in the beginning had been made good, and then he had sinned or broken covenant with God. The weaknesses of subsequent generations were certainly dwelt upon in the Bible, especially in the Old Testament. It was not, then, such a far step to the general notion that earlier generations of men were better than later.

Classical antiquity could not be worshipped by the Puritans, for plainly the great writers of old were not Christians; the church fathers had to be approached cautiously, for surely in their teachings they had more than once gone beyond the Bible.

36 Cotton, *An Exposition Upon The Thirteenth Chapter of the Revelation*, 65.

With concentrated fervor, the Puritans looked for satisfactory heroes. Sixteenth-century Protestants, known by their voluminous publications and also by personal reputation to the first generation of New Englanders, were naturally thought to be better Christians and scholars than the seventeenth century was producing. According to the same trend of mind, the first mature colonists who came to New England were better men than their sons. Both points could be easily proved by preachers who, always recalling the dicta of the Bible, eyed with filial deference the virtues of their fathers, and with parental sternness the sins of their sons. Unfortunately, there was something pecularily depressing in this rapid and apparently visible declination of human nature. If they could have admitted the superiority of the great thinkers of classical antiquity, if they could have believed in the complete authenticity of the teachings of the church fathers and the great medieval Christian leaders, then the old decay-of-nature theory might have consoled them with the reflection that no one is responsible for having been born in a worn-down world.[37] But the Puritan, unsolaced by any theory which shifted the blame from himself, had to face the bitter and discouraging conclusion that never, even in his maturity, strive as he might, did he equal his own father in wisdom or spirituality. Even if the men of each rising generation were not hypocrites, deceiving themselves or their neighbors, they were apparently more and more prone to carnal sin; finally weary at last of men who broke their covenant with him, God would desert his chosen people for other shores.

According to this same belief, the original Christian church, inspired by Christ and his Apostles, had at first been better in spirit and doctrine than all subsequent churches. The first churches in New England had been patterned as closely as possible after the suggestions in the New Testament and had been fashioned by better men than their successors could hope to be. Therefore, toleration, which carried with it the constant threat of change, was the permission and encouragement of sin; for any wandering away from the original dogma was sinful, so

---

[37] For an interesting discussion of the prevalence among non-Puritans of the decay-of-nature theory, see Richard Foster Jones' *Ancients and Moderns* (St. Louis, 1936), 23 ff.

sinful that the influence of Catholicism must be suspected. The
Roman Catholics had succeeded once in corrupting Christ's
church and in robbing it of its true-hearted simplicity. Naturally, the machinations of these allies of the devil were always to be hated and guarded against.

It was fear, then, not of ultimate damnation, but of the
day-by-day spiritual degeneration of man which lent fire to the
preaching of the period. Never once, in any printed sermon,
is there any hope expressed that changes may be for the better
or that life may be improving; the early ministers of New England, raising their eyes from the Bible only to see the sins of
their people, were never touched by the awakening idea of progress that was stirring minds in England and America throughout the century. Even the realization of their dearest dreams,
the success of the church, so well earned by the countless sacrifices of emigration to a new land, seemed calamitous, as the natural relaxation after accomplishment showed itself in a looser
morality and a growing tolerance.

5

What, then, was the solution to all these difficulties which
the saints faced? What cure could the ministers offer to sinful
New England, so rapidly slipping into a moral slough? The
answer was the good old one: have faith in God. Man must
be humble; he must shift his thoughts and confidence from himself to his Creator. As he reconsiders his past and present life,
he must repent his many sins. Important as these steps to heav-
en were, the emphasis was always upon faith as man's comfort
and soul-saver.

One dramme of faith is worth a hundred thousand worlds to a weary burthened soule.[38]

And why should not man have faith in a God who is infinite,
merciful, generous, and wise? In order to appreciate God's
mercy, man has but to remember that some are saved, although
all deserve damnation. Let him note who are saved. Poor and
rich, simpleton and scholar may be chosen—worldly condition
and intellectual ability mean nothing to this merciful God. Let

38 Hooker, *The Soules Implantation*, 12.

man note what God has generously given unworthy man as a world: a marvelous creation, with seasons and days; oceans with ebbing and flowing tides; in the waters fish in due seasons and on land corn, flowers, grass, herbs, and fruit; in the earth ore and jewels. From the very "frame and fabricke" of this stupendous work can be seen the Creator's wisdom and power.[39]

Man's faith manifests itself in love, not only love of God and Christ, but also love of fellowmen. Although it is always to be remembered that "Love is the sinewes of society,"[40] man cannot love his neighbor as much as himself. But then God never commands his people to do the impossible. The Bible merely tells man to love his neighbor *as* himself—that is, with the same protective, diligent love. Of course, a good man loves his brother's soul more than his own life. And if God is honored more by your brother than by yourself, then you must be willing to lay down your life for that brother.[41]

The man of faith and love is also the man of prayer. Theoretically every Puritan acknowledged the subjective value of prayer as a spiritually elevating exercise:

The work of Prayer is not to move or remove God, he is in one mind, he is still the same; but to move or remove our hearts neer to the Lord; and then we have prayed to purpose, when by Prayer our hearts and spirits are in a more celestial frame; . . .[42]

Prayer, accordingly, is the golden key to comfort, peace, and assurance, having its value in its effect upon our own souls. Naturally, this philosophical evaluation of prayer was rarely recalled. Usually the efficacy of prayer was considered more objectively:

Now Prayers are the Soules Ambassadors, that are sent to Heaven to negotiate great things with God for us, and they will do what they are sent about.[43]

39 Thomas Hooker, *The Immortality of the Soule: The Excellencie of Christ Jesus, Treated on* . . . (London, 1646), 19; *The Unbeleevers preparing for Christ*, 87; *et alii*.

40 Thomas Hooker, *The Paterne of Perfection: Exhibited in Gods Image on Adam: and Gods Covenant made with him* . . . (London: R. Y. and F. Clifton, 1640), 104.

41 *Ibid.*, 86-102.

42 Thomas Cobbett, *A Practical Discourse of Prayer* . . . (London: Printed by T. M. for Joseph Cranford, 1654), 6.

43 Whiting, *Abraham's Humble Intercession for Sodom* . . . , 14.

For this success, supplications obviously had to be made with faith in God's Almightiness and with due humility, as man was but a vile beggar asking much from God's excellency. After a saint had determined that his request was reasonable, importunity in pleading was desirable — man could not ask too often, in too great variety, or with too much holy eloquence. Although wise men prayed constantly, they also made special use of moments when the Lord might be looking at them with a softened gaze:

And when we have been doing for God, if we take advantage of time and of our hearts to speak to him, he will be doing for us; if we give anything to him, he will assuredly give us something that is better if we ask it.[44]

The constant stream of prayer that man should send to God did not need to be vocal; man could silently lift up his heart to his maker, and such "short turnes with God and Jesus Christ"[45] ought to be frequent. In time of trouble or temptation, however, man usually made use of short ejaculatory apostrophes to God. Public or church prayer was held at more stated times— on the Sabbath or on days of special services. Family prayer also was regular: morning and night the master of the family (or the most able substitute or a particularly holy guest) heard the confessions of members of the household and led the group in prayer. On the other hand, closet prayer—the individual, unostentatious, private appeal of man to his Creator—could be fitted into man's daily work at all opportune times.

If most of this praying was for God's intercession to help his chosen people out of their difficulties, it was also the saints' duty to pray against the enemies of God and of his elect. Subconsciously aware that by this practice they were dropping from the higher idealism of their faith, the ministers frequently justified these unchristian prayers of imprecation by the numerous anathemas in the Psalms, and congregations were warned not to delight in such prayers and not to direct them against particular people.

Considered spiritually, then, the community's problem of reform and the individual's problem of salvation had the same

44 Cobbett, *A Practical Discourse of Prayer*, 219.
45 *Ibid.*, 45.

constant, triplicate solution—faith, love, and prayer. Only occasionally did the ministers offer more practical advice to their listeners. While the saints had to be willing to make any sacrifices in this world for the next one, they were not supposed to offer their otherworldly interests as an excuse for neglecting their work here. Let each man do his task, urged Jonathan Mitchell, and do it quickly, thoroughly, whole-heartedly.[46] Samuel Whiting went beyond this good counsel of labor. He pleaded that men be not only energetic in their daily work, but also honest. There had been, as a matter of fact, so much unjust dealing in trade, so much promise-breaking, that from one of New England's own pulpits had come the amazing accusation:

New England hath many godly men in it, but but a few honest.[47]

The unnamed and courageous preacher was correct enough in one sense, as Whiting sadly admitted, but there could be no true godliness without common honesty.

But whether the solution to New England's problems was to be found in a spiritual turning to God or in a moral industriousness and honesty, there was one necessary means to the end, and that was a powerful ministry.[48] And by a "powerful ministry" was meant men of courage, willing to speak the truth to their congregations and unwilling to flatter them. Insincere preachers, speaking from their heads only, touched the ear only with generalities; true preachers spoke from their own hearts to the hearts of listening sinners—and the message was the unvarnished word of God, the holy hatred of sin.

46 Mitchell, *A Discourse of Glory*, 256.
47 As quoted in Whiting's *Abraham's Humble Intercession for Sodom*, 107.
48 Hooker, *The Soules Implantation*, 58-70.

IV

PRACTICAL TEACHING: POLITICS AND WAR

As the Puritans believed that even the smaller details of life could be established and governed by consulting the Bible, in all probability the preaching contained not a few practical interpretations of various Scripture lines that were applicable to daily life. Some remnants of this social comment have survived. Shepard, for instance, at one time examined at considerable length the sanctification of, or the right way to keep, the Sabbath.[1] The discussion is surprisingly liberal in tone. All necessary cooking may be done in order that people and animals may be comfortable; of course, wherever possible, all labor should be reserved for other days of the week. One unbreakable rule is that nothing should be done on the Sabbath for profit, and in all ways the spirit of holiness should be kept. On another occasion, Shepard censured the way artillery drills were being conducted—the men came when they wanted and did their work carelessly, though the officers were wont to "speak, charge, cry, yea, strike sometimes." Shepard gives a double reason why all church members ought to reform immediately and be an example to the rest: as Englishmen they ought to endeavor to be perfect in the art of military tactics and as Christians they ought to be more than ready to defend Christ's churches and servants.[2]

With less dignity, a number of ministers inveighed against the fashions of the day, a favorite subject for pulpit invective down through the ages.[3] Even the Reverend John Eliot took his mind off converting the Indians and establishing the perfect commonwealth in order to censure the wearing of long hair and wigs.[4] Another man whose thoughts one might think to have been on more vital problems was Thomas Hooker, the

1 Shepard, "The Sanctification of the Sabbath" in *Theses Sabbaticae*, 31-50.
2 Thomas Shepard, *Subjection to Christ* (London, 1652), 121-122.
3 *Cf.* G. R. Owst, *Literature and Pulpit in Medieval England* (Cambridge, 1933), Chapter VII; *Preaching in Medieval England* (Cambridge, 1926), 94.
4 J. Eliot, *The Historical Account of John Eliot*, in Massachusetts Historical Society *Proceedings*, 1st series, VIII, 27.

founder of Hartford.   Nevertheless, he at least twice attacked
the would-be stylish members of his congregation, with their
long hair, "loose locks," and fashionable clothes.   Furiously he
cries out for them to abandon these fashions and to let "God
dispose" of their clothes and hair—or afterwards they would
"fry and roar in the fashion."[5]   Chauncy, too, has an extended
argument against long hair.   No quoting of the Nazarites' being commanded to nourish their hair is going to satisfy him, as
he is convinced that modern people, supposedly living under the
rule of the New Testament, let their hair grow "out of pride,
vainglory, effeminacy, and the like sinful motive, and for sin-
ister ends."   Anyway, for a man to have long hair is to brand
him as having "correspondency with ruffians & swaggerers &
cavaliers yea the vilest persons in the country, yea Indians &
Pagans."[6]   A little later hair drops out of the discussion, but
the attack was still directed against the over-fashionable.   Danforth in 1670 speaks of "gorgeous attire" and "pomp in Wilderness" as signs of the degeneracy of the times.[7]   Hubbard about
the same time complains of the "effeminate childish pride in
habit and attire" that he sees before him; and he expresses additional contempt for those men and women who were dress-
ing out of their class—the peasant trying to equal a prince, the
maid vying in display of finery with her mistress.[8]

While such passages are amusing to later readers, they are
far from typical of the surviving sermons, which were printed
to help the heaven-bent, rather than to reprove the worldly.   Indeed, tirades or withering comments of this nature are surprisingly infrequent.   Apparently the ministers, in their calmer
good sense, followed their own creed: no one was going to hell
or heaven because of his haircut, although that haircut might
be indicative of the direction in which he was bent.   A man's
salvation depended on humiliation and faith, plus God's will.
These were, at best, perplexing subjects for any human being
to comprehend, and reading and re-reading of sermons dealing
with these weighty problems would help clear troubled minds.

5 Thomas Hooker, *The Soules Humiliation* (London, 1637), 164-165; also *The
    Application of Redemption*, 310.
6 Chauncy, *Gods Mercy*, 24-28.
7 Danforth, *A Brief Recognition of New Englands Errand* . . . , 17.
8 Hubbard, *The Happiness of a People*, 56.

The question of women's fashions and men's hair-dress was relatively trivial—easily disposed of by a few searing remarks.

Economic problems formed another pulpit topic that seldom found its way into print. How much of this type of discussion there was remains doubtful, but at least one preacher, the Reverend Hugh Peter, used his sermons for this purpose. It is to be noted that these discourses were not published, although Governor Winthrop, always an admirer of Peter's public spirit, considered their content important enough to enter it in his *Journal*—incidentally, without the Biblical proof of the points involved. According to Winthrop's account, Peter, while preaching in Boston and Salem during November, 1635, urged the settlers "to raise a stock for fishing," so that they would be independent and no longer at the mercy of the seamen.[9] By the next spring, energetic Peter had a new list of proposals for the improvement of the religious and economic interests of Massachusetts; the most surprising suggestion was that something be done to secure employment during the long winters for everyone, and most particularly for women and children, as he feared that so much idleness would be the ruin of church and commonwealth.[10] Again in February of 1641 Peter was demonstrating his "singular activity for all occasions" by trying to promote the building of ships.[11]

Not only Peter responded with good advice to the emergencies of the times; Winthrop also reports Cotton as devoting at least one sermon to the ethics of trade. It seems that in November of 1639 one Mr. Robert Keayne was fined for overcharging in some business deals. As Keayne was a prominent citizen, a connection of Governor Dudley, and a brother-in-law of the Reverend John Wilson, this judgment must have caused considerable comment. Therefore, on the next lecture day after sentence had been pronounced, Cotton endeavored to explain the rules of fair trading. A man may not sell above the current price—that is, such a price as is usual in the time and place and such a price as another customer who knows the worth of the commodity would give for it. In other words, a man may not

9 Winthrop, *Journal*, under date of November 26, 1635, I, 165.
10 *Ibid.*, under date of May 15, 1636, I, 179-180.
11 *Ibid.*, under date of December, 1640, II, 20.

sell as dear as he could, nor buy as cheap as he could; and he may not take advantage of another's ignorance or necessity. Secondly, if a man lose some of his merchandise by casualty of the sea or other calamity, he may not make good the loss by raising the price of the rest; to do so would be to refuse to accept the judgment of providence. On the other hand, if a commodity is scarce, the price of it may be raised, because now it is the hand of God upon the commodity and not upon the person dealing in it. Thirdly, if a man pays too much for any goods, he must accept his loss, which would be due to his own want of skill; to raise the price in re-selling would be making another pay for his fault. Fourthly, a man may not ask more for his commodity than his usual selling price, even if time is allowed for payment.[12]

If such interesting ideas as these were not deemed worthy of print, political discussion was another matter and held to be on a decidedly higher level. In the seventeenth century no man separated his religion from his politics; the two were closely bound together, with the adherents of each creed trying to fashion the government after their own beliefs. As a result of this policy, the status of any church was more or less at the mercy of whatever party was in control of the government. This conception of the mutual dependence of church and state obtained particularly in the colonies, which were virtually theocracies. Then, too, the very survival of these comparatively weak settlements in the New World was a problem which could not be ignored by men who fully realized that the controlling powers in England, even under the Commonwealth and much less under the crown, were never in complete sympathy with the ideas of the colonists. The ministers early met the challenge by trying to inform their congregations about the proper way to react to emergencies and about the political privileges and duties of those most fortunate of men, New Englanders. For example, in the hard winter of 1621 the newly settled colony at Plymouth

12 Winthrop, *Journal*, under date of November, 1639, I, 317-318. In this sermon Cotton evidently was following Luther's arguments in his *Long Sermon on Usury* (1520) and his tract *On Trade and Usury* (1524), perhaps as they had been reiterated in William Ames' influential manual *De Conscientia et eius iure vel casibus libri quinque* (1631), Bk. V, Chaps. xliii, xliv. *Cf.* R. H. Tawney's *Religion and the Rise of Capitalism* ... (New York: Harcourt, Brace and Co., 1926), 94, 126-131, 216-217.

was having its difficulties. The Pilgrims were struggling to pay off their debt to the English company which had financed their adventure; in order to do so, they had pledged themselves to put the fruits of their industry into a community store of assets. As a result, some men toiled, while others lazily mocked at them, for all would share alike the benefits of their diligence. Furthermore, because all were not willing to participate in the struggle, the colony was in danger of collapsing through want of commodities. Elder Cushman, preaching on the text "Let no man seek his own, but every man anothers wealth,"[13] begged for cooperation and charity. Every man should work, should accept with good grace the available coarse fare, and should be willing to share his bed, suit, and food with his less fortunate neighbor. No one must be forced to beg, lest he lose his "majesty," the image of God; society must offer him the necessities of life. Although Cushman himself thought the community life ideal, he did not urge it on religious or ethical grounds. His argument was purely practical; the time had not yet come to give individuals their portions and to let each family shift for itself; the colony must be given a fair chance—

And as you are a body together, so hang not together by skins and gymocks, but labour to be joynted together by flesh and sinewes.[14]

Thus the very first New England sermon which happened to find its way into print was one concerned with an economic problem and was devoted to saving a colony from disaster. Other preachers did not hesitate to render what they believed to be the same service to their congregations. When need arose, a minister used his pulpit efforts to propose a solution to some pressing political or economic difficulty; such discussions were naturally fit subjects for dispute on election-days. Nevertheless, not every preacher honored with the privilege of delivering the yearly sermon at this important time, took full advantage of his opportunity. Some, more pacifically minded, resorted to the old theme of New England's falling away from her pristine glory, and her sad need of reform. But two more definite problems were always with the people and were recog-

13 I *Corinthians* 10:24.
14 Robert Cushman, *A Sermon Preached at Plimoth in New-England December 9, 1621* (London, 1622), 18.

nized from time to time by their ministers. How much control should the magistrates have over religious matters? And what were the rights and privileges of the ruled as well as of the rulers? The Restoration, of course, added a third question. What, if anything, should the New England colonies do in order to avoid reprisals for their support of the Commonwealth?

The first question was closely tied up with the ministers' fear of toleration, but the problem was always stated as if it were a question of whether or not both tables of commandments[15] should be legally enforced. In other words, were the magistrates to have control over man's religious duties to God, as the latter were outlined in the first group of commandments? Or were the duties of the magistrates limited to compelling man to fulfill his ethical duties to his fellowmen, as outlined in the second group of commandments? It was natural that the clergy should approve of the magistrates' having full power to carry into effect all the Lord's commandments, as this meant that only one type of church organization was legally permissible. The Puritans, moreover, could see no hardship in this, as Norton shows in his definition of liberty:

If you ask what Liberty is? You may look at it as a Power, as to any external restraint, or obstruction on mans part, to walk in the Faith, Worship, Doctrine and Discipline of the Gospel, according to the Order of the Gospel.[16]

Here was a subject on which the ministers had no doubts. Shepard, for example, argued that any limitation of the magistrates' jurisdiction to non-religious questions was both sinful and dangerous, as it was really casting away Christ's power to deprive the magistrates of the ability to punish sins of the first table. The churches could not act for themselves, because, no

15 *Exodus* 31:18; also *Deuteronomy* 4:13, *Exodus* 32:19, 34:1, *Deuteronomy* 10:15. In Protestant churches the first four commandments, which have to do with man's piety, are usually considered as the first table; the next six, which have to do with man's probity, as the second table. The fifth commandment of filial duty, however, used to be considered as more closely allied with the religious precepts of the first four commandments than with the ethical ideas of the last five. *Cf. A Dictionary of the Bible,* edited by James Hastings (New York: Charles Scribner's Sons, 1898), I, 581-582, s.v. "Decalogue." The Roman Catholic Church (with Augustine and Luther) has followed the Massoretic Text in uniting the first and second commandments and dividing the tenth commandment. The first table then consists of three commandments, the second of seven. *Cf. A Commentary on the Bible,* edited by A. S. Peake (New York: Thomas Nelson & Sons, n.d.), 185.

16 Norton, *Three Choice and Profitable Sermons,* 7.

matter how flagrant the offence might be, their officers had only spiritual, not magisterial power over their members. Besides, the offenders might not be church members and so would be outside the censure of the church. The spread of heresy could be the only result of such laxity.[17]

Shepard discusses the matter quite calmly, probably because he could not imagine rational Puritans not agreeing with him, but by the 1660's the perfect union of clergy and magistrates was breaking down, and the theocracy was threatened. In the 1670's Samuel Arnold passionately defends the right of the magistrates to enforce both tables, basing his argument on the Old Testament and pointing out that nothing in the New Testament was contradictory. Any man who pretended to be religious, to believe in the Bible, had no choice of opinion.[18] As far as Arnold could judge, only acknowledgedly lost souls outside the pale of the church might raise the issue. A little later in the same decade, Shepard's son, the second Thomas Shepard, looking back upon the good old days of prosperity and happiness when magistrates and ministers worked together, sees all too much reason to fear that the great sin of toleration will allow everyone, even those trying to be godly, to be corrupted by erring members of the community.[19]

The second political question was more complicated, as it involved not only the proper choice of rulers, but also the ethical problem of whether bad rulers and their laws had to be obeyed. Shepard's election sermon of 1638,[20] based on "Then sayd all the trees to the Bramble come raine over us,"[21] was directed toward the solution of the first difficulty. To start with, Jotham's fable is placed and explained briefly: the olive tree stands for prudent men, the fig for rich men, the vine for holy men, and the bramble for irrational, destructive men. Two points are

17 Shepard, *Subjection to Christ*, 97.
18 Arnold, *David Serving his Generation* . . . , 13-15.
19 Thomas Shepard II, *Eye-Salve, Or a Watch-Word from our Lord Iesus Christ* . . . (Cambridge: Samuel Green, 1673), 25-31.
20 Shepard delivered the election sermons of 1637 and of 1638. The latter, preserved in a manuscript volume containing the notes of forty-seven sermons, was printed in 1870 in the *New England Historical and Genealogical Register*, XXIV, 361-366. See also Lindsay Swift, "The Massachusetts Election Sermons," in Massachusetts Colonial Society *Publications*, I, 388-451.
21 *Judges* 9:14-15.

evident in the allegory: first, men of holy hearts are not always willing to be governors; and second, the temper of multitudes in free states where government depends on popular election is apt to change quickly, and from best to worst. In fact, if all the trees were allowed to choose, the chances would be one thousand to one that they would choose a bramble; in other words, if the vote were not limited to church members, the populace would certainly make a bad choice of rulers. But even church members may err in judgment; and once in office, a bramble governor "accepts" tyranny and ruins his people (especially those who have helped him into office) by making a breach in their religion, by acting for his own benefit or profit, by favoring another religion, by slandering the ministers and magistrates, and by undermining the very principles of government. Mindful of this list of threatened evils, the people certainly should be careful in their choice and "maintayne the privilege to death" that their governor be of themselves, a member of some church. Also let him be well known—no newcomer barely arrived—and chosen with the voluntary assent of the freemen. And if, despite these cautions, a bramble should reign, the people are to cut him down, together with all that bear him up.

Undoubtedly, much of the fire and force of Shepard's attack is due to the colony's late experiences with Governor Vane, who was elected to office soon after his arrival in Massachusetts and who promptly lent his support to the Hutchinson-Wheelwright faction. Nevertheless, the sermon is doubly significant. The Bay Colony leaders were firmly convinced that the vote should be limited to church members. Furthermore, as early as 1638 they felt the need of publicly defending the restriction, perhaps because of Hooker's theories of the free franchise and his consequent removal with his followers to Hartford. Even more important is Shepard's attitude in demanding that all governors be New Englanders. The colony was already feeling independent of England and sensing that its very survival depended on this separation.

In the same year that Shepard was defending the theocracy from malcontents within and from English interference,

Thomas Hooker delivered at Hartford a more famous sermon,[22] one that has since been celebrated as the harbinger of American democracy. Hooker had not newly come upon the ideas he expressed in this discourse; on the contrary, he had written of them to friends sometime before, and these opinions had probably been among his chief reasons for migrating with his flock from Cambridge to Hartford, safely without the Bay Colony's bounds. He may even have preached earlier on this same subject.[23] But on May 31, 1638, he is known to have delivered a sermon on the text "Take you wise men, and understanding, and known among your tribes, and I will make them rulers over you." Only the barest outline of what he then said is known, but some of his headings unmistakably show the trend of his thought:

Doctrine. I. That the choice of public magistrates belongs unto the people by Gods own allowance.

II. The privilege of election, which belongs to the people, therefore must not be exercised according to their humors, but according to the blessed will and law of God.

III. They who have power to appoint officers and magistrates, it is in their power, also, to set the bounds and limitations of the power and place unto which they call them.

Reasons. 1. Because the foundation of authority is laid, firstly, in the free consent of the people.

2. Because, by a free choice, the hearts of the people will be more inclined to the love of the persons (chosen) and more ready to yield (obedience).

3. Because of that duty and engagement of the people.

Hooker's political ideas are supposed to have been the guiding spirit of Connecticut's body of laws, promulgated the following year, the first democratic constitution in America. Even here in these few lines a number of important points have been suggested. Since the limitation of church membership is not mentioned, the right to participate in the government has been implicitly given to all the people. The franchise ethically belongs to all the people, for in them is "the foundation of society";

22 Connecticut Historical Society *Collections* (Hartford, 1860), I, 1-20; printed from a volume of sermon-notes taken down in cipher between April 19, 1638 and April 29, 1641 and edited by J. Hammond Trumbull.

23 William De Loss Love, *The Colonial History of Hartford Gathered from the Original Records* (Hartford, 1914), 73, 74.

and, from a practical viewpoint, the people will obey with a better spirit if they have a voice in the government. But the people themselves are not to allow their decisions to be affected by any light reason; the will of God must be consulted and followed. In other words, Hooker does not deny that the church, as the interpreter of God's laws, should be allowed to influence men's votes; he does believe that the church should not be permitted to control suffrage. The third part of Hooker's discourse is almost as fundamental to American democracy as the principle that the people have the power to vote for their rulers. The people also have the power to establish and limit the authority of those in office. How much Hooker's ideas were in advance of some contemporary theories of government may be seen by noting one of the Reverend Samuel Arnold's sermons, preached in 1674. The thesis of this discourse is that a ruler ought never to obey the will of the people, which is very likely to be wrong; the good governor obeys only the will of God, presumably as interpreted by himself or by the church.[24]

There is no way of knowing Hooker's argument as to why the will of the people controls their officers, but some years later Davenport, another preacher with the courage of his convictions, discusses the same point. The New Haven pastor agreed with Shepard and the other Bay Colony conservatives that the vote should be restricted to church members[25] and that magistrates and all important civil officers should be chosen from this group.[26] Nevertheless, he believed with Hooker that those electing have control over those elected, although the reasoning that led the two men to this conclusion may not have been identical. There is a decided display of philosophy and logic in the syllogistic argument by which Davenport endeavors to demonstrate how the people retain this power over the men they have selected for office. The first step in his proof is the assertion that all living creatures have the right of self-preservation; secondly, that they give some of this right by "free donation" to their rulers; thirdly, that the people, nothwithstand-

---

24 Arnold, *David Serving his Generation*, 2-5.
25 John Davenport, *A Sermon Preach'd at the Election of the Governour, at Boston in New-England*, May 19th, 1669 (Boston, 1670), 5.
26 John Davenport, *A Discourse upon Civil Government* ... (Cambridge: Samuel Green and Marmaduke Johnson, 1663), *passim*.

ing, retain the right to measure out civil power according to the Word of God; therefore, they can set "bounds and banks" to a ruler's exercise of power; and if these conditions are violated, the people may choose another to rule over them.[27]

A little experience apparently taught the colonists that church members and old settlers did not necessarily have the qualities of leadership desirable in civil officers. The ministers' feeling from the beginning was that good leaders should be kept in office and that unnecessary changes should be avoided. Cotton early made this point,[28] perhaps with the thought in mind that the church would be better able to keep control of the situation if the men first chosen were allowed to retain their positions. Hubbard, some years later, remarked that treasurers might very well be changed frequently in order to avoid temptation; but he still clung to the idea that "supream rulers" should not be replaced without due cause, and he based this belief on a simple and practical reason, the difficulty in finding fit men, who are far from numerous at any time.[29] This statement brings him to the "tests" that should be applied to any proposed ruler. His discussion can be the more specific, since, under a consideration of valor, he has just disposed of the larger question of the attributes essential to leadership in general:

Valour is an inward virtue of the minde enabling us to persist in our duty notwithstanding the difficulty or danger thereof. They are not a little mistaken, that think nothing is required of valour, but a daring confidence to fight. *ut non poena martyrem, sic nec pugna fortem, sed causa facit.* It is a lawful striving as the Apostle tells us, that deserves the Garland, we must know therefore, that there are four ingredients necessary to the constitutioo [*sic*] of a valient minde.[30]

The four "ingredients" are magnanimity, confidence (or bold-

27 Davenport, *A Sermon . . . 1669*, 5-6.
28 In the election sermon of 1634 Cotton preached against the magistrates being reduced without due cause to private citizenship (Winthrop's *Journal*, Hosmer ed., I, 124-125, under date of May 14, 1634). By way of exception to the general feeling, the Reverend Ezekiel Rogers of Rowley in 1643 preached against the same man being chosen governor twice in succession (Winthrop's *Journal*, II, 97-98, under date of May 10, 1643).
29 Hubbard, *The Happiness of a People*, 21.
30 *Loc. cit.* Hubbard probably had in mind Augustine's comment in his sixty-first epistle: "Disputando & scribendo monstravimus, haereticos non posse habere martyrum mortem, quia Christianorum non habent vitam cum martyrum non faciat poena, sed causa." This is quoted in *Nannus Mirabellus Dominicus Polyanthea nova*, edited by J. Langius (Frankfort-on-the-Main, 1607), a contemporary book of excerpts and quotations.

ness), patience, and perseverance. But now Hubbard comes to the particulars of the character of an able ruler. First, and above all, any Puritan governor must be possessed by fear of the Lord and by the love of righteousness. And second to godliness is "humane learning" in the triple sense of experience, education, and study; no one but a "Weigelian Sceptick"[31] ever accounted Moses less fit to be a leader because he was learned. Third, constancy or steadiness of mind is essential; the people should always be careful to avoid choosing men with "Quicksilver tempers." Fourth, moderation is extremely important, as virtue often lies between two vices, truth between two errors; sometimes, too, following the strict letter of the law proves unjust in the issue and hence the saying, *"Summum jus est summa injuria."* Fifth, peaceableness, in the double sense of avoiding both war and contention in religion, is a sign of great wisdom. Sixth, all rulers should show "condescension," that is, humility of soul. And seventh, good rulers do not make hasty decisions; deliberation precedes each order or move.[32]

In the Reverend Jonathan Mitchell's similar description of the ideal ruler, the importance of such a governor's duty to the church stands out more definitely. Mitchell, preaching the 1667 election-day sermon on *Nehemiah* 2:10, comes quickly to the point that rulers are to seek the welfare of the people. As Junius Brutus said,

The people are not for the Rulers, but the Rulers for the people, to minister to their Welfare.[33]

But the welfare of the people depends primarily on the maintenance and furtherance of religion, with such temporal blessings as safety, honesty, prosperity, and tranquility subordinated to the religious issue. In other words, and Mitchell is again quoting, "Religion is the chief and last end of Civil Polity."[34] The trust put in rulers seems large indeed, when one remembers God's name is bound up with the welfare of his chosen ones. Therefore rulers must be compassionate, "studious and soli-

---

31 The reference is to the followers of Valentine Weigel (1533-1588), a Lutheran pastor and mystic.
32 Hubbard, *The Happiness of a People*, 27-33.
33 Jonathan Mitchell, *Nehemiah on the Wall in Troublesom Times* . . . (Cambridge, 1671), 7. Mitchell is quoting from one of William Buchan's books.
34 *Ibid.*, 3. Mitchell is quoting from Alsted's *Encyclopedia*, 1389.

citous of the Public Welfare." They must practise self-denial and patience, as Moses had before them. Their courage and constancy, their wisdom and prudence, should be much in evidence; and they can hope for little success if they are not "much in prayer."[35]

However pleasant and useful these characterizations of the ideal ruler may have been, the ministers could not deny that in practice those who were governing had the same faults and human weaknesses as had the governed. In a sermon[36] preached less than a year after his famous one advocating democracy, Hooker faced the problem that not all governors rule well. As he apparently confined his discussion to basically good rulers who have some weaknesses, his solution is one of moderation and good sense. The point is stressed that even very conscientious rulers may unconsciously err. Therefore, a governor should neither be too self-confident nor give way to self-abasement if he discovers the "blemishes" in his performance; and the public, instead of harshly censuring a temporarily weak governor, should seek help from heaven in advising him, for a less able man may occasionally offer seasonable advice to one that is far wiser.

Once it is admitted that the virtue and competency of even carefully selected rulers are open to question, the next problem presents itself. Must bad rulers and laws be obeyed? Shepard was the only minister whose detailed discussion of this somewhat embarrassing topic found its way into print.[37] The form of government does not seem important to him, and he disposes of this highly debatable subject somewhat summarily. He simply announces that any commonwealth ordered according to the sacred will of Christ, by such persons especially whose aim is to advance the Kingdom of Christ, is then the Kingdom of Christ; the form of government is only an ordinance of man and hence it is foolish to ask for warrant in Scripture. But in all governments known to history there has been a superior pow-

---

35 *Ibid.*, 2-22.
36 Connecticut Historical Society *Collections*, I, 21; printed from a volume of sermon-notes taken down in cipher between April 19, 1638, and April 29, 1641. As the cipher becomes unintelligible after a few lines, the sermon (based on *Exodus* 18:17, 18) is only partially available.
37 Shepard, *Subjection to Christ*, 112 *et seq.*

er vested in chief magistrates, princes, or chief courts of justice, as well as an inferior power controlling particular towns
or cities. All good Christians must give subjection to any government which is according to Christ's will, and all elected men
should be treated with respect. While it is better to suffer the
penalties of disobedience rather than to obey undoubtedly sinful laws, obedience to good laws, especially to town laws, is
essential. Admitting that these town regulations may not always be wise or foresighted and may lack publication and recording, still Shepard declares they must be obeyed if at all
possible. How to determine when legislation was good did not
seem to him difficult, as all such laws can either be found in
Scripture or plainly deduced from there, and they are always
to advance the public good. Such enactments are to be followed
by all honest men, even at personal sacrifice, for though ideally
laws should hurt no one, in practice some may temporarily cause
suffering. Carefully does this leader of his flock explain that
a penal law (apparently just a civil law) is about things of small
moment and is not by way of command, "but with an *aut,* a dis-
junctive copula, and is indeed rather a proviso than a law."
Hence such a law may be broken if the trespasser is willing to
pay the penalty. But "mixed laws," which have their source
or intent in Scripture, are on a different level. Such rulings as
provide for keeping hogs out of corn and for preserving peace
in town are to be kept carefully, and it is worse for a man to
encourage or permit his servants to break the law than to do
so himself.[38]

However careful Shepard might be to inculcate in listeners
a spirit of obedience to town-laws and to town-officers, despite
petty inconveniences that might have to be borne, he did not
hesitate to face larger problems courageously and resolutely.
Not only are "bramble" governors to be cut down. Naturally,
in any Puritan's opinion, earthly princes are of little importance or glory, born on a dunghill,[39] in fact, in comparison to the
Son of God. When considered in relationship to the bliss and
felicity of the saints, all crowns are nothing in this world—and
less than nothing in the next. While God's elect are chosen irrev-

38 Shepard, *Subjection to Christ,* 130 *et seq.*
39 Thomas Shepard, *The Soules Invitation unto Jesus Christ* (London, 1655), 240

ocably, kings and governors and viceroys come and go, proof, surely, that there must be one great King who rules these lesser potentates. And here is Shepard's answer to the knotty problem of law versus conscience: what could be more sinful, more essentially lawless, than to disobey Christ's laws under color of love for any other king?[40]

In one sense the preachers' response to the third political problem of the day, the quandary of the colonies at the Restoration, is part of this same weighing of two duties that had a tendency to conflict: obedience to law and obedience to conscience. The ministers of the different churches were far from being in harmony about what New Englanders should do in the prolonged crisis of the early 1660's. The Reverend John Higginson, in the election sermon of 1663, apparently still disturbed over the Restoration and what it might mean to the American colonies, takes the middle course of combining religion and common sense, but with religion in the final analysis out-weighing, at least by implication, all other considerations. He urges the people to do their best, behave peaceably, pray humbly, and believe in God as the maintainer of their cause, the church. And in making their choice in matters of public affair, to consider the final outcome of an issue; *"Summum jus"* may mean *"summa injuria,"* he points out, and so *"Salus populi suprema Lex."* All should remember that, in general, every New Englander had three outstanding loyalties: faithfulness to the cause of religion, according to every man's duty to God; faithfulness to the king, according to the oath of allegiance; and faithfulness to the local government, according to the oath of fidelity.[41] Twenty-odd years later—Higginson "sweated" in his pulpit for seventy-two years, if his elegist can be believed — this same earnest, dull preacher was still urging his listeners to have faith in Christ and to obey the magistrates, unless, of course, the latters' orders did not agree with God's commands as given in Scripture.[42]

Of a different spirit at this troublesome time was the New

---

40 Shepard, *The Parable of the Ten Virgins,* I, 22, 79, *et alii.*
41 John Higginson, *The Cause of God and His People in New England* (Cambridge: Samuel Green, 1663), 20-21.
42 John Higginson, *Our Dying Saviour's Legacy of Peace* (Boston, 1686), *passim.*

Haven leader, John Davenport, who in 1661 both directly and by implication urged his people to stand fast in their belief in God:

For, as, naturally, beams come from the Sun, and branches from the root; so, by spiritual discourse, one truth issueth from another; and, as the Sun and its beams, the roots and branches, are all of one nature; so the grounds of comfortable truths, and reasons taken from those grounds, are both of the same divine authority in themselves.[43]

The saints are to have hope despite evil times and evil tidings, even when

all things are turned upside down, and the mountains, Princes, and great Potentates, render themselves terrible to the Church and people of God, and the profane multitude rage against them, like the roaring of the waters, and they can have no rest in their dwellings;[44]

and when only evil men seem to prosper. The reformed churches of Europe might be in dire straits; their English brethren might be "under reproach," called "fools and phanaticks," by the many profane men temporarily masters of the situation. Nevertheless, every New England Puritan should remember:

But, if he is a fool that will suffer himself to be laughed out of his coat, much mure [sic] is he a fool, and a mad man, that will suffer himself to be laughed out of heaven, that will hazard the losse of his soul, and salvation to free himself from the mocks and scoffs of a prophane and sinful World.[45]

Just as indicative of Davenport's unreconciled attitude toward the restored English government is his plea that hospitality be extended to the regicide judges Whalley and Goffe, who had sought refuge in the colonies. From other evidence it is apparent that Davenport himself entertained these men for some time and then saw that they were harbored safely in the neighborhood and at Malden; not stopping with this kindness, he also wrote a cautious letter to conceal their whereabouts in the colony.[46] Nor did he hesitate to plead from the pulpit for their protection, strengthening his instructions with a most apt selection of Biblical texts. Let the faithful fear only God—a fear great enough to make all other fears seem inconsequential

43 John Davenport, *The Saints Anchor-hold, in all Storms and Tempests* . . . (London: Printed by W. L. for Geo. Hurlock, 1661), 51.
44 *Ibid.*, 179.
45 *Ibid.*, 197-198.
46 Massachusetts Historical Society *Collections*, 3rd series, VIII, 327-330; Isabel MacBeath Calder, *The New Haven Colony* (New Haven: Yale University Press, 1934), 222-226.

—and do their duty to their fellow-believers, as God had pre-scribed:

Withhold not countenance, entertainment, protection, from such, if they come to us, from other Countreys, as from *France* or *England,* or any other place. *Be not forgetful to entertain strangers: for thereby some have en-tertained angels unawares. Remember them that are in bonds, as bound with them, and them which suffer adversity, as being your selves also in the body.* Heb 13:2, 3. the Lord required this of *Moab,* saying, *Make thy Shadow, as the night in the midst of the noon day, i.e.* provide safe and comfortable shelter and refreshment for my people, in the heat of persecution and opposition raised against them, *hide the out-casts, bewray not him that wandereth. Let mine out-casts dwell with thee Moab, be thou a covert to them from the face of the spoiler, Isa.* 16. 3, 4. *Object.* But so I may ex-pose my self to be spoiled or troubled? He therefore, to remove this objec-tion, addeth, *for the danger is at an end, the spoiler ceaseth, the treaders down, are consumed out of the land.* While we are attending to our duty, in owning, and harbouring Christs witnesses, God will be providing for their and our safety, by destroying those that would destroy his people.[47]

Mitchell was another preacher who believed that the col-onists should govern their actions by keeping one dominant end in mind: the preservation of the church. "Honesty is the best policy," he tritely remarks, but New Englanders must remem-ber that the very existence of their dearly beloved church is at stake:

To that scope *Nehemiah* bends all his Actions and Endeavours; and *Finis est mensura mediorum,* the End serves to measure, regulate, direct and limit the means, and shew what should be done. That *Maxime* of the Romans was and is a Principle of right Reason, *Salus Populi Suprema Lex,* (The welfare of the People is the Supreme Law) and is engraven on the Forehead of the Law and Light of *Nature.* Hence it is owned and con-firmed by the *Scriptures,* as we see in the Text; and it is easily deducible from the Law of God: and that the Law of God enjoyns, that in Humane Civil Affairs, things be managed according to right Reason and Equity; so that Rulers, as they are for the people, so they are to make it their main business and the scope of all their Actions, Laws, and Motions, to seek the welfare of the people. There is Sun-light for this Maxime, and it was never doubted or denied by any that held but to Rational and Moral Principles. Hence the Law being Supreme, it limits all other Laws and Considerations. Hence it is impossible that a people or their Rulers should be bound by any other Law, or Customs, or Consideration whatsoever, to do anything that is really and evidently contrary to this. If it is indeed contrary or de-structive to the welfare of the people, (of the Community they stand charged with) it is impossible they should be bound in Conscience to do it.[48]

47 Davenport, *The Saints Anchor-hold,* 198-199.
48 Mitchell, *Nehemiah on the Wall,* 11-12.

In this appeal Mitchell is falling back upon the familiar Aristotelian and Roman maxim that the Puritans had used repeatedly against the crown.[49] The welfare of the people is all important. The preacher is positive that this welfare and the survival of the church, as it had been established in New England, are one. This seems, to modern minds, an arbitrary decision; but any Puritan, having based his argument on the Bible, would have been certain of his ground. He would have been positive, as Mitchell was, that the glory of God's name was "bound up" with the well-being of his people, to whom had been entrusted the "Holy Ordinances of God, The Truth of Religion, The dispensation of the glorious Gospel, the helps of everlasting Salvation." And apparently Mitchell was quietly determined to ignore the fact that interpretations of "the welfare of the people" might vary, even in the minds of some of his contemporaries, or that almost any desired change might be advocated as for the *"Salus populi."*

The Reverend John Norton was just as eager as Mitchell to preserve the colonies and the church. While it was his theory that the crown must be placated in every way, this preacher saw that outward change would not be enough and, morally, could not be urged upon the people; the alteration first had to take place in the very thought of New Englanders:

Suffer not your mindes to be prejudiced against the present, and ancient Government of our Nation: ... It is not a Gospel-spirit to be against Kings: 'tis neither Gospel nor English Spirit for any of us to be against the Government by Kings, Lords and Commons. ... God make us more wise and religious then so to carry it, that they should no sooner see a Congregational-man, than have cause to say, *They see an Enemy to the Crown* ... We have severe Observers; Tongues are not untaught to inform against us. It is but wisdom to give no cause, especially such as our own Consciences cannot testifie for, and such as all Orthodox Churches in the Protestant world will testifie against. In matters of the State-Civil, and of the Church, let it be shown that we are his Disciples, who (*Matth.* 22.21) said, *Give unto Cesar the things that are Cesars, and unto God the things that are Gods:* and in matters of Religion, let it be known that we are for Reformation, and not for Separation.[50]

Care not to give new offense in any way would not be enough, Norton was certain. There would have to be an apology made

49 Haller, *The Rise of Puritanism*, 366-368.
50 Norton, *Three Choice and Profitable Sermons*, 12.

for past misunderstandings, especially as some of the enemies
of the colonists in England had undoubtedly represented them
as "disaffected to government." Silence was not sufficient; the
apology would have to be more positive than that, and then New
Englanders might once more be found to be "faithful to that
Order of the Gospel" for which they were outcasts.[51]

One other great double problem is always before any people
—the reason and justification for war. The early ministers were
inclined to accept the idea of war as the natural consequence of
sin; in other words, war was one of God's ways of punishing a
people who turned from him temporarily. Certain sects, particularly some Anabaptists and later the Quakers, denied the
justification of war, but there is little comment on this phase
of the subject in any of the Puritan sermons preached before
the 1670's. But in the early 1640's the distresses of the English
civil war shocked these other Englishmen, far from home, but
not distant in their sympathies. After all, these were their own
brethren involved, twice their brethren, in fact, by race and by
religion. The Reverend William Hooke, preaching around
1641, showed the most vehement feelings on the whole subject
of war; he is not primarily concerned with the question of its
justification, for all his mind seems to be occupied with the
dreadful effects of war, most especially of civil war. His passionate description of the horrors of the field of combat, [52] with
its agony and noise, with its maimed and killed, is equalled only
by his tale of the aftermath. "The day of battle is a day of
harvest for the devill," but that is only the beginning of the misery involved. Think of the suffering and want of each slain
man's family. Even more dire are the results of war if they
are seen in a larger perspective:

Alas, Alas! this is but Warre thorow a Crevice. Beloved, do but consider; There is many times fire without warre, and famine and pestilence
without warre, but warre is never without them: and there are many times
robberies without warre, and murthering of passengers, ravishing of ma-
trons, deflouring of virgins, cruelties and torments and sometimes barbarous

51 *Ibid.*, 15-16.
52 William Hooke, *New Englands Teares, For Old Englands Feares* . . . (London, 1641), 10-11.

and inhumane practices without warre, but warre goes seldome or never without them.[53]

Hooke was shocked at the calamities of war and at the moral collapse that was apt to accompany it. Some years later, the Reverend Samuel Nowell expressed much the opposite opinion. To him, war seemed part of the natural course of events, and he could see no objection to thorough preparation for the inevitable. Nevertheless, the very fact that he had to defend war and war preparations may be considered as significant of New England's peace-loving temper. This new anti-war spirit, says Nowell, is a "strange piece of dotage befallen this crazy-headed Age, that men should not use the sword: the best of men have done it."[54] God himself is a Man of War; how many examples there are of this in the Old Testament! The wisest of rulers, the holiest of people have waged war; man has but to recall the wars of Israel. The law of nature, too, teaches self-preservation.[55] It must be remembered that the colonies might be attacked at any time. Who could doubt that every European nation had its eye on every successful, prospering settlement? There was also constant (if unspecified) danger from Rome, and the Indians would be of no help, rather an added danger, in a crisis. Nowell, as a practical man, could see but one solution: New Englanders must be trained to protect themselves, to recover any possessions taken forcibly from them, and to punish those who wronged them.[56] Another justifiable cause of war would be the defense of friends and allies. The men of New England must look to their arms; and the horse division must be especially encouraged and increased, if there was to be any hope of success in military combat.

Somewhere between the stand of Hooke, the pacifist, and of Nowell, the military tactician, was the viewpoint of such a man as the Reverend Urian Oakes. He had no heart to discuss the problems of war, for he thought that most of man's pug-

---

53 *Ibid.*, 12.
54 Samuel Nowell, *Abraham in Arms: Or, The First Religious General with his Army* . . . (Boston: John Foster, 1678), 5.
55 This same law-of-nature theory had been advanced in a previous artillery election sermon, John Richardson's *The Necessity of a Well Experienced Souldiery* . . . (Boston, 1675), 8.
56 Here Nowell was following the discussion of just and unjust wars in Grotius' *De Jure Belli ac Pacis* (1625).

nacity should be occupied in fighting sin. In his mind, every Christian, secure only in the love of Christ, through whom victory would come, was a soldier fighting against the evil within himself.

> Every true Believer hath constant fighting work before him. There is no end of his warre in this world, nor any time wherein He may give over fighting.[57]

Even when he was preaching an artillery-election sermon in 1674, Oakes devoted nine-tenths of his time to the evils of the day that ought to be crusaded against. Only at the end of his discourse does he mention war in what might be thought to be the accepted sense of the word on such an occasion. Still reluctant to desert the "good fight" for these lesser avocations of man, he asserts openly, "I am no Friend to warre, but an unfeigned lover of peace."[58] Nevertheless, military preparation must go on; war skills are necessary for survival. In his refusal to forget religious and moral issues in any preoccupation with the problems of war, Oakes seems to have been typical of most early New Englanders. War might be a necessary evil, and as such must be prepared for; but it was to be avoided on practical grounds, if for no other reason. As Hubbard, the historian of the Indian wars remarked, war was "welcome to none, but those who never made trial of it."[59]

---

57 Urian Oakes, *The Unconquerable, All-Conquering and more-then-Conquering Souldier: Or, The Successful Warre which a Believer Wageth with the Enemies of his Soul* . . . , 5.

58 *Ibid.*, 37.

59 Hubbard, *The Happiness of a People*, 31.

V

THE FORM OF THE SERMONS

Of all the many extant sermons probably few, if any, are preserved exactly as they were preached. This dissimilarity between the recorded and the spoken version of the same discourse does not mean that the latter was originally an improvisation to meet the demand of the moment. Nor were many sermons the result of sudden inspiration on the preacher's part. As a rule, all sermons were sedulously prepared; only very occasionally do we read of a visiting minister being called upon to preach extemporaneously. John Cotton, ever brilliant—or so his grandson's report makes him out—could, on getting a new idea, preach so well that his congregation could not detect the difference between his studied and his unstudied efforts.[1] One other minister, the Reverend John Wilson, was especially noted as having this rare gift of being able to preach satisfactorily without prolonged and specific preparation. On one occasion the latter was asked, while visiting another Puritan minister at Assington, England, to say something about the first chapter in the first book of *Canticles,* a passage which had just been read in morning prayer. Cotton Mather reports:

and from a paragraph of meer proper names, that seemed altogether barren of any edifying matter, he [Wilson] raised so many fruitful and useful notes, that a pious person then present, amazed thereat, could have no rest without going over to America after him.[2]

Later, when the chosen preacher failed to appear at a crowded Boston meeting, this same Mr. Wilson stepped into the breach and delivered a lecture which, taken down in shorthand by a listener, was afterwards deemed worthy of print.

But such examples of complete dependence on inspiration and remembered learning are rare; nearly always a congregation expected and got from its preacher what John Eliot, undoubtedly with *Exodus* 27:20 in mind, called "beaten oyl" for the sanctuary. To say that a man's sermons were well stu-

1 Mather, *Magnalia*, Book III, 25.
2 *Ibid.*, Book III, 46.

died was to pay him the highest compliment. Before going into
the pulpit every minister diligently prepared his heart and mind
by prayer and reading. For example, the renowned Thomas
Shepard, famous for the spirit of his work rather than its scholarship, devoted three days a week to preparation for the Sabbath and scorned any minister who had not his sermon fully
prepared by Friday night or early Saturday afternoon.[3] Undoubtedly, this habit of intensive and extensive spiritual and
mental preparation for the pulpit was taken as a matter of course
by men who, with Calvin and Luther, tacitly placed the sermon
on almost the same respected level as they did Scripture.

Sometimes before learning his forthcoming sermon *mem-
oriter,* a minister in the course of his preparation made a fairly
complete copy of it, as Ramus[4] and the ancient rhetoricians had
advised orators to do with their speeches. The Reverend John
Davenport was known for this habit of writing out his sermons
more largely than many of his peers; even more laborious was
Samuel Danforth, who wrote his sermons twice over. More
commonly, a minister merely made lengthy notes—that is, he
wrote his headings and sub-headings and then depended on his
memory and his knowledge of the Bible to fill in the proofs
and reasons and uses of his doctrine. At first there was a decided feeling that such written aids to the memory should not
be actually used in the pulpit, but the Reverend John Warham,
who preached for many years (1636-1670) at Windsor, Connecticut, introduced the custom of consulting such notes during the actual delivery of the sermon. Apparently Warham
preached so well that others imitated his practice, although a

3 Shepard in his *Four Necessary Cases of Conscience* (London, 1651) directly
   states (p. 5) that he commonly spent three days a week preparing his heart
   for the Sabbath. William Greenhill and Samuel Mather, in their life of
   Shepard prefaced to the latter's *Subjection to Christ,* speak of the long and
   early preparation made by Shepard for his public labors and then quote him
   as saying on one occasion: "God will curse that man's labours that lumbers
   up and down in the world all the week, and then upon Saturday in the afternoon goes to his study; when as God knows, that time were little enough to
   pray in and weep in, and to get his heart in frame, &c." Cotton Mather, in
   his *Magnalia* quotes this passage and stresses Shepard's early and careful
   preparation. In the face of these statements, Morison in his chapter on
   Shepard in *Builders of the Bay Colony* (London, 1930) curiously enough
   says: "He [Shepard] could never get his sermons prepared in time, but
   would meditate and procrastinate until there was left only the fag-end of a
   Saturday night and early Sabbath morning." (pp. 132-33).
4 *Scholarum dialecticarum, seu Animadversionum in Organum Aristotelis libri
   XX,* Recens emendati per Joan. Piscatorem . . . (1584), 603.

careful distinction was maintained between using and reading notes; a read sermon was always disdained,[5] and Luther's ideal of careful preparation followed by free delivery was faithfully upheld.[6]

There must be considerable variation in how closely the published sermons resemble their original oral form. The printed discourses that approach most accurately the actually delivered ones are, of course, those taken from the minister's own copies of his work, either written out before or after the occasion. Still, the spoken sermon may have varied slightly from the version that has been preserved. If the printing was done from the copy made before preaching, who can doubt that the latter was changed or improved when preached? On the other hand, if a copy made afterwards was used for publication, might not the minister have done a little revision on seeing his words in black and white? But more usually printing was done from notes, not from complete sermons; a minister "revueved and renewed, and fitted for the press" his lengthy notes of a course of sermons. How much he saw fit to change remains an unanswerable question. Sometimes, too, he deliberately put his sermons into book form, with only the chapter divisions to hint at the content of individual sermons. So Thomas Shepard redrafted, for the benefit of Harvard students, his conclusions on the fourth commandment, the result being a practical guide to the keeping of the Sabbath.[7] A few years earlier he had altered a group of sermons on *John* 16:8, 9, 10, 11 into a series of questions and answers to be published with a catechism.[8] Peter Bulkeley took his sermons on *Zechariah* 9:11 and rewrote them into a well-known instructive book, *The Gospel Covenant,* first published in 1646; five years later the book was reprinted with additional changes and chapter headings supplied by its author.

As long as a preacher prepared his own work for the press, we can be reasonably sure that we are reading his main ideas truly presented, even if many bursts of eloquence and references

5 Mather, *Magnalia*, Book III, 121.
6 Luther, *Table Talk*, 127-128.
7 *Theses Sabbaticae* (London, 1659).
8 *The Doctrine and Conviction of Sin, and Righteousness, and Judgment.* Published with *A Short Catechism* (Cambridge: Samuel Green, 1654).

to contemporary affairs may have been omitted. But sometimes a friend or disciple elaborated on a more famous minister's notes to produce a book for the press, or a faithful listener would make notes during the church service. In either case, the scribe was apt to mix, all unconsciously, his own beliefs with those of the professed author of the book; or, at best, the original argument would not be given in full or accurate detail. For example, a number of eager listeners took notes of John Cotton's sermons on *Acts* 7:8, some writing more at length and more exactly than others. An early edition[9] was then published from one of the shorter versions. Luckily one of the longer versions was kept, and the author was given the opportunity to correct these notes, which were then prepared for the press by the Reverend Thomas Allen, the Norwich pastor. The resulting volume[10] was one-third longer than the first publication of the same sermon-series. Thomas Hooker was less fortunate. Some of his sermons were taken down by an unskilled hand and published without their author's consent. In the preface to another of Hooker's many books, Dr. Thomas Goodwin avers that as a result of this mischance Hooker's normally clear thinking had been on occasion

utterly deformed and misrepresented in multitudes of passages, and in the rest, but imperfectly and crudely set forth.[11]

Similarly, Thomas Shepard makes his complaint about one of the earlier publications appearing under his name:

That which is called the *Sincere Convert* I have not the book; I once saw it, it was a collection of such notes in a dark town in England, which one procuring of me, published then without my will or privity; nor do I like to see it. He that published it, confesseth it came out altered from what was first written.[12]

Many of these early volumes, whether prepared by the authors themselves or by fellow ministers or by lay admirers, suffered from their printing. At first all work had to be sent to England; consequently no proof-reading usually was done by the author, although his friends at home may have been of

---

9 John Cotton, *The Covenant of Gods Free Grace* (London, 1645).
10 John Cotton, *A Treatise of the Covenant of Grace* (London, 1659).
11 Goodwin, prefatory epistle to *The Application of Redemption*.
12 Letter (dated Dec. 27, 1647) to Giles Firmin, published in the latter's *Real Christian* (London, 1670), 214.

some assistance in this respect. How unsatisfactory such long
distance publication proved to be is noted by Governor Winthrop
under the date of July 28, 1642:

Now came a book of Mr. Cotton's sermons upon the seven vials. Mr. Hum-
frey had gotten the notes from some who had took them by characters, and
printed them in London, he had 300 copies for it, which was a great wrong
to Mr. Cotton, and he was much grieved at it, for it had been fit he should
have perused and corrected the copy before it had been printed.[13]

Later, an increasing number of books were published at Cambridge and then at Boston. Although this arrangement allowed
more opportunity for emendation, a great many sermons, both
English and American publications, including much of John
Norton's and Thomas Shepard's preaching, continued to be
published posthumously by grieving survivors. The text of such
books naturally was uncorrected except by friends, who may
not have had the time or the ability to do what at best would
be an unsatisfactory job. Undoubtedly much of the apparent
confusion and difficulty of Shepard's polemic style,[14] as well as
a general formlessness to be seen in many of his longer treatises,
is due to bad printing and no correction.

While the sermons suffered much in transcription and in
printing, it is still possible in most cases to discern what they
must have been like in their original form. Of course, the occasion on which a sermon was to be delivered influenced its content to some degree. It must be remembered that the average
minister preached once or twice on the Sabbath, depending on
whether the church had but one ordained leader or had both a
pastor and a teacher. Very occasionally, too, a church had
co-pastors, usually a younger man still in his full strength and
an elderly one worn out by many years of service. In addition
to their Sunday preaching, many ministers, for the benefit of
their own congregations and the more zealous members of neighboring churches, conducted, usually on Wednesday or Thursday, weekly or fortnightly lectures or "lecture sermons."

13 Winthrop's *Journal*, II, 69-70.
14 The Reverend Alexander Whyte in his *Thomas Shepard Pilgrim Father and
    Founder of Harvard* (Edinburgh: Oliphant, Anderson and Ferrier, n.d. 1912)
    makes much of the difficulty of reading the New Englander's books. Dr. Whyte
    found not only that Shepard used "execrable" and "atrocious" English, but
    also that he "at his very best wrote an all but unrecognizable English" (10,
    11, 13).

This regular weekly and biweekly preaching made up the bulk of the minister's work, but there were also an additional half-dozen or more times during the year on which preaching was in order. Election days, both for civil and military offices, were solemn occasions on which the Lord's wishes, as interpreted by his ministers, were to be heeded. Moreover, in a world entirely governed by Divine Providence and one in which no element of chance entered, every calamity and every deliverance from trouble was interpreted in terms of how well New England was keeping her covenant with God. Therefore, in times of stress, sometimes the colony's officials, either the governor or the court, or sometimes individual churches would appoint fast-days on which all were to abstain as completely as possible from food, to wear their plainest clothes without ornament, and to refrain from both "lawful employments" and sports and recreations, "yea even the pleasure of married life."[15] Church services, as well as special prayer and self-examination, characterized these days, which were held whenever catastrophe jeopardized the survival of the feeble settlements. Sickness, naturally never unknown, was especially prevalent during the years between 1644 and 1649 and again between 1658 and 1666. Occasionally famine threatened, particularly in the first years when the colonies' delicate economic balance could be easily upset by a crop failure or by the arrival of newcomers without adequate provisions or by the delay of ships expected with necessary supplies; a little later, pests destroyed a number of crops. Sometimes the danger from hostile Indians seemed particularly menacing. But not only impending disasters called for days of humiliation upon which intervention could be sought. Often help for the future was felt to be needed, especially when a new church was to be gathered or a new minister settled in some pastorate that was temporarily vacant. In fact, any number of problems called for divine guidance, which was to be pleaded for most humbly. When a difficulty was satisfactorily solved, a day of thanksgiving sometimes was appointed. So the Boston church in 1632 fasted for the safe arrival of their minister, the Reverend John Wilson, who had gone back to England to bring over his wife and whose return with her was overdue. His

15 Thomas Thacher, *A Fast of God's Chusing* (Boston: John Foster, 1678), 4.

ship came in the day before the appointed fast-day, which was held as a thanksgiving. But such immediately local problems were not the only reasons for these special church services; sometimes the New Englanders showed a broader sense of the world's welfare and some realization of how European events would influence their own lives. For instance, Massachusetts in 1632 also celebrated the news of the victories during the past year of Gustavus Adolphus, who in his championship of the Lutherans and Calvinists in Germany had saved the Protestant cause in central Europe. Some years later, England's troubles during her civil war called for a number of days of humiliation.[16]

Naturally, in planning his sermons for these various occasions a minister allowed his thoughts to be governed to some extent by their purpose. Sabbath-day sermons were apt to be more directly inspirational and moral, while week-day lecture sermons had a tendency to be more doctrinal and informational about controversial points of belief. Thomas Shepard devoted his Thursday lectures for four years to the dangers of falling under the pernicious influence of Arminianism or of Antinomianism,[17] and John Cotton's week-day sermons at Boston discussed at great length the evils of Catholicism.[18] These two lecture-series are excellent examples of the dogmatic and polemical uses to which this type of sermon could be put; on the other hand, the difference between Sunday and week-day sermons is often only a matter of emphasis and tone. More easily distinguished are election-day sermons, as they habitually tended to bring in the question of civil government. The interest, however, lay less in political theory than in the fit character of rulers and in the mutual duty of the ruled and the ruler. Often, too, the minister saw the day as an excellent time for the community to consider their sins and the danger of divine punishment, if reform was not immediate. Artillery-election sermons, which were not delivered regularly until 1659 and not printed until 1672,[19] again brought up the problem of leadership and

16 William De Loss Love, *The Fast and Thanksgiving Days of New England* (Boston: Houghton, Mifflin and Company, 1895), 78-161, 177-191.
17 Shepard, *The Parable of the Ten Virgins.*
18 Cotton, *The Powring Out of the Seven Vials.*
19 Samuel G. Drake, *The History and Antiquities of Boston* (Boston: Luther Stevens, 1856), 236.

duty; but any question was apt to be clothed in the figure of a Christian, armored with Truth, going forth to fight the good fight against Satanic adversaries. Fast-day and Thanksgiving sermons were inclined to be more definite in their references to crucial problems that currently held the interest of all; but since these difficulties were usually explained as manifestations of God's wrath because his will was not being sincerely obeyed, the reproof of sin often dominated discourses of this type, too.

Variations due to the occasion are apparent in the content and tone, rather than in the form of the sermons, for the ministers practically always followed one fixed and standard pattern in their compositions.

Every sermon began with a definite Biblical text. While the necessity of preaching on an appointed day of humiliation or celebration or election called for an appropriate passage as a starting point, in their regular preaching the ministers often worked and reworked steadily through favorite parts of the Bible. Energetic John Cotton occupied the Boston, Massachusetts, pulpit for nearly twenty years, and Cotton Mather, using either his grandfather's own notes or Norton's contemporary account of Cotton's career,[20] is able to make this detailed report upon his ancestor's preaching:

Here, in an expository way, he went over the Old Testament once, and a second time as far as the thirtieth chapter of Isaiah; and the whole New Testament once, and a second time as far as the eleventh chapter to the Hebrews. Upon the Lord's-days and lecture-days he preached throu the Acts of the Apostles; the prophesies of Haggai and Zechariah, the books of Ezra, the Revelation, Ecclesiastes, Canticles, second and third Epistles of John, the Epistle to Titus, both Epistles to Timothy; the Epistle to the Romans; with innumerable scriptures on incidental occasions.[21]

Perhaps more typically, the Reverend Charles Chauncy, preaching successively at Plymouth, Scituate, and Harvard College, covered fewer parts of Scripture—the whole Gospel of John, the Acts of the Apostles, and the three Epistles of John—but he also "largely handled" the doctrines of Self-denial, Faith,

20 Norton, *Abel being Dead yet Speaketh; Or, The Life and Death of that Deservedly Famous Man of God, Mr. John Cotton* . . . (London, 1658), 22-23.
21 Mather, *Magnalia*, Book III, 23.

Justification, Adoption, and Sanctification, as well as many other occasional subjects.[22] Preaching in this way progressively through certain books of the Bible does not mean that a minister necessarily used a completely fresh text for each sermon. Often he lingered on a favorite or meaty passage, as John Warham did for twenty-seven sermons on *Romans* 5:1. With equal fervor of spirit, Thomas Hooker spent nearly a year on *Acts* 2:37, and Thomas Shepard, after four years on *Matthew* 25:1-13, congratulated himself that he had not, after the fashion of Papist commentators, squeezed the last bit of meaning out of it. Such detailed discussion called for a nice separation of the text into words and phrases, each of which could be used as the starting point of a distinct sermon. This dividing was considered one of the arts of pulpit rhetoric.

Once a text was selected, the preacher's immediate duty was to clarify it in all possible ways. Often the first step was to disclose the context, as the Reverend John Davenport placed *Acts* 2:36 as part of a sermon by Peter.[23] The Reverend Urian Oakes, even more conscientiously, in the process of unfolding *Deuteronomy* 32:29, analyzed the whole song of Moses. His listeners learned that it started with a "Rhetorical & pathetical Apostrophe" which is the "Exordium, Proem or Preface, wherein he labours to procure Benevolence, Attention and Docility"; then came the narrative, then a prediction of "the Apostacy, Idolatry, and horrible Ingratitude of Israel," then a "severe Commination of the deserved Chastisements and Punishment," and last a word of consolation with a concluding line.[24] Sometimes a minister felt that a rhetorical explanation of this sort was less necessary to the sense than a brief survey of the historical background of the text to be expounded. When the Reverend Samuel Hooker chose at a Connecticut election to preach on, "For it is time to seek Jehovah until he come and rain righteousness upon you" (*Hosea* 10:12), he first briefly considered the condition and history of Judea at the time of the prophecy.[25]

22 *Ibid.*, Book III, 137.
23 Davenport, *The Knowledge of Christ*, 2.
24 Oakes, *New-England Pleaded with*, 1-3.
25 Samuel Hooker, *Righteousness Rained from Heaven*, 1-6.

Even more often a preacher felt it necessary to "open" the meaning of certain words. The Reverend Thomas Hooker, when preaching from "Now therefore hearken unto me, O ye children, for blessed are they that keep my wayes" (*Proverbs* 8:32), took care to explain *hearken* as having the complex meaning of hearing, understanding, retaining, and subjecting the heart to the will of God; the *me* in the passage meant Wisdom of Jesus Christ, as shown by the beginning of the same chapter.[26] Similarly, the Reverend William Stoughton, using *Isaiah* 63:8 as his text for the election sermon of 1663, expatiated on the meaning of *to lie*, and his audience learned that the expression meant to deal falsely with the Lord—that is, to break the Covenant in deed or word.[27] Fairly often in the course of such explanations a minister found it necessary to refer to some authority, as the Reverend Charles Chauncy used Mercer[28] as the basis for reading "sons" as "some of your sons" in "And I raised up of your sons for Prophets and of your young men for Nazarites, is it not so, O ye children of Israel, saith the Lord?" (*Amos* 2:11).[29] The Reverend Samuel Hooker felt he had to draw upon the wisdom of Zanchius and Calvin as well as of Mercer in order to do justice to the various possible interpretations of *Hosea* 10:12 and the immediately preceding lines;[30] here, of course, he was dealing with a difficult passage, the text of which modern exegetical scholars consider to be very corrupt. Rather than appeal in this way to the authority of commentators, some ministers referred to other versions of the Bible to clarify a point. For instance, Jonathan Mitchell, discussing 1 *Peter* 5:10, noted that *but* becomes *now* in the Dutch and even in other English prayers, for both translations are used for the same Greek particle.[31] With a more impressive show of learning, the Reverend John Oxenbridge explained *Hosea* 8:4 by referring to the Hebrew, Arabic, Chaldean, Greek

---

26 Thomas Hooker, "Wisdomes Attendants: or the Voice of Christ to be Obeyed" in *The Saints Dignitie* (London, 1651), 124-126.

27 Stoughton, *New-Englands True Interest: Not to Lie*, 6.

28 Probably Guillaume Merchier (1572-1639), a schoolman and professor at Louvain.

29 Chauncy, *Gods Mercy, Shewed to His People*, 3.

30 Samuel Hooker, *Righteousness Rained from Heaven*, 2-6.

31 Mitchell, *A Discourse of the Glory*, 1-2.

(Septuagint), Syriac, and vulgar Latin renderings of the passage.[32]

No one of these methods of explication was used by any minister to the exclusion of the others. The Reverend William Hubbard, for example, taking the text "And of the children of Issachar, which were men that had understanding of the times, to know what Israel ought to do; the heads of them were two hundred, and all their brethren were at their commandment" (1 *Chronicles* 12:32), explained the historical background in some detail, referring to Sigonius as an authority on Hebrew government; he then construed "by a metonimy of the adjunct" *the times* to mean "things done in these times" and the familiar trope *Israel* to be understood as all holy people in covenant with God. Hubbard also felt called upon to define the word *understanding* as being two words in Hebrew which took in the meaning of *apprehension* and *judgment,* but the sense here was that of the Latin *prudentia.*[33] But even the most thorough elucidation of this type was done briefly, and, as a minister was interested only in the literal meaning of his text, he was able to "raise" his doctrine quickly.

In order to do this, he usually ignored the rest of the chapter from which his text had been chosen, and considered only the words or line or two upon which he was preaching. A most obvious illustration of this habit is to be seen in Samuel Danforth's *Cry of Sodom* sermon. Here the threatened fate of sinful Sodom and Gomorrah (*Genesis* 18:20, 21) is used to frighten iniquitous New England. Abraham's intervention and God's promised mercy if any righteous men were to be found are both ignored, although the congregation must have known well the whole familiar story. It is hardly possible that the Reverend Mr. Danforth's implication was that there were no righteous men in his congregation!

---

32 Oxenbridge, *New England Freemen Warned,* 1-3. He was probably using Brian Walton's *Biblia Sacra Polyglotta, complecentia Textus Originales Hebraeum (cum Pentateucho Samaritano), Chaldaicum, Graecum, Versionumque Antiquarum, Samaritanae, Graecae lxii. Interp. Chaldaicae, Syriacae, Arabicae, AEthiopicae, Persicae, Vulg. Latin. quidquid camparari poterat. Cum Textuum et Versionum Orentalium Translationibus Latinis . . .* (London, 1657). There were three earlier Polyglot Bibles, but Walton's was fairly inexpensive and much consulted by the clergy.

33 Hubbard, *The Happiness of a People,* 1-5.

Often the doctrine appears as a mere rewording of the text. "Seek ye the Lord while He may be found, call ye upon Him while He is near" (*Isaiah* 55:6) became, in John Oxenbridge's words, "If in seeking the Lord we would not miss of success, we must not miss the season thereof."[34] On the other hand, such a simple restatement was not always satisfactory to the Puritan mind. Old Testament texts were frequently seen in terms of the New Testament. A line from *Genesis*,[35] "And he believed in the Lord; and he counted it to him for righteousness," was considered in its later implications: "That it is by the Word and Promises concerning salvation by Christ, that men are brought to believe, or to become true believers."[36] Sometimes a minister allowed himself to shift the emphasis of the original line so that in his rewording of it some tenet of his belief, such as repentance or election, stood out more distinctly. Jonathan Mitchell took as a text the line "But the God of all grace, who hath called us to his eternal glory by Christ Jesus, after ye have suffered a while, make you perfect, stablish, strengthen, settle you" (1 *Peter* 5:10); this somewhat comforting statement was transformed into the less lucid but more Calvinistic one, "Eternal Glory in the world to come, is that which the faithful (the effectually called) shall be brought into (or obtain) by Christ Jesus (or by the Grace of God through Christ Jesus), after they have suffered a while in this world."[37]

Sometimes, too, the occasion of a sermon influenced the idea to be gotten from a particular line of Scripture. The Reverend Samuel Arnold, preaching the Connecticut election sermon of 1674, used as his text "For David, after he had served his own generation by the will of God, fell on sleep, and was laid unto his fathers, and saw corruption" (*Acts* 13:36). Arnold ignored the second part of the line and shifted the emphasis on the first part so that his doctrine became "The life of a Christian, especially of such as are in publick place ought to be a Serving of their Generation, and are to be ruled therein by the will of God."[38] That is, as the rest of the sermon makes very

---

34 Oxenbridge, *A Quickening Word*, 5.
35 *Genesis* 15:6; cf. *Romans* 4:3.
36 Richard Mather, *The Summe of Certain Sermons upon Genes. 15.6.*, p. 3.
37 Mitchell, *A Discourse of the Glory*, 3-4.
38 Arnold, *David Serving His Generation*, 2.

clear, no good ruler is governed by the will of his people. An interesting example of what was probably a more deliberately free use of the Bible is to be seen in the Massachusetts election sermon of 1669. The Reverend John Davenport chose as his text "The God of Israel said, the Rock of Israel spake to me, He that ruleth over men must be just, ruling in the fear of God" (2 *Samuel* 23:3). His doctrine reflects how the text could be applied not only to royal prerogative in old England but to the election of magistrates in New England: "That it is the Ordinance of God, in reference to Civil Government in Commonwealths, that some men orderly chosen should rule over other men: and in reference to the qualifications of Rulers, that they must be just, ruling in the fear of God."[39]

After the doctrine, came its "proof" or "reasons" or "causes." These arguments were all based on apposite Biblical passages, which were definitely referred to or quoted. Consequently, the body of a sermon usually contained a great many Biblical passages. Perhaps the average preacher in the course of a sermon might cite thirty or more lines from Scripture, using the Old Testament on the average of six times out of ten. A "strong text-man" would be much more liberal with his Scripture lines. Cotton Mather reports that the Reverend Samuel Danforth, who had some local fame as a "notable text-man," usually employed in each of his discourses from forty to fifty Scripture passages, each one distinctly quoted.[40] The same authority also notes that the Reverend George Phillips was such a distinguished Biblical scholar, reading both Testaments through six times a year, that he could find any line without hesitation and so had no need of using his concordance.[41] Perhaps his sermons, unfortunately never printed, reflected this combination of diligence and memory, but they can hardly have outshone the preaching of Davenport in this respect. In the fifteen and a half pages that contain one of the latter's surviving sermons,[42] there are at least eighty-nine Biblical citations and quotations.

39 Davenport, *A Sermon Preach'd ... 1669*, 3.
40 Mather, *Magnalia*, Book IV, 154.
41 *Ibid.*, Book III, 83.
42 Davenport, *A Sermon Preach'd ... 1669.*

Lest the congregation become confused, this part of the sermon was often divided and subdivided for the purpose of clarity, a method that Erasmus had strongly advised. For example, in an exceptionally well-organized sermon[43] but one that shows the general method employed or at least essayed, Davenport proved by six arguments that Jesus is "the only true Messiah." The first of these is based upon Christ as the perfect antitype of such "real" types in the Bible as Jacob's Ladder and the Passover and of such "personal" types as Adam, Noah, and Melchisedek, with ten of each sort of type enumerated; the second argument is made from Biblical prophecies, with general prophecies and specific ones separated and listed; the third, from genealogies, with an aside here on their value; the fourth, from miracles, wonders, and signs, with a discussion of the nature, purpose, and occasion of miracles; the fifth, from the agreement of the Gospel story with what had been prophesied; and the sixth, in continuation of the same reasoning, from the way in which Christ fulfilled the mediatorial office of Messiah which Scripture demanded.

The body of a sermon was rarely as simply developed as in the one just summarized. The very division and subdivision of points sometimes seem to make for confusion, although some of this may be due less to original obscurity than to faulty printing from poor or incomplete copies. But even without the complication of bad editing and faulty printing, the sermons differ a good deal in the lucidity of their structure; and the seventeenth-century habit of Sunday note-taking must have helped many a faithful listener to recall and study the steps in his pastor's development of an idea.

On the other hand, this part of the sermon, however important it might be felt to be, often was comparatively short. The minister devoted more of his time to the "improvement" or the immediate application of his doctrine. This emphasis on the everyday uses of a point of faith or doctrine stemmed back spiritually to Jesus's teaching, as it is shown repeatedly in the New Testament; but Ramus's arguments for the utilitarian application of judgment as opposed to scholastic esoteric

43 Davenport, *The Knowledge of Christ.*

abstractions" may well have encouraged the ministers to an extended consideration of the daily employment of religious precepts. That this development of the doctrine's application, even at the sacrifice of the rest of the sermon, was deliberate and purposeful, is shown by the Reverend Charles Chauncy's advice to a young minister:

Explain the words of your text clearly; bring proof of parallel scriptures; let your reasons be Scripture-reasons; but be most in application; which is spent in five uses, refutation of error, information of the truth, correction of manners, exhortation and instruction in righteousness. All of which you find in Tim. iii. 16, 17. And there is a fifth use, viz: of comfort, 1 Cor. xiv. 3.[45]

It is to be noted that this application of religious thought to a workaday world was usually, and somewhat disappointingly, general in tone. Specific emergencies and particular problems are infrequently examined. The "uses" of the doctrine in a given sermon might be two, three, four, or five in number, each carefully enumerated and so labeled that the content of the discussion is self-evident. The congregation might be told to learn and to apply to themselves the observations just made—this was "instruction"; or they might be urged to consider their past conduct in respect to this point of faith—"examination." If this scrutiny of their past and present ways showed any falling away from former standards, "reproof" was in order, or even more frequently, "humiliation," a realization of their own weakness and of their dependence on God's mercy. Perhaps "terror," the more definite threat of withdrawal of God's favor, was felt to fit the sinning congregation's condition, but "consolation" often showed them the means of returning to favor. "Exhortation," another fairly common use, might be nothing but a general plea for reform, more or less impassioned, according to the temper of the preacher; or some particular matter that needed reformation might be stressed.

An example of a sermon constructed with most of its emphasis on the application may be seen in the Reverend John Norton's election-day sermon of 1661.[46] Preaching on *Jeremiah* 30:17, a text which he called "A Divine Plaister for a Sin-sick

---

44 Ramus, *Dialectique* (Paris, 1555), 70.
45 A letter dated December 20, 1665, quoted in Mather's *Magnalia*, Book III, 83.
46 Norton, *Three Choice and Profitable Sermons*, 1-15.

Outcast," Norton has as his doctrine (p. 3) "When Sion for its sin is become an Out-cast (a subject of contempt) God takes occasion from her Calamity to give Repentance, that so he may bring upon her the Blessing of his own People." He then admits that the text has "paradoxes and riddles," but he decides to ignore them and to go on to "reasons." These are threefold: there is always sympathy between the Head and its members, God's name suffers when his outcasts suffer, and the outcast must be "capacitated" to receive the benediction of a Father. All three points are discussed but briefly; in the printed sermon this part of the discourse takes but two pages. Then begin the ten pages of "uses." The first of these is called "instruction," and five points are brought out: Zion is subject to apostasy; apostasy always brings calamity; but Zion's "maladie" is not curable by calamity; this sickness can only be healed by God's promise; and repentance is a signal of God's mercy. Having quickly learned their lesson, the members of the congregation are now ready for a more extended "exhortation," developed in six parts, which they must accept as God's plaster to restore them to a sound condition. First, they must learn to judge aright of liberty, which should mean liberty to walk in the order of the Gospel. Second, they must acknowledge the divine order; here Norton is really pleading for acceptance of a council's decision in controversies, but his argument becomes somewhat complicated. There are, he says, three types of judgment: discretive, proper to any believer; authoritative, proper to every church; and decisive, proper only to a council. Similarly, the supreme, "authentick" judge is Christ; the "regulative" judge is Scripture; and the "ministerial" judge is a council. Having settled this somewhat knotty problem to his own satisfaction and perhaps to his audience's confusion, Norton proceeds to his third use: "to sanctify God in his Providential Testimonies" against the abuse of liberty. Here the colonists are reminded of their many adversaries who would gladly deprive them of all liberty. The fourth use is for the elect to study the past examples of the "godly wise" struggling to continue their liberties; these archetypes may be seen in the Bible. With the fifth use, the earnest preacher becomes practical: New Englanders must walk in liberty, but must be careful not to give offence to civil authority. Here he gives his plea that the colony apologize to the restored government in old England. The sixth use, "a principal Ingredient of this healing Plaister," also is very definite in its good advice: New Englanders must take care that their practice follows their doctrine, or else their integrity and sincerity will suffer. The problem is faced honestly. Spectators, watching the colonies, ask, "Whether the Congregational-way be practical, yea or not?" And the answer has to be either that the Congregational way is not the way of God or that the colonists are unfit for that way, "for the behavior of the house of God." In a final two-page entreaty Norton reiterates the main points he has been discussing under "exhortation": the men of the congregation are urged to take advantage of the coming year and not to "betray liberty, under a pretence of liberty." Let them prove that they were not mistaken in themselves and their own strength. Let them not neglect an apology to the English government.

Norton's sermon shows the structure that a great many preachers essayed. He is a little more clear-cut in distinguishing his points than most of the ministers manage to be. The different arguments do not overlap, and he ties some of them together in a final summation and supplication. He is also much more practical and concrete in his application than most of his contemporaries. That is, he not only reminds the people to turn to God, but he also tells them to show this turning by definite actions. Norton had an exceptionally logical and lucid mind. There is, of course, one other easily detected reason for the clarity and superiority of this sermon in comparison with many discourses of the same type. Apparently the preacher was a little impressed with the importance of the occasion; he was preaching an election sermon in the critical year of 1661, when every Puritan must have been bewildered and distraught at the political changes that had taken place and might still take place.

VI

SERMONIC SIMILITUDES: A SIDELIGHT UPON THE PURITAN MIND

No matter what point of faith or behavior the ministers wished to establish, they clarified it by suggesting comparisons. Luther had advised all preachers to use examples and similitudes; the current Puritan preaching manuals urged this same method; and Cotton Mather, some years later, was still pleading with pulpit speakers to search for similitudes with which to clothe their ideas and "make them sensible to the lowest and meanest Capacities, yea, to all Flesh."[1] But the early ministers of New England really did not need extra encouragement to pursue this course, for they seemed to drop naturally into this way of appealing to the common sense of their listeners. In other words, the members of the congregation were asked to recall some fact or incident that by ordinary observation they knew to be indubitable; then they were asked to apply to the somewhat intangible concepts of religion the practical truth which they had just recognized as common knowledge. When any preacher needed to confirm the greatness of Christ, he spoke of kings. Would not ordinary men make great preparations for the visit of a king? Would they not beg most humbly for his favors? Accept gratefully and without question what he gave them? Could any believer, then, do less for the King of kings, beside whose glory earthly monarchs were "born on a dung-hill"? When any preacher needed to discuss the intimate yet sacred relationship of Christ and his church, he turned to the well-worn Biblical imagery of the bridegroom and his bride. The marital relationship is shown as one of dignity and affection. A man will forgive his wife anything if she be but faithful to him; on the other hand, a woman, once she realizes her husband's love for her, will do anything for him. Even if he leaves her temporarily, she will spend her time reading and re-reading his letters, sent to her from a distance, or she will de-

---

1 Cotton Mather, *Manuductio ad Ministerium Directions for a Candidate of the Ministry* (Boston, 1726), 104.

vote her energy to preparing everything for his return. Should the church have a less gracious, less holy spirit toward its Master?

These similitudes are doubly informative about the Puritan mind. Men who instinctively associated royalty with glory that went beyond words had an innate respect for kings that passing events could not easily shake. Men who habitually spoke of their dearly beloved church and Savior as bride and bridegroom had some respect for woman and for the dignity of marriage. Considered more objectively, the similitudes are certainly revelatory both of the people as a whole and of the ministers' relations with them. That these comparisons were a successful means of increasing the clarity of each sermon was due to the preacher's self-restraint. Each minister was faced with a constant double duty while appealing to the reasoning power of his followers . The logic of the whole sermon had to stand out, unconfused by side-issues; and each step in the argument had to be made vivid by illustration. Hence he always ran the danger of having his audience not see the forest for the trees. The solution was to keep the clarifying similitudes not only terse and plain but also within the experience of all. Every comparison must be one that every man in the congregation could at once understand, without any distracting moments of consideration. Any minister would have defeated his own aim if he had surprised or shocked his listeners by strange tidings or extraordinary allusions. Each conscientious servant of God was duty-bound to stay within the limits of the taste and knowledge of his flock. For his tropes, he had to draw, of course, upon nature and man, the great sources of imagery. And though seventeenth-century Puritan listeners were primarily interested in man, in his physical being, in his daily life, in history, nature was not entirely neglected.

The ministers saw the physical world through the eyes of the Bible. This limitation, which they considered a privilege, was true in both a larger and a lesser sense. At first they were all Ptolemaicists, of course; not only did the Bible speak of the earth as the fixed center of the universe, the sun as a moving body, but most of the early Protestants had been zealous against the Copernican theory.   Luther,[2] Melanchthon,[3] Calvin[4] had all aspersed the "upstart astrologer" and his disturbing new theory.   The New England preachers did not bother to do so. Cotton on just one occasion disproved the Copernican theory to his own satisfaction, by citing the usual procedure of throwing a stone in the direction of the claimed rotation of the world.[5] Most of the time he takes for granted that the Bible can be accepted literally on this matter as on all others.   This was the common viewpoint of the rest of the early preachers.   Shepard repeatedly uses the steady movement of the sun as a standard basis with which to compare other movements or developments.[6] Hooker speaks of the sun rejoicing like a giant to run its course, "because God commands it."[7]   No minister asserted in his pulpit his advocacy of the Copernican theory, although President Chauncy of Harvard seems to have adopted the new theory as early as 1659,[8] and presumably he was not at this time alone among the clergy in accepting the change; but as late as 1671, the end of the period under consideration, Mitchell was still extolling the sun as "that admirable work of God, travelling his dayly and yearly circuit."[9]

Obvious, if fallacious, comparisons, such as the steady progress of the sun, constituted most of the average minister's interest in natural science; in fact, only a very limited number of preachers ever went beyond a very infrequent aside on earthquakes or tides, two phenomena which must have forced themselves on the attention of all.   Now and then, however, there was felt a need for an interpretation of some Biblical command. Shepard, for example, saw some difficulty in determining the proper timing of the Sabbath.   Yet in his *Theses Sabbaticae* he explains with fair clarity the effect of longitude on the begin-

2 Martin Luther, "Tischreden" in the *Works* (Walch edition, 1743), XXII, 2260.
3 Philipp Melanchthon, "Initia Doctrinae Physicae" in *Corpus Reformatorum* (Bretschneider, Halle edition, 1846), XIII, 216-217.
4 *Cf.* Andrew Dickson White, *A History of the Warfare of Science with Theology in Christendom* (New York, 1897), 126.
5 Cotton, *A Briefe Exposition of the Whole Book of Canticles*, 14.
6 Shepard, *The Sincere Convert, passim; The Parable of the Ten Virgins, passim.*
7 Hooker, *The Paterne of Perfection*, 26.
8 Morison, *Harvard College in the Seventeenth Century*, 216-217.
9 Mitchell, *A Discourse of the Glory*, 121.

ning of any given day, and notes the variation of "four" hours in time between Old England and New England. The effect of latitude on determining the Sabbath bothered him a little more, and he could only hope that in Russia and other northern countries, "wherein for about a month's time the sun is never out of sight," the inhabitants measured their natural days by the motion of the sun."[10] It is to be noted that this explanation occurs in Shepard's volume of discourses rewritten for the benefit of Harvard students, and there is no way of telling whether or not this discussion was in the original sermons as they were delivered from the pulpit. But the chances seem to be that it was an interpolation intended for the future ministers busily studying at the college; certainly this is the only time that the Cambridge pastor dwells even briefly on a scientific problem.

Sometimes, too, his text started Cotton talking about natural science, a field of some interest to him, for he felt that all should study "the nature, and course, and use of all Gods workes" in order to honor properly the Creator; moreover, although his own remarks are rarely of a practical type, he believed man might well benefit himself by this sort of knowledge.[11] The first chapter of *Ecclesiastes* led him to a number of large problems and induced him to give a brief summary of the Aristotelian theory of the four elements and the stability of the world, to defend the Ptolemaic geocentric theory against the newer ideas of Copernicus, and to attempt an explanation of the original of all waters.[12] Perhaps his audience was more interested in some less abstract concepts that he advanced during his explication of *Matthew* XVI. Here he comments on the movement of the stars, on eclipses of the moon and sun, on rainbows and weather-galls, and on the sky as a means of foretelling the weather.[13] His repetitious explanation of morning and evening red skies is typical of his conscientious struggling with a scientific problem:

The best reason given, that I meete with in this case is this, the brightnes of the clouds in the evening is a signe, they say, of the rarity or thinnes

10 Shepard, "The Morality of the Sabbath," in *Theses Sabbaticae*, 148-151; also "The Beginning of the Sabbath," in *Theses Sabbaticae*, 13, 31.

11 John Cotton, *A Briefe Exposition upon Ecclesiastes* (London, 1657), 25.

12 *Ibid.*, 11-13, 14, 17.

13 John Cotton, *Gods Mercie Mixed with His Iustice* (London, 1641), 120, 126, 133, 113-114.

of the ayre, in which these clouds are, and is thorowly pierced by the beames of the Sunne, and easily shed or driven away, and so the matter of foule weather is remooved: The cleere brightnesse of the cloud in the evening is a signe that the cloud is rare and thinne, and the body of the cloud pierced thorowly, by the beames of the Sunne, whence it is that the matter or cause of foule weather is discipated. And so for a reason of the other; If the morning be red and lowring, you say it is a signe of a stormy day: So also I say, the reason of this is not easie for every man to discerne, but these men resolve upon the conclusion, whether they know the reason or no. But the reasons I meete with in nature are these in this case; they say, there is some rarity in some part of the cloude, but in that it is cloudy, it is a signe there is thicker matter in the cloude then the Sunne beams can readily pierce through; and therefore because of the heaviness of the matter, the Sun beams cannot drive those clouds away, nor are able of a sudden to dissolve and discipate them into winde or raine; but in time they make account winde and raine will follow, but the clouds being lowry and sad, shew an easinesse in the clouds, now to dissolve themselves and to water the Earth, and in the end will burst foorth into raine and winde that day."[14]

It is to be noted that Cotton carefully qualifies his statements, letting his listeners know not only that there are other theories, but that the event does not always follow the sign. He has the instincts of honest scholarship and shows no sign of being adverse to scientific inquiry; in fact, he welcomes any knowledge that may help to explain God's universe or to clarify the Bible. Nevertheless, in his approach to all these questions, Cotton is no scientist even in embryo,[15] but a Puritan theologian who is also a seventeenth-century scholar. He reads in his Bible of certain natural phenomena; he observes them happening about him. In his intelligent desire to know more about reasons and causes, he reads more than one authority on each point, and then selects the answer which appeals to him *a priori* and which offers no seeming contradiction to any Biblical text.[16]

In the smaller sense, too, the ministers were apt to see the world only through the Bible. The world was simply part of God's ordered universe, another example of his power and good-

---

14 *Ibid.*, 113-114.
15 For an interesting discussion of the Puritan attitude towards science, with especial emphasis upon Cotton, see Theodore Hornberger's "Puritanism and Science," *The New England Quarterly*, X (No. 3, September, 1937), 593-615.
16 One other minister, the Reverend Samuel Danforth, was sufficiently interested in science to write *An Astronomical Description of the Late Comet or Blazing Star, Together with a brief Theological Application Thereof* (Cambridge, 1665). From the present form of this discourse it is impossible to tell how much of the scientific discussion had been originally delivered from the pulpit; even the "theological application"—that New England should reform—has completely lost its sermonic style.

ness, and was interesting only as such. The New England scene hardly broke in upon their consciousness. The rivers of the sermons are vague rivers of the love and goodness of God, or, perchance, rivers of tears, or even streams of corruption that need damming. The wells are wells of salvation into which the bucket of prayer must be dipped. The birds are, for the most part, kites and eagles, carrion crows and doves. "Kites look downward, but Eagles look upward," observes Whiting, and then remakes his point by remarking, "Carrion crows are much upon the Earth, but Doves fly high toward Heaven."[17] Of course, people differ in position and duty in this well-regulated world, and to elucidate the truth of this somewhat obvious statement, Hubbard asks:

In the firmament of the air, may we not see the lofty eagle in his flight far surmounting the little choristers of the valleys?[18]

Man can learn in other ways from watching the habits of birds. The latter, for instance, know enough to worship regularly their Creator:

The very Birds, morning and evening (and some also (as the Nightingale) in the night also) are in their manner lifting up their notes unto their maker, and maintainer.[19]

Again, the migratory habits of birds make Shepard wonder at their instinctive sense of self-preservation, in contrast to human dullness in not realizing the necessity of turning immediately to God for spiritual survival:

Doth the *stork know when winter is near, and not you your season?*[20]

Yet occasionally a preacher's interest seems to have gone beyond his Bible reading or his need for a fit simile. Bees and honey held a particular fascination for Shepard. Using the obvious allegory of bees for men,/honey for grace, the hives for life, he speaks repeatedly of bees gathering honey, of smoking-out bees, and of tasting honey; and he notes epigrammatically, "The full soul loathes the honey-comb."[21] Butterflies and bees often came to the minds of various ministers as an apt com-

17 Samuel Whiting, *A Discourse of the Last Judgement* (Cambridge, 1664), 158.
18 Hubbard, *The Happiness of a People*, 9.
19 Cobbett, *A Practical Discourse of Prayer*, 234.
20 Shepard, *The Parable of the Ten Virgins*, Pt. I, 214; *cf. Jeremiah* 8:7.
21 *Ibid.*, Pt. I, 85.

parison of the lazy and the diligent, but Hubbard's is the most pleasing:

The prudent husband man uses more to be delighted in the busie, active yet sable Bee, than in the gaudy Butter fly, which it may be ranges all over the field to get only fine colours wherewith to paint her wings, from those flowers whence the other diligent creatures fetch both wax and honey, wherewith they both build their houses, and furnish them with provision to feed themselves, and refresh their owners, while the other are but the object of childrens sport.[22]

Hooker, while not neglecting bees or butterflies, found that apples afforded him a number of parallels with more important matters. But, despite his steady interest, he was no expert in pomology:

Take but an Apple, there is never a man under heaven can tell what tast it is of, whether sweet or soure, untill he have tasted of it; he seeth the colour and the quantity of it, but knoweth not the tast: so there is no man under heaven discerneth more of grace than he findeth in himselfe.[23]

Now and then, but very rarely, some such slight interest in his surroundings led a minister to comment on differences between the Old and New World. Hooker, on one occasion, starts with a common proverb, and then elaborates upon it pleasantly:

Birds of a Feather wil flock and fly together. As here in *New-England*. The Color of some Birds is very strange, by reason of the Climate, heats and colds: and that causes some wholly to differ from other. Yet if we see them flock and mate commonly together, we conclude, it is a Starling, not a Black-Bird, She keeps with such: though her color and Feathers be other, yet Nature and kind is the same.[24]

And Cotton saw this surprising variation in frog-life:

And like unto Frogs are they for their continuall croking; nothing but one kinde of tune: their own matters they never leave croking of, not like these Frogs here in *America* that have a severall tune in each part of the yeare, but they are alwayes in one, or two, or three at the most; either the Catholique visible Church, or the Pope the Judge of controversies, or of visible succession.[25]

Perhaps, however, he wanted to see this distinction between the old country and the new, for Cotton's monotonous frogs are always Jesuits, just as his locusts are the other Catholic orders.

But one part of nature did impress the ministers—the ocean.

22 Hubbard, *The Happiness of a People*, 56.
23 Hooker, "Culpable Ignorance" in *The Saints Dignitie*, 209.
24 Hooker, *A Comment upon Christ's Last Prayer*, 418-419.
25 Cotton, *The Powring out of The Seven Vials*, 35.

Perhaps the long and difficult sea-passage lingered in their memories. And how large a part the ocean played in the lives of the early colonists may be seen by the frequency of allusion to maritime pursuits. Time and time again practically every minister resorts for his imagery to the sea and ships and sailors. Quite naturally Shepard speaks of "fears on fears, as wave on wave," and of being "afflicted and tossed with tempests." And a dozen situations that have to do with sailing the Atlantic are brought into his discussions. Unscrupulous merchants send forth their boats, but perfidiously refuse to go themselves. Sailors make elaborate and necessary preparations for a voyage. Once at sea, mariners make use of any wind, or of a compass, or of soundings to find their way to port. An anchor is essential if anyone hopes to ride securely through storms. Another necessity is confidence in the master, who will save his crew if he be given enough liberty. Then, too, all sea-going men long to be on shore, and there is no pleasure like riding safely to harbor.[26]

Hooker was another preacher many of whose warnings take nautical form. The imagination, he feels, is like a vast sea, apt not to keep channel. Man should not expect in this life great joy without some sorrow:

Great revelations have great Humiliations go before them; the Eb is very low before the Tyde comes with greatest strength and height; otherwise the soul would never be able to bear such overbearing expressions of Gods Love, and communications of himself, but would certainly abuse them. If the Keel of the Boat were little and narrow, a large Sail would overturn it, not convey it to the Haven. Great assurances and Glorious Joyes, are too large a sail for a heart that is not widened with enlarged contritions and humiliations.[27]

Mariners carried away in a storm are forced by the rage of winds and fierce weather to wander away from their destination, but a godly, capable pilot keeps his course despite the wind or tide. Even a clever mariner has difficulty in getting a boat through a narrow channel. A ship with fair sails and strong masts still needs a wind in order to go; so a soul may have God's ordinances, but needs his spirit as well. Or again, the soul is a little bark, supplied with the sense of God's love and mercy as a

26 Shepard, *The Parable of the Ten Virgins*, I, 32, 37, 42, *et alii*.
27 Hooker, *The Application of Redemption*, the Ninth and Tenth Books, 336. For another passage on tides, *cf. The Soules Union*, 34.

sail that carries it on a Christian course; alas, if the sail is too big, the boat is capsized. After a ship has broken up, any piece of board is seized and made use of by the drowning sailors. A humble spirit is the best anchor to keep a man's spirit quiet; on the other hand, if a boat accidentally runs aground, neither tacking nor other efforts by the mariners will help, until the wind and spring tide bring it safely to port.[28]

Hooker and Shepard were not alone in their predilection for similitudes from the sea. Other preachers use much the same imagery, with slight variations. Elder Cushman, always a realist, notes somewhat tritely that a man rowing a boat faces one way, but goes in the opposite direction—and perhaps the same is true of man in his religion.[29] As the ship is borne along swiftly if her sails are filled, Whiting comments, so man's desires would be gratified quickly if his prayers were filled with faith.[30] Eleazer Mather points out that the head of a family should be regarded as the pilot and able steersman, his children but unskilled passengers; but he fears that New England, for all that, is a sinking ship, about to be deserted by God.[31] Mitchell, a little more cheerfully, tells his congregation that the joys of the saints in heaven will be as an ocean in which they swim.[32] Hubbard emphasizes the need of a skilful pilot; only an experienced ruler can keep to the middle of the channel and prevent the boat's being shipwrecked. Again, only as long as those at the helm remain united in council and endeavour, will the ship not be wrecked.

A wise man alwayes sailes by the same compass, though not alwayes by the same wind.

And the body of the people is "not much unlike the body of waters, which are not apt to move of themselves"; and, alas, standing waters are apt to become corrupt.[33]

It may be justly said that most of these maritime images

---

28 Hooker, *The Application of Redemption*, the Ninth and Tenth Books, 141, 231, 234, 237, 310, 336; *The Soules Humiliation*, 71, 138; *The Soules Ingrafting*, 133; *A Comment upon Christ's Last Prayer*, 123; *et alii*.
29 Cushman, *A Sermon preached at Plimoth in New-England December 9 1621* . . . , 2.
30 Whiting, *Abraham's Humble Intercession*, 27.
31 Eleazer Mather, *A Serious Exhortation*, 26, 30.
32 Mitchell, *A Discourse of the Glory*, 33.
33 Hubbard, *The Happiness of a People*, 12, 15, 17, 26, 29, 52, *et alii*.

are closely connected with man and his struggles against nature. As one would expect to find in the strenuous life of seventeenth-century colonists, man and his daily difficulties in surviving and making a living are all important. Moreover, the Puritans were particularly frank about man's interest in himself, and they found their most apt illustrations in everyday life and existence.

Frequently the preachers saw that the human body, especially the illnesses it was prone to suffer, could be used for similitudes that would strike home to all. The Reverend Thomas Walley throughout an entire discourse,[34] the Plymouth election sermon of 1669, applied the terminology of physical sickness to the condition of New England's churches with their various diseases, which included lethargy (insensibility to sin), fever (a spirit of contention), and possession by an evil spirit (proclivity to sin). He went on to discuss the attendant evils of sickness and possible cures for the various ailments. Earlier ministers made less lengthy use of tropes taken from bodily conditions, but did not hesitate to employ metaphors and similes of this type. Such figures of speech from the body were well accepted in Elizabethan and post-Elizabethan days, as a glance at the work of the Spenserian and metaphysical schools of poetry will show; but the ministers probably were more influenced by the example of Augustine, who draws frequently on the human body and on sickness for exemplification of his points.

Hooker was particularly fond of analogies between the body and society as a whole, stressing the interdependence of parts of the body. His congregation was reminded of many of the physiological notions of the day, among them that the liver makes blood for the whole body;[35] that the veins carry the blood to all parts of the body in order to allow the bones to make bones of this necessary fluid, the sinews to make sinews;[36] that the hair (like the leaves of a tree) grows upon the moisture coming from the body, not upon the substance of the body;[37] and that the

34 Walley, *Balm in Gilead to Heal Sions Wounds: or a Treatise wherein there is a clear Discovery of the most Prevailing Sicknesses of New-England, both in the Civill and Ecclesiasticall State; As also sutable Remedies for the Cure of them* . . . .
35 Hooker, *The Soules Effectuall Calling to Christ*, 610.
36 Hooker, *A Comment upon Christ's Last Prayer* . . . , 417.
37 Hooker, "The Soules Union with Christ" in *The Soules Exaltation* (London, 1638), 18.

heart is the last part of the body to die.[38] Since humors were
the popular explanation of many physical conditions, Hooker
notes that wens are caused by superabundant humors of the
body and that these abnormal growths (like hypocrites) sap the
strength of the body.[39] Or he expatiates upon the similarity between the evil humors and the lusts that man might suffer from:

Look how it is with the bodie of a man, if one have a foul stomack, full of
very bad and noisome humors, commonly it breedeth a rheumatick eie, and
a sleepie and drowsie head; Just so it is also with the soul; if a mans heart
harbour any noysome lusts, if any sinfull corruption lodge there, the truth
is, it alwaies breeds a blear-eyed judgement, it sendeth up such streams and
mists into the understanding as quite dazeleth it, so that it cannot discern
the truth of God; . . .[40]

The ministers, not content with using physical imagery to
bring out the idea that all parts of the body (and of society) are
dependent upon each other, were always quick to make much of
everybody's knowledge that the whole individual suffers when
part of him is affected. By this palpable observation, the belief could be forcefully inculcated that the whole community
would pay for the malpractices or abuses of a few. If the
stomach were purged of its foul humor, Hooker remarks sig-
nificantly, the pain of "wind in the head," caused by rising
fumes, would be eased.[41] Cotton makes much the same comment about the suffering of even the worthiest New Englanders,
if the poorer and weaker settlers were to be allowed to sin:

So that (minde you) how the sins of the time rise from the contagion of
the hearts and lives of the people; That look as a man catcheth cold on his
feet, it fils the head with distempers: catch but cold in the lowest part,
abouth the ancles and feet; or suppose the stomach be somewhat annoyed
through ill dyet, or ill digestion, what then? It strikes up to the head pre-
sently; you cannot annoy the feet, ancles, or middle Parts, but the head will
feel both.[42]

But indigestion and colds were not the only illnesses that
the colonists experienced. Now and then the sermons reveal
the sharper tribulations that every family knew and at some
time had endured. People in the throes of consumption call for

38 Hooker, *The Soules Effectuall Calling*, 184.
39 Hooker, "The Soules Union," 19.
40 Hooker, "Culpable Ignorance" in *The Saints Dignitie and Dutie*, 200.
41 Hooker, *The Application of Redemption*, Books IX and X, 234.
42 Cotton, *The Powring out of the Seven Vials*, 13.

meat and then are unable to eat it.[43] "Green" wounds are easily cured,[44] but limbs suffering from gangrene must be amputated, else the whole body will be infected.[45] Ulcerous sores must be deeply purged so that they heal and the bandage may be painlessly removed.[46] There was a disease named Pica, the victims of which fed upon coal and ashes (charcoal), apparently because such a diet best suited the noisome humors in the stomach.[47] Pregnant women, too, were apt to want to eat coal,[48] and the sharper the throes of child-birth, the more speedy the mother's recovery.[49]

The sermons tell not only of suffering, but also of possible remedies. There were two general ways of alleviating the pangs of illness. Aqua vitae (alcohol, brandy, or ardent wine infused with spices and herbs)[50] was a recognized help in all cases of fainting and weakness. And a different type of aid for the sickly or feeble consisted of rubbing with oil to restore life and warmth to benumbed parts of the body. Almost all other suggested cures depended on the current belief in the curative powers of herbs. But, although herbalism was extremely popular in the period, the preachers make a very limited number of references to its use, perhaps because false and ignorant herbalists pretended to knowledge they did not in reality possess;[51] there may have been a good deal of uncertainty in many minds about the exact virtues of particular herbs, especially as enthusiastic herbalists claimed that practically every plant cured innumerable diseases.

Nevertheless, here and there in the sermons, especially in Hooker's preaching, a casual reference shows the common cures of the day. Rhubarb and "dock-wood" are mentioned as pos-

---

43 Shepard, *The Parable of the Ten Virgins*, 89 *et alii*.
44 Hooker, *The Application of Redemption*, 329.
45 Hooker, "Wilful Hardness" in *The Saints Dignitie*, 42.
46 Davenport, *The Saints Anchorhold*, 172-173.
47 Hooker, *The Application of Redemption*, 641.
48 Cotton, *Christ the Fountaine*, 168.
49 Hooker, *The Application of Redemption*, 421.
50 For the various meanings of the term *aqua vitae*, see *An Illustrated Medical Dictionary*, edited by Frank P. Foster, M.D. (New York: D. Appleton & Co., 1891), Part 2, p. 356, *s.v.* "aqua." Alchemists used the term for mercury and for wine distilled with mercury as well as for spirit of wine. *Cf. Lexicon Alchemicae sive Dictionarium Alchemisticum* (Frankfort, 1612), 51.
51 Shepard, *The Parable of the Ten Virgins*, I, 75.

sible aids for a "chollerick" stomach.[52]   Since rhubarb is a member of the dock (*Rumex*) family, dock-wood may refer to burdock, the stems of which formerly were used as a vegetable and as a blood-purifier. Children, who even in the seventeenth century showed an unfortunate appetite for raw fruit, should be given "worme-seed" or the herb *Feniculus portinus* (also called *Fenciulus porcinus* and *Feniculus poeticus*),[53] because this was a certain cure for worms and other stomach ailments.[54]   Balsam was recommended as a general panacea,[55] but there is no way of knowing whether Hooker had in mind the herb balsam or costmary (*Tanacetum balsamita*), a pleasant scented plant which had been introduced into England from the Orient in the sixteenth century; perhaps he was using the term "balsam" in the more general sense of any healing or soothing agency.   On another occasion, Hooker, urging that all distressed sinners accept the Word of the Lord, aptly points out the advisability of sufferers' taking a little mithridate, for if they "take hot water into a windy stomacke the winds will stirre on one side, and the water on another side, and distemper the stomacke."[56]   Most mithridates or antidotes for poison were in the form of electuaries made from dried herbs combined with honey.   Still other very effectual remedies that Hooker recalled were "powder of scorpions" and "mercury water," both medicines being capable, in his opinion, of acting against the most poisonous humors.[57] Scorpion-powder may have been made from scorpions, as scorpion-oil was a popular cure for venomous scorpion bites; or the powder may have been pounded from dried scorpion-grass (*Myosotis*), which also was supposed to be effectual against the sting of a scorpion.   "Mercury-water," despite its misleading name, was only the juice of the herb *Mercurialis,* a stomach cleanser.[58]   Physic, doubtlessly home-made of herbs—for every home apparently had its bottle of "Kitchen-Physick"[59]—was fre-

---

52 Hooker, *A Comment upon Christ's Last Prayer*, 417.
53 *An Herbal* (1525). Edited and Transcribed by Sanford V. Larkey, M.D. and Thomas Pyles (New York: Scholars' Facsimile and Reprint, 1941), *s.v.* "Feniculus portinus," and page 32.
54 Hooker, *The Application of Redemption*, 9-10, 200-201.
55 *Ibid.,* 155.
56 Hooker, *Foure Learned and Godly Treatises*, 208-209.
57 Hooker, *The Application of Redemption*, 101.
58 *An Herbal (1525)*, *s.v.* "Mercurialis" and p. 45.
59 Both Hooker and Shepard mention this a number of times.

quently mentioned as a necessary means to good health; an effective purge first made the patient sick and then helped to cure him. All bitter things were considered cleansing, on the principle that the stomach would abhor them and therefore expel them rapidly; sweets, on the other hand, were nourishing.[60] Some of the other suggested health aids were not so strenuous as those just mentioned. Dying men, said gentle Shepard, had to be tenderly nourished "by conserves and alchemies and spirits of gold."[61] Conserves in those days usually were made of the tender leaves and tops of such herbs as scurvy-grass (*Cochlearis*), wormwood (*Absinthium*), and rue (*Ruta*), or of such fruits as barberries or aloes. Alchemies would be the juices of any plants considered of a beneficial nature. And the "spirits of gold" would have been one of various distilled liquid preparations made with powdered gold or, more probably, with some other yellow mineral.[62] Distillation was a familiar process in the medicine of the time; Hooker comments that five drops of distilled liquors are more powerful than five spoonfuls of the unaltered substance.

Although the ministers did not hesitate to draw parallels between man's physical being and his spiritual state, and between the human body and society, they were far more apt to illustrate their points by references to man's daily life and occupations. Again they were following in the Augustinian rhetorical tradition, for the Bishop of Hippo enlivened his exegesis with innumerable details borrowed from local habits and daily life.[63] The frequency with which the preachers resorted to the allegory of the bridegroom and his bride to show the relation of Christ to his church, has been noted. When they wished to show the relationship of man to God, they turned just as naturally to child-parent imagery. These pictures, far from stern in tone, reflect tender paternal affection. The way a man becomes possessed of Christ is charmingly explained:

As it is with a little child that is not able to goe of it selfe, the father takes the child in his hand, and then it is able to goe. The child holds, the father,

60 Hooker, *The Application of Redemption*, 361.
61 Shepard, *The Parable of the Ten Virgins*, 170 *et alii*.
62 Foster's *An Illustrated Medical Dictionary*, Part 2, p. 508, *s.v.* "Aurum."
63 *Cf.* Louis Bertrand, *Saint Augustin*. Translated by Vincent O'Sullivan (London, 1914), 286-294.

not because it hath any power of it selfe, but because the father holds him, so we hold the Lord Jesus Christ, because we are holden of him: for the humbled soule stands possessed of Christ, because Christ makes him his care, and his charge, and takes possession of him, and therefore he comes to an interest in Christ.[64]

A good and kindly father tries to persuade his fractious child to eat a substantial meal:

As it is (in reason) with a childe happily when the father entertaines him at the table, he gives him a little sweet-meat, as some conserve, or the like, and it is so sweet that he can taste nothing but that, and his minde is still upon it, that he may receive more of it: the father commends this and that, and praiseth a third, and extols a fourth dish, but yet the childe cryes, more of this because he felt the sweetnesse of it, and was marvellously contented with, and he loved it.[65]

Then, too, a father is by his very nature forgiving, winking at his son's imperfect services as long as the young man "desireth and endeavoureth to doe better."[66] How different is the fate of a child serving not his own father, but a hard master.[67] A son or daughter kept at home will naturally inherit more richly there-fore; but how affectionately is a good son welcomed home, after his father "hath sent him on a great journey to doe some busi-ness, & the weather falleth foul, and the way proveth danger-ous, and many a storm, and great difficulties are to be gone through"; so God will greet his faithful children after their long travail on earth.[68]

Fathers were not the only members of the family to be gently helpful with children. Sometimes, too, an elder brother would watch over a younger one with loving care and kindness:

As if an elder brother should set a child one of his younger brethre to get his father a poesie of flowers, and the child out of ignorance, should gather some weeds and put them in it: And the elder brother gathers out the weeds, and sprinkles the flowers, and then presents them in the child's name to the father. So does Christ to us, while we gather up petitions here and there, and as we think for the best and some truth and work of grace there is in them, yet some weeds of sinfull folly, then Christ takes them out of our hands and pulls out the weeds and sprinkles them with the blood of his

64 Thomas Hooker, *The Soules Ingrafting* (London, 1637), 87.

65 Hooker, "Spiritual Love and Joy" in *The Soules Implantation*, 202-203. For other examples of spoiled Puritan children, see Richard Mather, *The Summe of Certain Sermons*, 5, and Cobbett, *A Practical Discourse*, 185.

66 Hooker, "Grace Magnified" in *The Saints Dignitie*, 111.

67 Shepard, *The Parable of the Ten Virgins*, 21, 31, *et alii.*

68 Hooker, "The Activities of Faith" in *The Saints Dignitie*, 186-187.

crosse, and the merit of his sufferings, what he hath don and suffered for us. And so by this means it is not possible that our prayers should be rejected.[69]

The most affectionate father needs to discipline his erring son. The ministers here employed one of the oldest sermonic illustrations, that of a parent temporarily hiding from his child and then reappearing to comfort his wailing offspring, who by this time is supposed to have learned his lesson about false security. This story, which was current at least as early as the *Ancren Riwle,* is told again and again in medieval instructional and pulpit literature,[70] as well as in later sermons. For instance, Thomas Goodwin, one of the more noted English Puritan preachers, has this theme running through, and now and then definitely worded, in a number of sermons on *Isaiah* 50:10, 11 which he preached in the late 1620's and which were first published in 1636 under the suggestive title *A Childe of Light Walking in Darkness*;[71] Goodwin's point is to show why God allows his elect to suffer from attacks of despondency about their spiritual state.

In all versions of this incident, the basic kindness of the parent is always emphasized lest the point of the tale be lost, and the audience begin to wonder at the strange and arbitrary will of God. How well the Puritans kept the tender spirit of the original exemplum can be seen by comparison with the *Ancren Riwle* version:

Ure Louerd, hwon he iðoleð þet we beoð itented, he plaieð mid us, ase þe modor mid hire ȝunge deorlinge, vlihð from him, and hut hire, and let hit sitten one, and loken ȝeorne abutan, and cleopien, Dame! Dame! and weopen one hwule, and þeonne mid ispredde ermes leaped lauhwinde uorð, and clupped and cussed, and wiped his eien. Riht so, ure Louerd let us one iwurðen oðer hwules, and wiðdraweð his grace, and his cumfort, and his elne, þet we ne iuinded swetnesse in none þinge þet we wel doð, ne sauur of heorte.[72]

Chauncy is briefer and more restrained:

The Lord intends to make us more watchful, for future times: . . . As the

---

69 Cotton, *Christ the Fountaine*, 223-224.

70 Hope Emily Allen, "Some Fourteenth Century Borrowings from "Ancren Riwle'," *The Modern Language Review* (1923), XVII, 1-2.

71 Published also in 1638, 1643; in *The Workes*, 1681-1704; and in *The Works* (Edinburgh: James Nichol, 1861), III, 227-350—note especially 244, 312.

72 *Ancren Riwle* (Camden Society, 1853), 230.

Mother hides herself behind some tree or wall, to make the Childe watchful, and to cry after her, and search, and hang upon her armes: so doth God.[73]

Hooker, on the other hand, gives his incident a little more individuality:

I have seene the father deale so with the child; when the father is going on in his journey, if the child will not goe on, but stands gaping upon vanity, and when the father calls, he comes not, the only way is this, the father steps aside behind a bush, and then the child cries and cries, and if he gets his father againe, he forsakes all his trifles, and walks on more faster and more cheerfully with his father than ever.[74]

However affectionate parents may be, children, unfortunately, react in different ways to correction. One child, still stubborn, "snuffles, and falls into a swoune with griefe." But the better-spirited youngster accepts a blow and goes on his way quietly without any sort of fuss.[75] In school, too, children are naughty and manage to annoy their elders in various ways. If a schoolmaster is angry when he sees blots on exercises, picture his emotion if the recalcitrant pupil "blurs and blots" his face and soils his clothes.[76] And boys instinctively resist the learning process, going to school one day, staying away a week, later running away from their apprenticeships; alas, just so are men wilfully ignorant, "truant scollers in Gods Schole, so many runnagate apprentices from the meanes of Salvation."[77]

Another source of homely imagery was the daily indoor life of a family, especially the mistress's duties. What could be closer to the people, more domestic in tone, than this picture which Hooker presents while urging everyone to watch his own heart and keep it free from impurity:

You may conceive it by a similitude, if a pot be boyling upon the fire, there will a scum arise, but yet they that are good housewives, and cleanly, and neat, they watch it, and the scum riseth up, they take it off and throw it away, happily more scum will arise, but still as it riseth they scum it off.[78]

Spinning, too, provided some obvious images, especially to illustrate the virtues of moderation. Too fine a spinning of thread, Hubbard says positively, "doth but draw the wool be-

73 Chauncy, *Plain Doctrin*, 67.
74 Hooker, *The Soules Ingraffing*, 132.
75 Hooker, *The Soules Humiliation*, 187.
76 Whiting, *Abraham's Humble Intercession for Sodom*, 220.
77 Hooker, "Culpable Ignorance" in *The Saints Dignitie*, 199.
78 Hooker, *The Saints Dignitie*, 4-5.

yond the staple" and will never hold in weaving."[79] And although every day in a housewife's life must have been a busy one, wash-day seems to have presented some peculiar difficulties, if Cotton reports accurately:

> And so an Huswife that takes her linning, she Sopes, and bedawbs it, and it may be defiles it with dung, so as it neither looks nor smels wel, and when she hath done, she rubs it, and buckes it, and wrings it, and in the end all this is but to make it cleane and white; and truly so it is here, when as Tyrants most of all insult over Gods people, and scourge them and lay them in hee, or Dung, so as the very name of them stinks, yet what is this but to purge them, and to make them white, and it is a great service they doe to the people of God in so doing . . . ."[80]

The daily occupations of men were also found to offer many convenient parallels with spiritual life. Figures from warfare —the all-conquering Christian spirit, its armor, its aids, its foes —were put to good use, especially in artillery-election sermons. Frequently, too, the preacher could not resist the standard comparison of man's not untroubled passage through this world with a traveler's strenuous journey, and from time to time congregations were reminded that they should remember that this world was but their inn, soon to be left behind, not their permanent home. Another of the more popular pictorial fields, but one undoubtedly taken more from the Bible than from observation, was offered by the goldsmith's trade. The blowing of the fire that melts the ore, the hammering of the gold, the testing of it by taste and touch, the separation of the precious mineral from alloys, were familiar and colorful comparisons.[81] Closer to everyday seventeenth-century life was the observation that when much counterfeit gold is about, each man has his own scales with him and does not rely only on inspecting and rubbing dubious coins. Because there is many a "cozening chapman" and adulterator, practical men in good times and bad always taste wine and other commodities before buying them, just as they test corn and fields before purchasing them. Why, then, should not sensible men be equally careful about what doctrines they accept? Shopkeeping also offered many neat metaphors. Since a large, well-kept store obviously preserves mer-

79 Hubbard, *The Happiness of a People*, 29.
80 Cotton, *Christ the Fountaine*, 71-72.
81 Hooker and Shepard both use these comparisons repeatedly.

chandise and displays it to the best advantage, why should not every man be careful of the condition of his heart?[82]   Observe how one man, no matter how diligent, cannot own and manage successfully two stores.   A good Puritan must devote all his energy to being saved, and, anyway, notes Shepard, with an amusing lack of logic, shopkeepers who have lost their businesses are never willing to try their hands at more menial or more arduous tasks.[83]

Part of this feeling that man's daily achievements and failures made the most telling illustrative material is shown in the ministers' fairly steady interest in man as he is portrayed in history.   But just as the preachers feared to distract their congregations by citing whatever aids they had used in interpreting the Bible or in clarifying their doctrine, so, too, they hesitated to mention names, either of recorders or of characters, in the little illuminative quotations or stories that they occasionally substituted for the more familiar similitudes from daily life.   "As the poet says" or "as the heathen says" was often the only acknowledgment made for a borrowed illustration, which in turn was apt to have as its subject a "certain" king or general.   Here again the ministers were following the advice of Perkins, who had urged all earnest preachers of the gospel to avoid "humane testimonies," and, if it were impossible or too inconvenient to avoid them entirely, to leave out the names of the writers.[84]

Despite the ministers' good intentions not to mention any book but the Bible, any character not in the Bible, here and there in the sermons are to be found a few names of famous men and of the lesser men who wrote about them.   A familiar authority was Josephus, whose works had been especially recommended by Perkins as offering corroboration of such important Biblical stories as those of the flood, the death of Herod Agrippa, and the promised Redeemer of Jewish expectation.   Eusebius of Caesarea, the "Father of Church History," was another writer for whom Perkins had expressed his esteem, noting that Eusebius's ecclesiastical history was especially valuable in two

82 Hooker, The Souls Ingrafting, 97 et alii.
83 Shepard, The Parable of the Ten Virgins, I, 111, 154, et alii.
84 Perkins, The Arte of Prophecying, 664.

respects: in it were preserved the titles and a few extracts from the works of Melito, Bishop of Sardis, the rest of whose work has perished; and the sixth book was devoted to a study of Origen and his work. The ministers referred not only to Eusebius, but also to Socrates, whose great admiration for Eusebius had led him to continue the latter's work down to his own time, and to Sozomen, Socrates' less skilful contemporary, who also purposed to continue the work of Eusebius; still another fifth century authority occasionally cited was the historian Theodoret, whose numerous and varied works included ecclesiastical history and biographies of early ascetics. Three early British and English writers—Gildas, Bede, and Alcuin—were recognized sources of information, both for ecclesiastical and civil data. It is to be noted that the works of all these early authors were the better known because of the fact that they had been printed and reprinted during the sixteenth and early seventeenth centuries. The ministers must also have been familiar with many later ecclesiastical historians, but only a few are cited by name: Carolus Sigonius, a learned Italian antiquarian whose best known work was *A Treatise of the Commonwealth of the Hebrews* (1593); Peter Cunaeus, a Leyden professor who was another authority on the ancient Jews; Paolo Sarpi, who wrote under the pseudonym Pietro Soave Polanus, an Italian writer whose *The History of the Church since the Dayes of our Saviour Jesus Christ* (1624) was a popular book throughout the period among the religiously inclined; Heinrich Bullinger, better known for his exposition of the New Testament, but whose detailed chronicles of the Swiss reformation and of the rise of the Anabaptist sect were early translated into English; John Dury (Duraeus), a contemporary seventeenth-century Scotchman who made a study of the current state of the various Protestant churches in different parts of Europe; and that more famous contemporary, Hugo Grotius, whose interests included the annals not only of the Belgians, but also of Goths, Vandals, and Lombards.

But the ministers did not confine themselves to historians who were primarily concerned with religious matters. The sermons also show that Herodotus, Thucydides, and Plutarch were read. The latter was well known in many circles during the

seventeenth century. Probably this popularity, as far as the
Puritans were concerned, is not to be explained only by the ex-
cellence of the North translation, which was to be found at an
early date in a number of New England libraries; Plutarch's
taste for moralizing, his desire to find and reveal "the signs of
the soul in men," certainly helped to make him well-liked. An
occasional reference is also made to some of the Latin historians; Caesar, Livy, Lucan, Tacitus, Justin all contribute quotations or anecdotes. The ministers, moreover, were interested
not only in Greek and Roman times. Some of the more noted
later chroniclers are referred to. In fact, the ministers must
have gained a surprising variety of information from their reading of such sixteenth-century historians as Philip de Commines,
the French writer whose reputation is attested to by the fact
that his *Chronique et Historie* and *Chroniques du roy Charles
Luytresme* were reprinted twice before the mid-seventeenth century; Francisco Lopez de Gomara, the Spanish historian whose
Historia General de les Indes and *Chronica de la Nueve Espana
con la Conquista de Mexico* were so popular that they achieved
many editions in Spanish, French, Italian, and English; and
Albert Krantz (Crantzius), the author of *Chronica Regnorum
Aquilonarium Daniae, Sueciae, et Norvegiae* and of *Saxonica:
De Saxonicae Gentis Vestusta Origine.*

Literary references not purely historical in nature are few
in the sermons, but here and there an allusion to a classical writer
shows that the ministers occasionally ventured into broader
fields, or recalled having once so wandered. The interest is always predominantly in character studies or in quotable senten-
tious wisdom, but at least the ministers were familiar with quotations from such varied writers as Epictetus and Ennius, Cato,
Cicero, Virgil, Horace, Ovid, Seneca, and Hadrian, although no
one of them is mentioned more than a very few times in the whole
surviving body of pulpit literature. The ministers' taste and
their choice of illustration need no comment in most of these
cases; as English university men, the ministers would have been
very familiar with the works of Cicero, Virgil, Horace, Ovid
and Seneca.[85] Ennius, moreover, was probably known mostly

85 Morison, *The Founding of Harvard College*, 60-78.

through Cicero's enthusiastic regard for him. Seneca, both in
the original and in the Lodge translation, was extremely popular
during the seventeenth century, and his Stoic philosophy is supposed to have had an especial appeal to Puritans. In addition,
the ministers would have had their attention directly turned to
him by Calvin's frequent use of Senecan quotations. And as
for the last of the writers mentioned, it was Hadrian's brief
death-bed prayer—

> Animula vagula blandula
> hospes comesque corporis,
> quae nunc abibis in loca
> pallidula regida nudula,
> nec ut soles dabis jocos

that seemed valuable to the ministers.[86]

Not only did the average preacher make sparing use of historical and literary references, but he also gave as tersely as
possible those that he did permit himself. Apparently the reasoning behind this practice was that the more educated members of his congregation would automatically recall, perhaps only
roughly, perhaps with some exactitude, the context of the quotation or the details of the anecdote without any unnecessary
help from the speaker; and that those listeners without formal
education should not have their minds distracted by unessential
details which would mean little to them. Consequently, there
is a consistent air of brevity about all such allusions. So Oxenbridge gives a brief paradox from Cicero: "All wise men are
Freemen, all Fooles Servants."[87] Hubbard has one of Livy's
apothegms, both in the original and in English: "Oft doth the
remedy prove worse than the disease. Infaeliciter agrotat cui
plus mali venit a medico, quam a morbo."[88] Thomas Shepard,
Junior, quotes from Seneca without bothering to translate:
"Bene facere, & male audire regium est."[89] Although Seneca's
works are known to have been in a number of colonial libraries,
a note in the margin shows that Shepard here was only requot-
ing from John Reynolds's *The Triumphes of God's Revenge*

86 Leonard Hoare, *The Sting of Death and Death Unstung* (Boston, 1680), 6.
87 John Oxenbridge, *New-England Freemen Warned and Warmed . . .* (Cambridge, 1673), 20.
88 Hubbard, *The Happiness of a People*, 14; the reference is to Livy, preface
to Book I.
89 Shepard, *Eye-Salve, Or a Watch-Word from our Lord Iesus Christ unto his
Churches*, 45.

against . . . Murther . . . in Thirty Tragicall Histories (London, 1629).

Not all the allusions are quite so brief as these; sometimes a minister lingered for a moment or two with a favorite author. Cotton liked Epictetus's comparison of the body and clay, although some of the old Greek teacher's irony seems to have been lost on its way to New England:

Epictetus came forth one day, and saw a woman mourning for breaking her Pitcher, the next day he came forth, and saw another weping for her son, and he said, *Yesterday an earthen Pitcher broken, and to day a mortal body dead;* as if it were the same to have a Pitcher broken, and to dye.[90]

Shepard in the course of the argument of one of his sermons finds occasion to translate a few apt lines from Horace:

Let us comfort ourselves against this with God's promises: let us do as the covetous man in the Poet, who being mocked as he went in the streets, went home and looked into his closet, and there seeing his bags of gold, rejoyced in his wealth and scorned all their reproaches; so when we are mocked and scorned of men of the world, let us looke into the Bible, and we shall find bags of promises, true treasure; and therein let us rejoyce.[91]

Some years later, the Reverend Samuel Nowell, a little impressed by how close a "heathen" approached the thought of the Psalmist, also paraphrased Horace at some length:

It is Hope that animateth all our work. The heathen that had not true peace of Conscience, yet had some sense of the natural Conscience excusing, and doe express it in a strange manner. What is it such a man needs to fear? It is not all the violent storms he can be in or hazzard by them: not the cruelty of Tyrants, nor though the world should rush together. It is but a Heathen speech, but expresseth a strange apprehension they had of the benefit of peace of natural Conscience: they knew not peace with God. A man that is whole and sound within, may better look Death in the Face, than any other, from any other Consideration. The Psalmist expresseth

---

90 John Cotton, *A Practical Commentary* (London, 1656), 82.

91 Thomas Shepard, *The Saints Iewell* (London, 1642), 11. Undoubtedly Shepard had in mind Horace's *Satires*, Book 1, Satire 1, line 61 *et seq.*

> At bona pars hominum, decepta cupidine falso
> Nil satis est, inquit, quia tanti, quantum habeas sis.
> Quid facias illi? jubeas miserum esse libenter
> Quatenus id facit: ut quidam memoratur Athenis
> Sordidus ac dives, populi contemnere voces
> Sic solitus: populus me sibilat: at mihi plaudo
> Ipse domi, simul ac nummos contemplor in arca.

it in another manner, Psal. 112.7. He shall not be afraid of evil Tidings, his heart is fixed trusting in the Lord.[92]

Quotations and paraphrasings were, then, occasionally resorted to for illustration; but in their search for adequate illumination of difficult points, the ministers were a little more apt to borrow from history or poesy a definite anecdote about some famous person, and to retell the story as tersely as possible. So Oxenbridge relates the remarkable courage and perseverance that Demosthenes showed in the face of all odds while fortifying Pylus against the Spartans and other Lacedaemonians; the sermonic reference is brief to the point of being elliptic:

Now shall not we hold the Lands and Liberties which our God hath given us, . . . and indeed for your just bounds it will be great weakness to shorten them, for that Enemy is the worst, as *Sparta* found by the *Athenians,* seizing on Pylus a near and neglected island.[93]

Cyrus's feat in taking Babylon by changing the channel of the Euphrates was an exploit that held the attention of Hubbard, who, in the course of his argument for unity among the colonists, says briefly:

Cyrus is said to have overthrown the impregnable city of Babylon, by drawing the great channel of Euphrates, into several small rivulets, which had they continued in one main stream, he could never have done.[94]

When John Norton wished to stress the difference between life eternal and death and how the newly-freed soul would be gone from the dead body, he thought of an unpleasant detail in the story of cruel Mezentius:

It is said of one, that he would bind a dead corpse to a living man, and so he would torture them. This new man is bound to a dead corpse: there is

---

92 Nowell, *Abraham in Arms*, 16. Nowell is referring to Horace's *Odes*, Book III, Ode 3:

> Iustum et tenacem propositi virum
> Non civium ardor prava iubentium,
>   Non vultis instantis tyranni
>   Mente quatit solida neque Auster.
> Dux inquieti turbidus Hadriae
> Nec fulminantis magna manus Iovis
>   Si fractus illabatur orbis,
>   Impavidum ferient ruinae.

> *Cf.* Book I, Ode 22—the "Integer Vitae" has the same thought.

93 Oxenbridge, *New-England Freemen*, 24. The story is told by Thucydides, Book IV, Chapter 3 *et seq.*

94 Hubbard, *The Happiness of a People*, 17. The story is told by Herodotus, Book I, Chapter 191, as well as by other historians.

no part of the Understanding Will, or Affections, throughout the whole man, but this dead corpse is there.[95]

Other characters step out of the annals of the past and have their brief moments of service in various sermons. Zaleucus, the king and law-giver of the Locrians, keeps his own law that all adulterers be blinded, but saves his sinning son by sacrificing one of his own eyes for one of his son's.[96] Themistocles, the Athenian general, in vain demands tribute from the Andrians.[97] Pericles has to remind himself yearly that he is ruling Athenians and, therefore, free men.[98] Aceas the Scythian rebukes Philip II of Macedon for his false pride in his fighting men.[99] The Cynic Menippus makes his wise apology which healed the breach between citizens of different ranks.[100] Fabius Maximus Quintus, the illustrious Roman general, stresses the value of slow deliberation in all matters of any consequence.[101] Tiberius listens to Sejanus, Caesar to Brutus, Augustus to Maecenas.[102] Caesar keeps his presence of mind in danger and encourages his boatmen.[103] The convert Theodosius foolishly insults the Saracens, so soon to be victorious.[104] And Amphilochius, Bishop of Iconium, urges Theodosius to repress the Arians.[105]

As can be readily seen from this list of kings and generals, of brave men and foolish men, the ministers usually chose their historical exempla from ancient times. Only two Harvard graduates, Hubbard and Whiting, resorted to stories that had a medieval or modern background. Hubbard, for instance, casually told his congregation the tale of a Duke of Burgundy who

---

95 Norton, *Three Choice and Profitable Sermons*, 22. The reference is to Virgil's *Aeneid*, Book VIII, ll. 485-488.

   Mortua quin etiam iungebat corpora vivis,
   Componens manibusque manus atque oribus ora,
   Tormenti genus, et sanie taboque fluentis
   Complexu in misero longa sic morte necabat.

96 Chauncy, *The Plain Doctrin*, 44.
97 Hubbard, *The Happiness of a People*, 20.
98 Oxenbridge, *New England Freemen Warned*, 15.
99 Oakes, *The Unconquerable, All-Conquering & More-then-Conquering Souldier*, 30.
100 Hubbard, *The Happiness of a People*, 19.
101 *Ibid.*, 33.
102 Whiting, *Abraham's Humble Intercession for Sodom*, 23, 186.
103 Shepard II, *Eye-Salve, or a Watch-Word*, 9.
104 Hubbard, *The Happiness of a People*, 32.
105 *Ibid.*, 33.

lost his life and treasure in a miserable quarrel with some
Switzers over the toll upon a load of calf-skins.[106] A better anecdote related by Hubbard was that of an English captain, sent to
spy upon the enemy's camp; the brave fighting man proudly reported that there were enough of the foe for some to be killed,
some to be taken prisoners, and still others to run away.[107] Whiting, too, tells a good story of Henry the Seventh's cup-bearer
who had the misfortune to stumble and spill wine on the king's
garments. The king, furious at this clumsiness, asked his ser-
vitor if he had "done well in what he did." The reply came
promptly, answering irony with courtesy, and the king was
equally quick to meet devotion with generosity:

If your Majesty thinks it well done, it is well done. Sayest thou so, sayes
the king, then I say it is well done, and so pardoned him.[108]

More deliberately pathetic—and less moving—is Whiting's tale
of the convicted Cambridge thief whose main regret was that he
had not profited by the time he had spent in a particularly pious
Puritan home.[109]

The preachers realized that for their purposes emphasis
should be put upon the character of men as revealed by life's
emergencies, incidents which occurred in man's daily existence
or which had been recorded in history. After all, the points to
be illustrated had to do mostly with the nature of God and his
relationship to man, of men's proper attitude toward and duty
to his Creator and his Saviour, all concepts that should be expressed most easily through the terminology of man and his
virtues, of the devotion and service that man showed or should
show to his fellow-man. The fact that few similitudes are taken
from the arts does not in itself demonstrate that the Puritans
had little interest in these fields; on the other hand, if the preachers had been imbued with aesthetic ideas, the latter would undoubtedly have crept into their speech. But the culture of men
as shown by their accomplishments in the arts, was relatively
unimportant inasmuch as it did not furnish obvious illuminative material. Nevertheless, the ministers' scattered comments

106 *Ibid.*, 30.
107 *Ibid.*, 22.
108 Whiting, *Abraham's Humble Intercession for Sodom*, 19.
109 *Ibid.*, 41-42.

on music, art, architecture, and the stage offer an interesting
side-light upon Puritan aesthetic values.

It is an old commonplace of criticism that the Puritans
hated music, and encyclopedias, histories, and kindred reference
books reiterate this falsehood, always citing as proof the Round-
heads' destruction of church organs during the English civil
wars. It is true that the Puritans objected to contrapuntal music
and to the use of instruments in church, on the ground that
both types of elaboration detracted from the clarity of the service; and without this clarity, there could be no appeal to reason
but only to emotion. But in the orthodox Puritan view, music
per se was to be regarded as one of the good gifts of God, even
though it might be occasionally stolen and put to perverted use
by the devil. Luther certainly approved of psalm-singing and
of the congregation sharing in this part of the church service.[110]
Calvin, too, was not unappreciative of the powers of melody, for
he wrote:

Music hath a secret and almost incredible power to move the heart.[111]

American Puritans did not depart from this accepted view of
the virtues of music when it was correctly employed. John Cotton put in print his agreement with the idea that Psalms should
be sung in church and that instruments should be permitted in
the home.[112] At least two other ministers were fond enough of
music to own instruments for their own pleasure: the Reverend
Edmund Brown of Sudbury bequeathed in his will a "base vyol"
as well as a number of books on the subject; and the Reverend
Nathaniel Rogers of Ipswich left a "treble viall."[113] Later Cotton's son-in-law, Increase Mather, enthusiastically recommended music as "of great efficacy against melancholy discom-
posures."[114]

110 Prefaces to Johann Walther's *Geystliche Gsangbüchlin* (1525) and other
     sixteenth-century hymn collections. *Cf. The Hymns of Martin Luther*, edited
     by L. W. Bacon . . . (London: Hodder and Stoughton, 1884), xxi-xxvii.

111 Calvin, Preface to Liturgy in the *Annales Calviniani* (Brunswick ed.), VI,
     p. xvi.

112 John Cotton, *Singing of Psalms, A Gospel-Ordinance* (London, 1647).

113 Morison, *Harvard College in the Seventeenth Century*, 115.

114 Increase Mather, *Remarkable Providences Illustrative of the Earlier Days
     of American Colonization* (London: Reeves and Turner, 1890), 187. For an
     interesting discussion of the Puritan attitude towards music, see Percy A.
     Scholes' *The Puritans and Music in England and New England* . . . (London:
     Oxford University Press, 1934).

Theoretically, then, the ministers approved of music in its proper place and with some limitations in its church use. But the scarcity of musical imagery in the sermons suggests that music played but a minor part in their lives and for them was far from being "the universal language of mankind." The type of allusion certainly shows little aesthetic sensibility to lyric pleasure. True, there is no direct adverse criticism of music or of the enjoyment of music; in fact, few comments are as derogatory in tone or connotation as Chauncy's picture of sinners, heedless of their doom, "singing and chanting to the sound of the viol."[115] On the contrary, to at least two ministers, Thomas Cobbett and Samuel Whiting, a similarity between prayer and music repeatedly suggested itself. For example, in protesting against lip-prayer and loud protestations, Whiting notes:

Every mournful Ditty is not good Musick with me; nor beast-like roaring Melody in the ears of God.[116]

But usually the preachers did not comment at all upon the virtues of music, but contented themselves with remarking upon the difficulty of tuning an instrument.[117] So the Reverend Edward Bulkeley of Marshfield and Concord says:

To play on Musicke is pleasant, but it is hard to set the Instrument in tune to play well; It is hard to get the heart in tune, in a Spiritual lively humble frame.[118]

More definite and more knowing is Hubbard's recognition of the tuning problem:

The best way to keep an instrument in good tune, is to leave the strings upon a Sharp, they being naturally able to fall of themselves, and mankind is continually bent to declining.[119]

Even more practical in tone is Hooker's comment, which puts instrumental music on a definitely serviceable level:

The Musitian will first string his instrument before hee play with it: the waggoner will have his wheeles prepared, otherwise they draw heavily:

115 Chauncy, *The Plain Doctrin*, 43.
116 Whiting, *Abraham's Humble Intercession*, 7.
117 *Cf.* Cobbett, *A Practical Discourse of Prayer*, 319, 341, 345, 346, *et alii*.
118 Edward Bulkeley, *A Thankfull Remembrance of Gods Mercy* (Cambridge: Samuel Green, 1676), 10.
119 Hubbard, *The Happiness of a People*, 44.

so if thou wouldst have thy heart make musicke before God, tune it with righteousnesse, and then thy practice will go chearfully.[120]

The saddest remark of all, but one that pays high compliment to the harp by implication, was made by Jonathan Mitchell while drawing a comparison between the earthly and therefore temporal pleasure of communion with God and the eternal glory to come:

By the time your Harp is well in tune, and begins to sound well, you are fain to lay it aside: Wordly [sic] ocasions, Bodily necessities take you off, and interrupt your talk with God, and with his Word, and with your own Harts.[121]

Limited as musical references in the sermons are, they far outnumber allusions to and images taken from the pictorial arts. Once in a great while a preacher expresses some such elementary idea as this platitude of Shepard's:

A picture long a drawing is exact, another soon done is lightly done.[122]

And Shepard, whose critical acumen seems to have stopped with the problem of whether or not a work of art was "exact," once used a fairly interesting simile:

The wind is like an exact picture, it looks every man in the face that looks on it, if God speaks in it.[123]

Then, too, there was only the very slightest interest in the story of art, and scarcely an artist's name, real or mythical, is to be found. Scholarly Cotton vaguely refers to Pygmalion as loving his own picture[124]—perhaps the learned Boston divine in a moment's aberration was confusing Narcissus's admiration of his own image with Pygmalion's passion for his creation, Galatea. Mitchell, in more detail and using Caussin as his source, gives the story of Zeuxis, the "elegant" painter who explained his diligence by announcing that he was painting for eternity.[125] Of course, neither Cotton's nor Mitchell's reference shows any feeling for art except as it may be used for moral illustration.

Architecture, too, was seldom resorted to as a means of

120 Hooker, *The Paterne of Perfection*, 114.
121 Mitchell, *A Discourse of the Glory*, 72.
122 Shepard, *The Parable of the Ten Virgins*, Pt. I, 194.
123 Thomas Shepard, *A Treatise of Ineffectual Hearing the Word* (London, 1654), 167.
124 Cotton, *A Discourse upon 1 Cor. 14:40*, 9.
125 Mitchell, *A Discourse of the Glory*, 78.

clarifying a point, despite the precedent of the striking concept
of Christ as the cornerstone of the church, a noted passage in
Isaiah, repeated in the *Epistle to the Ephesians.*   But that this
was not an entirely neglected field of illustration is shown by
Hubbard's recurrent use of architectural figures in one of his
sermons, *The Happiness of a People.*   Near the beginning of
this somewhat lengthy discourse, Hubbard offers this piece of
general wisdom:

In a curious piece of Architecture, that which first offers it self to the view
of the beholder, is the beauty of the structure, the proportion that one piece
bears to another, wherein the skill of the Architect shews itself.[126]

He then goes on to apply this architectural idea to God's creation of man—the head as the watch-tower, the eyes as windows;
but he quickly loses himself in discussing the ears as the Daugh-
ters of Music, ever ready to give audience to messages, and
soon he is discussing the senses as the "Cinque-ports" in and
about the head.   Towards the end of the sermon, however, Hubbard returns to his architectural tropes, this time applying them
more directly to his point:

Rulers indeed if they are built like arches, that clasp in all around together,
the more weight there is laid upon them, the firmer they stand, but being
disunited, or not joynted in well together, they weaken the authority of each
other and hasten the ruine of the whole.[127]

Having re-interested himself in this type of figure, Hubbard
also remarks:

Corner stones [rulers] ought carefully to endeavor not only to keep up,
but unite the whole building together.[128]

In contrast to the general scarcity of architectural tropes
is the fairly frequent use made of the theatre for exemplification.   Rather surprisingly, in view of their well-known anti-
pathy to the drama of their own day, the Puritans did not hesitate to resort to a comparison of the world and its transient
inhabitants with a stage and its actors.   This far from novel
similitude, which is to be found more aptly in a number of Eliza-

126   *The Happiness of a People,* 11.
127   *Ibid.,* 43.
128   *Ibid.,* 43.

bethan plays,[129] has a long and honorable secular history,[130] being attributed to so early a philosopher as cheerful Democritus. The preachers, however, had better and more definite precedent for their use of this type of simile and metaphor. The same analogy of the stage to life interested a number of the church fathers, apparently especially those who had come under the influence of the schools of heathen rhetoric or who were converted to Christianity fairly late in life. The eloquent Chrysostom used the picture of actors slipping off the stage and abandoning their masks to bring out the changes that death would bring to many that seemed to be prospering in this world, but who would then be judged by their works, not their appearance of righteousness.[131] Isidore of Pelusium, Chrysostom's disciple, saw a similar comparison,[132] as did Synesius of Cyrene,[133] famous for his insistence upon the parallel importance of heathen and Christian literature.

How fully the works of these early writers were known to the preachers remains undemonstrable, but certainly all Puritan scholars would be familiar with Augustine's repeated comment that man's whole life of temptation is a stage play, with God as the spectator.[134] Later religious writers, including John of Salisbury,[135] the distinguished twelfth-century classical scholar, were attracted by this notion that life was a drama. And Erasmus, another writer certainly well-known to reading Puritans, expanded the parallelism between life and a play, pointing out that each had an author to control the action of the players and determine their fate.[136]

That the theatre had various emotional connotations for different ministers is very obvious from the use that they make of this trope, but, with their knowledge of the learned tongues, they must have been very aware that the very word "hypocrite"

129 *As You Like It*, 2.7.139; *Bussy d'Ambois*, 1.1. *New Inn*, 1.1.
130 *Cf. Notes and Queries*, Ser. 6, Vol. 4, pp. 148, 311; also note by Felix E. Schelling in his edition of Jonson's *Timber* (Boston, 1892), 121.
131 "In Lazare Homine" in *Opera* (London, 1612), Book I.
132 *Epistolae* (Paris, 1638), Book I, ep. LXV, 20.
133 "De Providentia" in *Opera* (Paris, 1638), Book II, p. 106a.
134 Psalm CXXVIII, "Expositions on the Book of Psalms by S. Augustine," in *A Library of Fathers of the Holy Catholic Church* (Oxford: John Henry Parker, 1857), VI, 46; also Sermon 178, Section 8, in *Opera* (Basle, 1529).
135 *Polycraticus* (Lugd. Bat., 1595), Book II, Chapter 8, pp. 142, 146.
136 *Encomium Moriae*, translated by Chaloner (1577), Dviii, verso.

comes from the Greek word for a stage-player. It is to be noted that whatever antagonism some ministers felt was directed against the actors, not against the theatre as an institution; and even this feeling was not universal. Shepard shows no prejudice against the stage, but, perhaps influenced by Augustine's neat phrase, *"Theatrum mundus, spectator Deus,"* says that it does not matter what their fellow-actors think so long as God, the great spectator, esteems them. On another occasion the Cambridge pastor urges the members of his congregation to do their duty before they are "turned off the stage." And in discussing hypocrisy he quietly suggests that "a stage player that acts the part of a king wants the glory of a King."[137]. With far more feeling, Hooker applies this same comparison to the question of carnal hypocrisy:

Looke as it is among stage-players, the stage-player puts on brave aparell, and comes on to the Stage, and resembles the person of a King, and acts the part of a Monarch, but if you pull him from the stage, and plucke his roabes from his backe, he appeares in his owne likenesse, so it here, a carnal Hipocrite, a cursed dissembler is like a stage player, he takes upon him the person and profession of a godly, humble, lowly man, and acts the part marveilous curiously, and hee speakes bigge words against his corruptions, and he humbles himself before God, and he heares, and prayes, and reades, but when God pluckes him off the stage of the world, and his body drops in to the grave, and his soule goes to hell, then it appears that he had not the power of godlines, he was only a stage player, a stage professour.[138]

In another condemnation of this same sin of hypocrisy, Hooker speaks just as acrimoniously and even more fully of a hypocrite as a "stage-player," using prayer and fasting as the stage upon which he acts his part so that others may see him and glory may come to him.[139] Cobbett was another preacher in whose mind hypocrites and actors were closely associated:

In hypocrisie there is affectation, hypocrites are stage-players, which albeit they are illiterate dunces many of them, yet will be highfloun sometimes in their expressions, their mouth speaketh great swelling words when they speak to me or God, or else they faile of their use and aime.[140]

Some years later Mitchell makes use of the same similitude, but in a far more philosophical spirit:

137 Shepard, *The Parable of the Ten Virgins*, Pt. II, 53 *et alii*.
138 Thomas Hooker, *Four Learned and Godly Treatises* (London, 1638), 8-9.
139 Thomas Hooker, "Spiritual Love and Joy," in *The Soules Implantation* (London, 1637), 236-237.
140 Cobbett, *A practical Discourse of Prayer*, 315.

This lower World was made but to be a Stage for men to act their parts on for a few ages, and then taken down: Hence it stands but on Crazy shows it may and will e're long fall on heaps: It is like a Tent or Tabernacle that stands on stakes thrust into the ground. But the third Heaven stands on strong unmoved foundation, Heb. 11.10.[141]

These, then, were the typical similitudes to which a Puritan congregation listened, at least with comprehension, presumably with appreciation. Abruptly introduced, with little by way of prelude, they do not seem unpleasing to the ear, especially when it is remembered that their function was not decorative but purely purposeful. Even in their brevity, they occasionally have the appeal of the picturesque or of the pathetic; nearly always they have a touch of humanity about them. The earnest preacher in his pulpit is truthfully presenting a bit of life as he knows it or has read about it. And not content with having so illuminated his point, he still does not depend upon the understanding of his listeners but always diligently explains the application of his illustration to the religious idea under discussion. This care is typical of his spirit of service to his congregation. No one is going to fail to comprehend every particular of his creed, but just as surely no one is going to be led astray by any mundane suggestions into worldly preoccupations. No one is going to wander from the all important subject of salvation, if his pastor can save him from such a pitfall.

141 Mitchell, *A Discourse of the Glory*, 69-70.

VII

THE PLAIN STYLE AND ITS VARIATIONS

There is, naturally, considerable variety in the style of the many ministers preaching in New England for a period of some fifty years, but there is also much similarity in this pulpit oratory, especially as it was emphatically dominated by its purpose and deliberately controlled by its sermonic form. Then, too, the use of the same type of illustration, taken for the most part from everyday life and so worded that the dullest member of the congregation could understand, gives their work a certain likeness, although the preacher's personality still is apparent in his use of this imagery. More fundamental is the unity given by the outstanding characteristic of all this Puritan literature, its sincerity. The general feeling was that words spoken from the pulpit were to be used purposefully, without waste, and were to be chosen so that the "meanest and weakest" in the audience could understand and profit. Learned obscurity and deliberate eloquence both were to be avoided, as they might distract the minds of the congregation from the point of doctrine or faith under explanation. In the words of one of the most popular preachers of the day, the leaders of congregations were not to waste their time and the community's patience by using "fine gilded sentences, where there is nothing but a jingling and a tinkling, nothing but a sound of words."[1]

This fine level of effective simplicity the first ministers constantly aspired to and most of the time attained. In the last decades of the seventeenth century human vanity seems to have won a victory over any such spiritual dedication, and many a preacher, forgetting the greater art of seeming artlessness, could not resist showing his Harvard education and the many hours he spent closeted with his books. But during the first years of their existence the congregations were in this respect more fortunate. To the average listener, versed as he was in Puritan terminology and in his own minister's thought processes, the dis-

1 Hooker, *The Soules Implantation*, 65.

courses must have been extremely comprehensible. Occasionally some weakness in the construction of a sermon series or some confusion resulting from the rewriting of such a series, is now apparent. Sometimes, too, the modern reader may feel that the preacher's logic is somewhat circuitous or superficial. There is an occasional tendency to argue that a just God by his very nature has certain attributes, and, having these attributes, is therefore a just God; or that man by his sinful nature fell from grace, and, having fallen, was therefore obviously sinful. Nevertheless, although this circular reasoning may be felt by the modern non-believer in Puritanism, individual points of doctrine and usually individual sermons remain lucid in the sense that there is rarely any doubt about what the minister thought and wished his reader to think.

The language is simple and plain, easily understandable. In fact, the ministerial policy of "preparing the milk for the meanest and weakest" went far beyond merely shunning pompousness and forced elegance. There was a decided attempt made to avoid euphemisms. As Hooker says, in the mouth of a good preacher "a spade is a spade, a drunkard is a drunkard." It is, he adds, Satan's policy to cozen the world with colors, "painter or tyre-maker like." The beautiful ways of godliness then are termed "simplicity" or "exactness," Puritanism is named "hypocrisy," and vices have a veil cast over them so that drunkenness becomes "good fellowship," covetousness becomes "frugality," and cowardice becomes "discretion." No minister can in this way make godliness seem lovely, or sinfulness seem truly odious. A certain "heat of heart" is required for good preaching; as a strong physic either kills or cures, so with a powerful ministry.[2]

Despite this advocacy of strong, household language, the sermons maintain a tone of quiet dignity. Frequently, however, some homely expression gives life to the familiar argument. Thomas Shepard sharply cautions his congregation "But if back and belly, thine and mine, be chief in request, this will ruine you."[3] Thomas Hooker in a mordant moment could accuse his flock of not caring as much for God's commands as does

2 Hooker, *The Application of Redemption*, 205-215.
3 Shepard, *The Parable of the Ten Virgins*, I, 7.

"a frothy headed maid for a clout."[4] With equal scorn he held
up to contempt those easy going souls who thought they could
have faith "with a wet finger."[5] The comforting idea that there
is "some hard knot in every Worldly pillow"[6] appealed to Jonathan Mitchell as he pleaded with his people to think only of
spiritual values. In like vein, John Wilson complained that
Quakers, Ranters, and Seekers did not even try to arouse men
to a realization of their sins, but instead had "soft Pillows to
put under men's Elbows."[7] Many similar colloquialisms may
have been lost whenever a sermon was prepared for printing.
Apparently even with the dignity of the pulpit in mind, a minister was not afraid to drop into this homespun phraseology.

The sermons themselves offer good evidence that a preacher
certainly reached down to the members of his church more often
than he flew above their heads. Grandiloquence he never indulged in, and any parade of human learning was felt to be
definitely out-of-place. The limited comprehension of the simply educated man was always kept in mind, and even when a
minister found himself breaking Perkins' dictum that for spiritual preaching "neither the words of arts, not Greeke and Latin
phrases and quirkies must be intermingled in the sermon,"[8] he
as a rule quickly translated, either verbatim or loosely, the bit of
Hebrew or Greek or Latin that had slipped in. So Thomas
Shepard, while urging his people to think more of the common
welfare and less of themselves, gives Luther's *"Venter in omni
religione potentissimum idolum"* and then paraphrases "When
the belly is served, Christ must be destroyed."[9] Sporadically
through many of the sermons such evidence of the preacher's
reading may be found, but the great majority of the early ministers remembered that the sermons were meant for an audience
which, for the most part, knew only English. True, an occasional scholar—such as the Reverend Charles Chauncy, the Harvard president—could not resist giving evidence of his linguistic
ability. The learned Chauncy, sometime professor of Hebrew

4 Hooker, *The Application of Redemption . . . The Ninth and Tenth Books*, 139.
5 Hooker, *The Soules Effectuall Calling*, 462.
6 Mitchell, *A Discourse of the Glory*, 171.
7 John Wilson, *A Seasonable Watch-Word* (Cambridge: S. Green and S. Green,
   1677), 6.
8 Perkins, *The Arte of Prophecying*, 670-671.
9 Shepard, *Subjection to Christ*, 65.

and Greek at the English Cambridge, took care to make a prefatory statement in a volume of his collected sermons that his preaching was planned "for the Capacity, and Understanding of the Weak and Ignorant."[10]   Notwithstanding this noble aim, he could not resist defining important scriptural words by giving the original Hebrew or Greek.

Despite occasional displays of scholastic vanity of this type, the first ministers with amazing consistency bore their audiences in mind and rarely permitted the fact that a large part of their preparatory reading was not in English to thrust itself upon their listeners.   Indeed, most of the preachers made a deliberate attempt to express themselves adequately in plain English.   Increase Mather, always a respectful son even if he did not follow his father's practices, has this to say about the Reverend Richard Mather's way of presenting his ideas:

His way of preaching was plain, aiming to shoot his Arrows not over his peoples heads, but into their Hearts and Consciences.   When he studiously avoided obscure phrases, Exotick words, or unnecessary citation of Latine Sentences, which some men addict themselves to the use of.   Mr. *Dod* was wont to say, That *so much Latine was so much flesh in a Sermon*: So did this humble man look upon the affectation of such things in a *Popular Auditory* to favour of Carnal Wisdome . . . . And much approved that of Austin: *If* (said he) *I preach Learnedly, then onely the Learned and not the Un-learned can understand and profit by me; but if I preach plainly, then Learned and Unlearned can undestand, so I may profit all.*[11]

This studied restraint upon the part of the ministers was, of course, in sharp contrast with the stylistic manner of their successors in New England's pulpits.   Critics have often noted that a pedantic habit of extremely frequent citation and quotation from the learned tongues was one of Cotton Mather's more obvious rhetorical weaknesses.   Even Chauncy's successor at Harvard, the Reverend Leonard Hoare, betrays in his work this growing tendency to find that one language was not sufficiently expressive—or impressive.   Hoare, coming to America as a lad, attended Harvard; then he continued his studies at Cambridge, England, and preached in a number of the home pulpits until he was silenced after the Restoration; finally he

---

10   Chauncy, *The Plain Doctrin*, title page.
11   Increase Mather, *The Life and Death of that Reverend Man of God, Mr. Richard Mather* . . . (Cambridge: S. G. and M. J., 1670), 31-32.

returned to Massachusetts with that second influx of ministers that came in the 1660's.   His ornate, prolix style is a harbinger of the changing pulpit fashion, and thrice in one sermon he breaks unnecessarily into Latin. For example, he casually quotes the proverb *"Ex malo corvo malum ovum"*[12] and allows the following passage on sin and death to illumine the sense, which becomes clear enough. Similarly, the context each time gives the meaning of his quotation, but Hoare's free interpretation of Perkins' advice would have shocked the ministers who first established New England's churches.

This level of practicality, this air of convincing plain men by plain preaching, did not preclude an occasional appeal of a more emotional nature.   Some of this warmth of feeling was devoted to discomforting such members of the congregation as might be allowing their thought to wander from the accepted creed of the churches.   Here and there, a bitter remark or a vituperative attack of greater length betrays the speaker's sensitivity concerning the threat of Catholicism.   As we have seen in discussing the apparent fear of the infiltration of Catholic or Arminian thought,[13] Cotton, Shepard, Hooker, and many another minister thought such warnings essential.   Any number of caustic comments of this sort could be quoted, but no one disposed of the Catholic clergy more briefly and more effectively than did the Reverend William Hooke when he charged:

O monsters among men these Prelats are, trained up by Tygers, whom no incestuous offspring of *Lot* can parallel by a thousand degrees.[14]

Such onslaughts upon various phases of Catholicism are fairly frequent in a great many of the sermons, especially in the earlier ones. A little later, however, some of this condemnation was directed against a different threat to the churches—or, as some of the ministers were able to persuade themselves, the same menace in a different form: "Quakerism is Popery in a new dress, or rather Popery and worse,"[15] declared the excitable Reverend John Norton.   The Reverend John Wilson, who shared

12 Hoare, *The Sting of Death and Death Unstung*, 5-6.
13 *Cf.* pp. 51-54.
14 William Hooke, *The Priviledge of the Saints on Earth* (London: John Wilkins, 1673), 6.
15 John Norton, *The Heart of New-England rent at the Blasphemies of the Present Generation* . . . (London, 1660), 81.

Norton's perturbation about this particular danger to the church-es, devoted in 1665 one of his sermons to an attack on the "Dreamers" of his day, that is, Quakers, Ranters, and Seekers. He objected, with natural vehemence, to these intruders who dared to scorn the services of the regular ministry; but, fairly enough according to his way of thinking, he blamed the mem-bers of the church, first, for their laxity which had opened the way to this heresy, surely a punishment from God, and, second-ly, for their listening to the new doctrines. Censure is mixed with somewhat pathetic entreaty as he recalls the first great generation of preachers, almost all of whom had passed away, and as he urges the colonists to listen only to himself and to his brother pastors, duly ordained leaders:

O hearken not to these and those Dreamers; God will tell you one day you had your *Cotton* and your *Norton,* and your *Hooker,* and your *Shepard,* and your *Rogers,* and these and those, you had my Ministers, . . . hearken not therefore to these or those Dreams or Dreamers, but stop your ears against them: as the Adder that keeps her self from being charmed, she is said to stop her ear with the ground on which she lyeth, and the other ear with some other part of her body; so in this case stop your ears against them, and take heed in this case: else Conscience will fly in your faces an-other day, and say I told you of it, and I checked you for it, and you would not regard.[16]

Not all of a preacher's fervor was spent in raging against possible heresies among the elect. Once in a while, too, a min-ister became fairly impassioned in the course of making the usual entreaty that his congregation reform their ways and get true faith, that all endeavor "to close with Christ." Depending on the individual preacher's ability, these pleas range from the sim-ple and effectual call to the wordy and confused one which does little more than show the speaker's ardor. So Chauncy, al-ways an able man in the pulpit, skilfully beseeches his listeners:

Wee are singing and chanting to the sound of the Viol, while God sounds an alarum, by the trumpet of warre. Wee are *dancing* in jollity, while God is *marching* in Battalia. We are drinking in the Wine, and strong Drink, while God is letting out our Blood. Wee are devouring the Crea-tures, while wee are devoured of the Creator. Wee are joyning Sexes in Marriage, while God is separating soul from body. Swimming in pleasures till we are drowned in the floud; and no man takes warning, . . . Let thy tears run down like a river, day and night, give God no rest, cease not to

16 Wilson, *A Seasonable Watch-Word,* 7.

complain to him.   Let thy heart like *Noahs* Dove, find no place to rest on, till thou hast gotten Christs satisfaction to bee thy souls Ransome.[17]

It is in such appeals as this that the influence of Biblical cadence and balance becomes most apparent. But not every preacher could keep his emotion under such rhetorical control.   For example, with less stylistic art than Chauncy displayed, but with at least equal warmth and earnestness, Oxenbridge harangues his congregation:

What: Jesus Christ to stand without knocking and calling, till the dews of evening fall upon him.   How oughtest thou now to make haste?   He knocks by common Mercies, and by Special Mercies, such and such Successes, and such Prosperity, will not all this provoke thee to get on from the Bed of Security, and to embrace him?   How farre did Jesus Christ come to Redeem Thee? he came from Heaven to Earth to Redeem thee. Thou art undone, and thy Inheritance lost; and Christ thy kinsman come to Redeem thee.   He opens not his Purse for Silver and Gold, but he opens all the Veins of his heart to let out his heart-blood to Redeem thee and thine Inheritance.   *Lo, I come*!   Shall not Joseph be made to run when he comes from the Dungeon?   Remember those loud cries upon the Cross, and his thirsting upon the Cross; and he tells thee of it: and what was this for, but to save thy poor Soul? the cry of Christ that made the Earth to quake, and the Mountain to break, and will nothing move and break thy heart and perswade thee?   It may be Jesus stands at the door, and in stead of opening the door, thou hast some churlish dog, some peevish Lust to drive him from the door; or thou hast some unclean Lust that maketh thee to stink, thy profane language, thy Atheistical thoughts, vain Conversation, are so many stones thrown at him: it may be when Christ is at the door, thou lyeth a-bed, and that with thy unclean harlotry Lusts; thou hast dealt so with him many a long day: but before he goes he looks back, to see if thou wouldst relent a little, and return, and therefore once more he calls thee; be not at rest this night till thou hast done something about this match, and closing wih Christ: *Isai.* 30.18.[18]

Here the Bible has been put to good use for illustrative material. Oxenbridge obviously is thinking in terms of *Luke* 12:36-40 (or *Revelation* 3:20)and *John* 10:32 as well as of the account of the crucifixion in *Matthew 27*.   Unfortunately, he has become involved in his own parable to such an extent that his message is lost in his exuberant verbosity.

While such passages of eloquence or attempted eloquence are not extremely infrequent, they seem almost like aberrations in the steady, reasoned progress of instruction and cor-

17 Chauncy, *The Plain Doctrin*, 43-44.
18 Oxenbridge, *A Quickening Word*, 16-18.

rection that makes up the great body of this sermonic literature. Nevertheless, within this ideal of a "plain and powerful" ministry, the personality of individual preachers was allowed to shine forth. It would be an exaggeration to claim that every sermon, read without noting its titlepage, could be ascribed definitely to its author. But the difficulty does not lie primarily in the obvious fact that some ministers were more colorless than their more fortunate brethren. The preachers that remain vague and indefinite for the reader perhaps do so because they published so few sermons, and, moreover, those few that have survived are in an abbreviated printed form. The more prolific writers are distinct personalities. Certainly no one would mistake Hooker's preaching for Cotton's, or Cotton's for Shepard's; and the sermons of all three are so unconsciously revelatory of their creators that even a casual reader, after a volume or two, would feel that he knew the author of each.

Of these three most important pulpit leaders, the most capable and forceful in his preaching was Thomas Hooker. In many ways this Hartford minister seems to have had the combined characteristics of the perfect intellectual leader and practical guide for a group of religious colonists. He makes all his important doctrinal and moral points again and again, never hesitating to repeat himself in the good cause of helping his congregation to see the truth as he so sincerely saw it himself. And each step in his argument, each concept, is carefully elucidated and made concrete not by one illustration but by two or three. Accordingly, his listeners learn first that wandering thoughts are like fluttering butterflies, gathering no honey from the herbs upon which they alight, and in the next sentence that they are like ships without ballast.[19] A less simple idea called for a longer series of similes. For example, in discussing the complicated question of the soul's union with Christ, he clarifies the problem by comparison with the father-child and husband-wife relationships, with the graft and the tree, and with lumps of dough being kneaded together.[20]

The intelligibility of Hooker's work depends not solely on

19 Hooker, *The Application of Redemption.* The Ninth and Tenth Books, 231.
20 Hooker, *The Soules Union with Christ,* 4-5.

his habits of multiple exemplification, but also on the variety of the analogues he offered. Of all the ministers, Hooker has the greatest diversity in his use of homely imagery, and every member of his audience, man, woman, and child, must have been appealed to as the preacher brought home his ideas by appealing to the common knowledge that he and his congregation shared about people and their occupations and pastimes. When he urged that all prepare for Christ's coming, he put his plea in language that any housekeeper would appreciate:

The Lord hath promised to come into our soules if we humble them, and make them fitting to receive his Majesty: and therefore Sweep your hearts, and cleanse those roomes, cleanse every sinke, brush downe every cobweb, and make roome for Christ: for if thy heart be prepared, and divorced from all corruptions, then Christ will come into the soule, and take possession of it. Remove therefore all corruptions out of the heart. And when thou hast swept every corner of the house, doe not leave the dust behind the doore, for that is a sluts tricke: doe not remove sin out of thy tongue, and out of thy eye, and out of thy hand, and leave it in thy heart.[21]

No point of Puritan theology is more delicate than that of how much man can do in the way of preparation for grace without Christ's aid, for all had to be urged to try for grace, although only the few could hope to succeed. On this question hangs the whole doctrine of election, and Hooker's handling of the problem is masterful in its simple approach through the terminology of play:

The ball must first fall to the ground, before it can rebound back againe; for the Lord Jesus must first dart in his love into the soule, before the soule can rebound in love and joy to him again, we must receive in grace before wee can rebound backe any love to God: as 1 *Tim.* 1.7 . . .[22]

Commonplace as most of these comparisons are, their very lack of pretension gives them a certain appeal, and his brief pictures, whether taken from everyday life or from the Bible, are most effective. Indeed, the only weak spots in his preaching occur when, not content to let well enough alone, he manages to over-elaborate upon his graphic descriptions. Hell may be a fearful punishment for evil-doers—the more vague, perhaps, the more fearful—but the damned among Hooker's listeners also heard that they would spend eternity not only endur-

21 Hooker, "The Preparation of the Heart" in *The Soules Implantation*, 50.
22 Hooker, "Spirituall Love and Joy" in *The Soules Implantation*, 182.

ing the other discomforts of hell but also reading, by the light of the flames, his sermons which they had refused to profit by in the happier climes of Connecticut.[23] Or, mindful of Jesus' complaint that he had wanted to gather the Jews of Jerusalem together "even as a hen gathereth her chickens under her wings,"[24] the New England preacher asked his audience to see Jesus and his call to grace as a hen clucking her chickens together.[25]

Conscientious and utilitarian in purpose as most of his work shows him to be, Hooker at times allowed the more spiritual and poetic side of his nature to shine forth and break the monotony of his discourses. Not by reason alone did any devout Puritan live, and the first Hartford pastor, even as he labored to convince his parishioners of the truth, knew that a little God-given faith transcended any such efforts that he might be able to make. Passages of religious exaltation are to be found in many of his sermons, and the following is distinguished from many a similar one only by its brevity:

If mine hands were all of love, that I could worke nothing but love, and if mine eyes were able to see nothing but love, and my minde thinke of nothing but love, and if I had a thousand bodies, it were all too little to love that God that hath immeasurable loved me a poor sinfull helhound.[26]

Here and there, too, above the steady plateau of his determined effort to persuade all to his exact way of thinking, rises a felicitous sentence, all the more striking because of its apparently unstudied poetic quality. He could say, casually,

One dramme of faith is worth a hundred thousand worlds to a weary burthened soule.[27]

Or he could reflect upon the "starre-light of reason" in which the natural or unsaved man walks, while the saint or saved man at least walks in the twilight that gives a hint of the greater glory to come,[28] walks with "a little rush-candle of holiness and purity, of grace and meekness" to guide his footsteps.[29]

23 Hooker, *The Application of Redemption*, 249.
24 *Matthew* 23:37.
25 Hooker, *The Unbeleevers Preparing for Christ*, 92; *The Application of Redemption. The Ninth and Tenth Books*, 317; *The Immortality of the Soule*, 14.
26 Hooker, "Spirituall Love and Joy" in *The Soules Implantation*, 179-180.
27 Hooker, "The Broken Heart" in *The Soules Implantation*, 12.
28 Hooker, *The Paterne of Perfection*, 54-55.
29 Hooker, "Spirituall Love and Joy" in *The Soules Implantation*, 214.

Always competent, occasionally a little inspired, Hooker as a preacher commands respect in any age. Less apparent is the reason for the homage enjoyed in his own day by John Cotton. Granted that Cotton Mather, never one to understate his case, may have exaggerated his ancestor's virtues and so helped build up the tradition of the family's greatness, there remains ample testimony in contemporary accounts to prove that few other men have been so esteemed in their own time. The Reverend John Cotton had a long and apparently successful career in both the old and the new Boston. His fellow ministers had only the highest praise for him, and it is interesting to note that among those who expressed commendatory opinions were such different men as Roger Williams the exiled rebel, Nathaniel Ward the outspoken critic, and William Hubbard the conscientious historian. There is even a note of worship in John Wilson's statement:

Mr. Cotton preaches with such authority, demonstration, and life, that me-thinks, when he preaches out of any prophet or apostle, I hear not him; I hear that very prophet and apostle; yea, I hear the Lord Jesus Christ speaking in my heart.[30]

The sermons, despite all this adulation of their creator, are disappointing reading, especially so when they are contrasted with the efforts of Hooker and Shepard. The reasons may be multiple. Their author was an ardent, almost fanatic believer in plain, "untrimmed" sermons.[31] In fact, he once wrote in protest against the practices of some ministers that "swelling words of humane wisdome make mens preaching seeme to Christ (as it were) a blubber-lipt Ministry."[32] Not only were his sermons therefore stylistically plain to begin with, but most of the printed ones were taken down in shorthand while they were being delivered and afterwards submitted to Cotton for his correction. This means of transcription perhaps eliminated many of his illustrations and figures of speech, and Cotton may have considered it vanity to reintroduce them into the printed versions. Then, again, he may well have been one of those great preachers whose evangelistic appeal is more dependent on the force of their living personality than their contemporaries realize. This dis-

30 Quoted in *Magnalia*, Book III, 25-26.
31 Mather, *Magnolia*, Book III, 25; also 15, 16.
32 Cotton, *A Brief Exposition of the Whole Book of Canticles*, 112.

crepancy between his oral and his printed work was true of the famous itinerant revivalist George Whitefield, whose kindest critics disparage his published sermons even as they marvel at the potent oratory by which he moved tens of thousands.[33]   And Cotton, for success in the more limited and more religious orbit of his fellow Puritans, would not have needed Whitefield's extraordinary power to hold an audience spellbound.

Lacking that companionable, one-with-his-listeners touch so pleasing in the preaching of many of his New England contemporaries, Cotton nevertheless shows himself in his surviving sermons to have been a man of rare intensity of feeling.   It is unfortunate that in so large a proportion of his recorded preaching this passionate energy should be devoted to denunciation. Far more frequent than passages of religious exaltation are his fierce condemnations of what he believed to be evil, for his zeal for reform led him to attack his parishioners' laxity in great matters and small.   Undoubtedly, his most bitter tirades are devoted to telling his congregation of the machinations of "the Pope and his crue."   In speaking of the Protestant reformers, he has a typical attack on Catholicism:

> Secondly, there was a noysome loathsomeness discovered, by these True Witnesses, and Martyrs of Christ, unto the people.   Whereby they began to see that the common sort of their Religious Orders were full of Idlenesse, of Ignorance, of Covetousness, of Hypocrisie . . . . A grievous malignant ulcer it was, and the more they stirred in it, the more they were vexed.[34]

But even his virulent anti-Catholicism did not satisfy all his propensity for fear and hate; in no weak terms he warned his people against the principles of Separatism,[35] against moving from Massachusetts to newer plantations that might be without the benefit of an adequate clergy,[36] against any sort of tolerance under which a man permitted his neighbor to live as he would,[37] and against hypocrisy of all types.[38]   Deliberate prof-

---

33 J. B. Wakeley, *The Prince of Pulpit Orators: A Portraiture of Rev. George Whitefield, M.A.* . . . . (New York: Carlton & Lanahan, 1871), 30-31.

34 Cotton, *The Powring Out of the Seven Vials*, 5-6.

35 *A Briefe Exposition*, 62, 180-181, *et alii*.

36 *An Exposition upon the Thirteenth Chapter of the Revelation*, 240.

37 *Christ the Fountaine*, 240-256.

38 *Gods Mercie Mixed with His Iustice*, 99, 108, *et alii.; The Powring Out of the Seven Vials*, 18-19; *The New Covenant, passim*.

anation of the Sabbath he believed to merit the death penalty.[39] He also found it necessary to direct his indignation to the correction of such lesser manifestations of the evil spirit as he saw by looking down from his pulpit: men wearing long hair, women coming bonnetless to church, women speaking in church, and many men talking at once in church.[40] New ideas and changes he distrusted, particularly "a new-fangled Trick of Ministers and People, when the Minister fits their itching ears with new-fangled Doctrin."[41] Every preacher should instead seek a new approach to the old doctrine. And what if sinners failed to heed the warnings of the Reverend John Cotton? He was not above an occasional threat. The judgment of the Lord would be felt, first upon their cattle, then on their servants and children, and then on their wives. If all this penalization of Boston's citizens through their possessions did not prevail upon them to reform their ways, then they themselves would be stricken with grievous diseases, first in their bodies and then in their souls and consciences.[42]

But Cotton was not only a man of righteous wrath; he was also a great student. His often noted twelve-hour day spent closeted with his books[43] was, of course, not without effect on his sermons. Not only is his Biblical learning apparent and often backed by references to earlier commentators or scholars, but an occasional passage betrays his other interests. Few other men have had as high a sense of the setting apart of the ministry, especially in their pulpit-duties. If the church was the Bride of Christ, the ministers were the breasts of the bride,[44] he said in the somewhat forced allegorical style of which he was very fond. Nevertheless, Cotton was one of the few early New England preachers that permitted themselves, while in the pulpit, to digress into discussions of matters which were not generally considered essential to the religious and political welfare of the colonists. His more than passing interest in the larger problems of science has already been commented upon.[45] That

39 *The Powring Out of the Seven Vials*, 21.
40 *A Discourse upon I Cor. 14:40*, 4.
41 *A Practical Commentary*, 68.
42 Cotton, *The Powring Out of the Seven Vials*, 13-14.
43 Mather, *Magnalia*, Book III, 26.
44 Cotton, *A Briefe Exposition of the Whole Book of Canticles*, 109 *et seq.*
45 *Cf.* pp. 101-102.

this interest in natural phenomena was general and far from specialized is shown in the course of his exposition of *Canticles* in which he has asides[46] on the chastity of doves and on the nature of pomegranates, of various herbs, and of sapphires, most of his information coming directly from Pliny and Fernelius. Easily explained is another of Cotton's deviations from the more customary discussion of doctrinal and spiritual problems. Luther had set an example of seeing in *Revelation* a history of the world. Accordingly, while listening to a weekday sermon-series supposedly in explanation of the thirteenth chapter of *Revelation,* Cotton's devoted audience also got a general review of late Roman, medieval, and sixteenth-century history. This survey, fairly broad in its scope, emphasized the fall of Rome under the barbarian attack, dwelling briefly upon the parts played by Constantine, Theodosius, Alaric, Genseric, Theodoric, Totila, and Odoacer; brought out Europe's state of ignorance in the nine hundreds; mentioned the deeds of Godfrey de Bouillon, the leader of the first crusade and capturer of Jerusalem; discussed in some detail the Waldensian and Albigensian heresies, with the consequent cruel penalties; and naturally included important sixteenth-century events in Spain and Holland.[47]

Until the end of the Puritan regime Cotton was much honored in Massachusetts, but far more appealing to later generations have been the personality and preaching of Thomas Shepard, the Cambridge pastor. Hooker to this day has considerable fame as the founder of Hartford and as an early democrat in an age of theocracy and autocracy. Cotton is often recalled as a member of the Boston Cotton-Mather dynasty, and his name still brings to mind the figure of a typical Puritan minister and scholar, narrow-minded but sincere. Shepard alone truly survived his own time, to be read and loved for three centuries. Jonathan Edwards, sometimes honored as America's greatest religious philosopher, found it profitable to make a careful study of *The Parable of the Ten Virgins,* one of Shepard's longer sermon series, and numerous citations from the latter are included in *The Treatise of Religious Affections.* Lesser American scholars, such as David Brainerd and Thomas Prince, were

46 Cotton, *A Briefe Exposition of the Whole Book of Canticles*, 41, 107, 159.
47 Cotton, *An Exposition upon the Thirteenth Chapter of the Revelation, passim.*

almost equally enthusiastic about the merits of Shepard. It is, perhaps, only natural that later New England thinkers should reverence Shepard's work . Far more surprising is the latter's popularity in Pennsylvania among the German colonists, for whose benefit an eighteenth-century German translation of some of his work was thrice reprinted.[48] Apparently, he continued to be read and studied in various parts of the United States well into the nineteenth century, for a three volume edition of his writings was published as late as 1853, an accurate, but incomplete gathering, accompanied by John Albro's detailed life of the author. But not only in America did this Cambridge pastor's reputation endure. In Scotland, James Fraser of Brea, a preacher of great renown in his own day and of distinguished memory, voiced his belief that in Shepard "the Lord had made the Interpreter one of a thousand."[49] Perhaps because of the plaudits of Fraser, Shepard continued to be used by Scotch divines. Among the last of these devotees was the late Alexander Whyte, noted preacher, minister of Free St. George's, and Principal of New College, Edinburgh. During the first decade of the twentieth century Dr. Whyte delivered a series of lectures on the New England preacher, and then published his material in book form. There is no denying that the result is a rather strange and inaccurate volume,[50] praising Shepard's spirituality and thought even while deploring his style. But the old doctor's sincere affection and admiration for his subject are apparent on every page.

What is the secret of Shepard's lasting appeal to religiously inclined men of different ages and nationalities? The little New England preacher was a gentle mystic, profoundly and continuously conscious of his Maker's presence, a mystic well content with this feeling of oneness with God and perfectly satisfied

---

48 Thomas Sheppards *Schmaler Weg zum Leben, oder die wahre Bekehrung durch Christum zu Gott* . . . (Pennsylvanien, 1838; also Harrisburg, 1839, 1850). The preface reveals that the anonymous editor was using Nicolaus Leydecker's translation, made in 1712 and reprinted in 1754.

49 James Fraser, *Memoirs of the Life of the Very Reverend* . . . (Edinburgh, 1738), 41, 44, 117-118, 179, 241, 275-276.

50 *Thomas Shepard Pilgrim Father and Founder of Harvard* (Edinburgh: Oliphant, Anderson and Ferrier, n.d., 1912). This book, written in Dr. Whyte's old age, abounds in factual errors and in misquotations from Shepard. The most amusing of Whyte's apocryphal and anachronistic anecdotes has Shepard collapsed in a jealous "swoon of sweat and tears," having just read one of Thomas Hooker's sermons in a copy of the *New England Gazette*.

with leaving the explanation of the final mysteries of life and
death, of salvation and damnation, to a benign, if awesome
Creator, who would at his own pleasure vouchsafe to his chosen
in heaven the right answers. A contemporary, in praising Shepard, wrote of his "inward acquaintance with God,"[51] and the
words well express that sensitive spiritual power that made him
tell his Cambridge audience of "the infinite unknown sweetness,
and mercy, and presence of God."[52] Melodiously, almost poeti-
cally, he found that time was "but a little spring or river which
runs into eternity, and carries all men living down with it to
eternity"[53] and that God is "the journey's end of all a man's
labours and life and travels."[54]

But Shepard could not often allow himself the more esoteric pleasures of religious meditation. He was a New England colonist and a Puritan minister, very much aware of his
community's needs. He took active part in the founding of
Harvard College,[55] he endeavored to build up the library,[56] and
his was the first proposal in America of a system of scholarships to help poor boys obtain an education.[57] But such public
spirited activities were incidental to his services to his faith.
He fought hard to combat Familism in his own church, with the
result that this was the only group to stay entirely free from
the Anne Hutchinson schism. Dutifully, and often dully, he
devoted much of his preaching to the plea, made again and
again, that his parishioners take care lest they deceive themselves about their spiritual state.

But even his least moving discussions are animated by his
peculiar charm. For Shepard was not only that rare combination, a mystic and an earnest worker; he was also a man who
knew instinctively how to be one with his audience. This feeling of harmony between listener and preacher was mostly due

51 Preface to Shepard's *The Sincere Convert.*
52 Thomas Shepard, *A Treatise of Ineffectual Hearing the Word* (London:
    Printed by T. R. and E. M. for J. Rothwell, 1652), 189.
53 Shepard, *The Parable of the Ten Virgins*, Pt. II, 48.
54 Shepard, *Subjection to Christ*, 17.
55 Samuel Atkins Eliot, *A History of Cambridge, Massachusetts 1630-1913* (Cam-
    bridge, 1913), 15.
56 Letter to Hugh Peter(s) in *New England Historic-Genealogical Register*,
    IV, 373-4.
57 *Historical Collections* (Edited by Ebenezer Hazard, Philadelphia, 1794), XI,
    17.

to his use of domestic similes that came within the understanding and experience of all. Every phase of religion, he seemed to find, could be quietly explained in terms of daily health and of home life. Thrice married, he was the father of a generous number of children, most of whom died in infancy. He himself was always in such precarious health that he often had to spend the long New England winters by his fireside,[58] leaving it only for his regular pulpit duties. It is not surprising, then, that his imagery is domestic in tone and frequently shadowed by the sick-room. Even the value of Christian fellowship materializes in his mind as a picture of many friends aiding a dying man, one rubbing him, another chafing his limbs, another holding him, still another fetching water. Regularly, too, such vital questions as Christian duty, forgiveness, and faithfulness are expressed in terms of marital difficulties and joys. But children and the parental relationship provided him with many of his most apt illustrations. Intimately, tenderly, he speaks of children who do not realize the intense love that parents have for their offspring, of infants who will cry if any but their mother feed them, of little ones that must be whipped if they will be up before dawn, and of little girls who carefully fashion dolls out of clouts. With pleasing detail he tells of little incidents in a child's life:

If a child be at board from his father's house, though he be at play with his fellows, yet if he sees horse and man come to fetch him, he is glad, and leaves his play and companions to go home to his father willingly; so here we are at board in the world, and we are at play, as it were, among his creatures, but when death comes, which is a horse and man, we should be willing to go to our Father's house, which is best of all.[59]

Slowly, surely, by means of these plain little illustrations from family life, Shepard found a way to express himself and his beliefs. He seems, in fact, to have been able to combine a mystic and utter faith comparable to George Herbert's with the tender humanity that inevitably makes the modern reader think of that later Englishman, Charles Lamb.

These three most prominent leaders, Hooker, Cotton, and Shepard, were men of outstanding personality, but other minis-

58 Thomas Shepard, *The Clear Sunshine of the Gospel* (London, 1648), Sabin's Reprints, Quarto Series, X, 8.
59 Shepard, *The Saints Iewell*, p. 12.

ters in New England pulpits were not without that individuality of style which added much to the value of their teaching. The most skilled and sustained rhetorician was the Reverend William Hooke. Although his career in the colonies, where he preached at Taunton and New Haven, was cut short by his return to England in 1656, his few printed sermons are sufficient to show that their creator was a man of definite talent. Naturally, his discourses now and then are evangelistical in tone, archaic in language. Nevertheless, in contrast to most of his contemporaries, Hooke does not seem to be primarily a seventeenth-century Englishman and Puritan, transplanted to a struggling new community and busily engaged in expounding the doctrines of his church. His call to all men is universal in its appeal and oddly timeless:

Brethren! Liberty is more precious than life, inasmuch as death is the common lot of all men, but servitude the portion only of men destined to misery.[60]

It is, however, Hooke's telling descriptive power that has made critics praise the literary merit of his few published sermons. His tirade against war is his emotional and pictorial masterpiece, rising in fervor as it proceeds:

Warre is the conflict of enemies enraged with bloody revenge, where the parties opposite carry their lives in their hands, every man turning prodigall of his very heart blood; and willing to be killed to kill. The instruments are flashing swords, ratling spears, skul-dividing Holberds, murthering pieces, and thundering Cannons, from whose mouths proceed the fire, and smell, and smoake, and terrour, death, as it were, of the very bottomless pit. We wonder now and then at the sudden death of a man, alas, you might there see a thousand men not onely healthy, but stout and strong, struck dead in the twinkling of an eye, their breath exhales without so much as, *Lord have mercy upon us.* Death heweth its way through a wood of men in a minute of time from the mouth of a murderer, turning a forrest into a Champion suddenly, and when it hath used these to slay their opposites, they are recompensed with the like death themselves. *O the Shrill eare-piercing clangs of the trumpets, noise of drums, the animating voices of Horse Captaines and Commanders, learned and learning to destroy!* (*Iob 39. 19.20, etc.*) *There is the undaunted horse whose neck is cloathed with thunder, and the glory of whose nostrils is terrible; how doth hee lye pawing and praunsing in the valley, going forth to meet the armed men? he mocks at feare, swallowing the ground with fierceness and rage, and saying among the trumpets, Ha, Ha, he smels the batell a far off, the thunder of the Captaines and the Shouting.* Here ride some dead men swagging in their deep saddles, there fall others alive upon their dead horses; death

60 Hooke, *New England's Sence of Old-England and Irelands Sorrows*, 27.

sends a message to these from the mouth of the Muskets, these it talks with face to face, and stabs in the fift rib: In yonder file there is a man hath his arme struk off from his shoulder, another by him hath lost his leg; here stands a souldier with halfe a face, there fights another upon his stumps, and at once both kils and is killed; not far off lies a company wallowing in their sweat and goare; such a man whilst he chargeth his Musket is discharged of his life, and falls upon his dead fellow. . . .[61]

Hooke's ability to use vivid description to oratorical advantage is outstanding, and his easy, flowing prose is exceptional. On the other hand, not a few of his fellow preachers, even though they lacked his smoothness of style, were scholarly, spirited men, capable of delivering many a well-turned, thought-provoking sentence and an occasional impassioned plea. There was the Dorchester pastor, the Reverend Richard Mather, strong in body and mind. The father and grandfather of two more famous Mathers, Increase and Cotton, Richard was a better preacher than either, for to him was given the great gift of being able to elucidate the tenets of his belief so that all his listeners and readers could understand them. He did this not so much by exemplification of his ideas, as by clarity and organization in his thinking, plus remarkable skill in the use of apropos Biblical citations. *The Summe of Certain Sermons on Genes.* 15.6,[62] an example of this development of a thesis, gives an extraordinarily affective exposition and résumé of what "salvation by faith" and all the ramifications of the doctrine meant to the Puritan. Moreover, the whole sermon series rises to a climactic summation in the last logically derived idea he submitted to the elect. The guilt of Christ's passion and death could be placed not upon Judas, nor Herod, nor Pilate, not upon the Jews, not upon the deeds of the wicked, but upon the sinning of God's chosen people, for whom Jesus had died.[63]

Mather was direct and vital in his thinking, but neither adjective could be ascribed to the brilliant mind of Cotton's disciple, the Reverend John Davenport of New Haven. The latter was a great text-man, citing and quoting Biblical lines often, but his study of Scripture led him into many by-paths of reading. As a result, like Cotton, to whom he owed his conversion

---

61 Hooke, *New Englands Teares for Old Englands Feares*, 10-11..
62 Cambridge: Samuel Green, 1652.
63 Mather, *The Summe of Certain Sermons*, 43.

to Puritanism, Davenport occasionally digressed into subjects which apparently interested him for the time being. Theories about the exact date of Christ's birth, for example, held his attention during part of one of his fast-sermons,[64] and in the course of one lecture series he gave a detailed summary of a recent book on the condition of Protestant churches in various parts of Europe.[65] Indeed, if the surviving sermons are typical of the rest of his preaching, Davenport, unlike many contemporary preachers, seems to have been unable to content himself with reiterating the essential concepts of his religion; instead, he allowed lesser points, sometimes political, sometimes theological, to hold him fascinated. Since so many of the Puritan sermons of the period strike the same notes of a plea for true faith or of an attack on hypocrisy in one of its many forms, these New Haven sermons are attractive in their very variety. Nevertheless, they reveal their author as a man of uncompromising notions, and one who would have made a stormy career for himself even in a more tolerant spot than seventeenth-century New England. He never succeeded in being quite one with his church or his colleagues, and was not above occasionally twisting the truth in order to get his own way—the better to serve the Lord, he would say. Perhaps the fundamental trouble lay in his inability to make himself accept any higher will than his own. In fact, his own words, in one of his many ponderable sentences, are unconsciously suggestive of their voicer's difficulty:

When mens wils are not subdued and conformed unto Gods will, they are, in times of affection, like sullen birds in a Cage, which beat themselves to death; like peevish forward children, which will be pleased with nothing, if there wills be crossed in anything.[66]

Another man of exceptional learning was the Reverend Charles Chauncy, who, when his distinguished career in England was cut short by Archbishop Laud, served the Plymouth church for a few years, moved to Scituate for a longer period, and finally became president of Harvard, a post he held for eighteen years. A great scholar, he was given to some slight parade of his knowledge of the learned tongues, but this weak-

64 Davenport, *Gods Call to His People* (Cambridge: S. G. and M. J. for John Usher, 1669), 18-20.

65 Davenport, *The Saints Anchor-hold*, 181 *et seq*.

66 *Ibid.*, 75.

ness was counterbalanced by a surprising lucidity and simplicity in his expression of important concepts. He casually explained, for example, that the temptations and anguish of Jesus Christ were comparable to "shakings of clean water, in a clean glass, the water remains pure still."[67] Such bright flashes abound in his work, and his style is never moribund, but extremely readable, being nearly always spirited, and frequently a little stirring. A man of but slightly concealed passion, he often enlivened his discourses by forceful phrases and epithets; scorners of the ministry and their services were "coveteous earthwormes";[68] wearers of long hair were "hairy wicked scalps";[69] and the boasted learning of the Schoolmen was nothing but "a very hodch-potch & mingle-mangle of heathenish Philosophy and Divinity."[70] Then, too, Chauncy had enough sense of the dramatic to make his statements effective and memorable by a very nice use of contrast. In an effort to account for the obvious but somewhat inexplicable fact that both good and evil men seem to suffer equally in this world, he manages to word concisely his belief in a planned universe:

God therefore stabs the wicked, as an enemy, with his Sword, but lances the godly, as a Surgeon his Patient, with the Lancet.[71]

Less reasoned, but more emotional is his cry against those who do not seek salvation:

O the misery of natural man! far surpassing that of a Beast; if a Dog bee chained hee howls, if a Swine bee bound hee cries, but sinful man laughs in the middest of his bondage; he counts it his liberty to live a slave to the Devil, and thinks to gratify his fleshly lust is liberty.[72]

There were many other able ministers serving the growing towns of Massachusetts. Prominent among them was the Reverend Peter Bulkeley of Concord, a preacher with an exceptionally clear and capable style. He gives the impression of having been an extremely diligent and conscientious worker, arguing his points without heat, but carefully balancing them so that all could understand each tenet of belief. Bulkeley's discourses may

67 Chauncy, *The Plain Doctrin*, 55.
68 Chauncy, *Gods Mercie*, 15.
69 *Ibid.*, 28.
70 *Ibid.*, 54.
71 Chauncy, *The Plain Doctrin*, 64.
72 *Ibid.*, 26.

have been a little lacking in charm, but the sermons of the Reverend Thomas Cobbett of Lynn and Ipswich must have been appealing, as their author seems to have combined an almost naive faith in the power of prayer correctly made at the opportune moment, with a certain loftiness of spirit that recognized fully that the subjective value of faith is far more important than any objective gains. Even more pleasing in personality was the Reverend Samuel Whiting of Lynn, who apparently was a preacher much of Shepard's mold—a lesser man, but with the same sweetness of manner, the same earnestness for the good of all. To pray for everyone, to pray steadily and fervently, never angrily, was Whiting's solution to most of this world's difficulties. Far from gentle and mild was the Reverend John Norton of Boston and Ipswich, whose words tumbled over each other in the vehemence of his attack on whatever he felt to be threatening New England's welfare. But his vast scholarship and his very intensity of manner do much to make his work palatable. Another man of wrath was the Reverend John Wilson of Boston. He had considerable fame in his own day as a poet and anagramist; he was also known as an especially spirited preacher, given in his latter days to spending most of his pulpit time in exhortations and admonitions to his wandering flock. Unfortunately, his one surviving sermon in print is supposed to have been delivered extemporaneously and was taken down in shorthand by a listening clergyman; hence his style, while direct and passionate, seems somewhat plain and lacking in Biblical and lay allusions of interest.

Some of the early Harvard graduates did not lag far behind their predecessors and contemporaries from the English universities. The Reverend William Hubbard of Ipswich has been somewhat scorned as a dull historian, lacking in originality; nevertheless, his sermons are far from boring. What they lack in organization, they make up for in content and apt historical allusion. A more deliberately erudite preacher was the Reverend Urian Oakes, pastor at Cambridge and president of Harvard College. Despite recorded testimony of his congregation's appreciation of his genius, some of his more labored sermons may well have appealed to the Harvard students and to his fellow-ministers, rather than to a mixed congregation of average intellectuality. A much more capable preacher than Oakes was the Reverend Jonathan Mitchell of Cambridge. Here was a clear-headed thinker who never allowed his scholarship to make his sermons the less pleasing. His work has a certain solidity and moderation about it, and his longspun discourses are saved from tediousness by his continual use of lively similitudes from everyday life. And one more particularly successful preacher must be named, a man respected as much for his potentialities as for his actual accomplishment in the pulpit. If an early death had not cut short his career, the Reverend Eleazer Mather might have developed into as distinguished a preacher as his father, Richard Mather. *A Serious Exhortation to the present and succeeding generations in New England,* the younger Mather's one printed book and the substance of his last sermons, shows him to have been effective and clear in style, establishing his ideas by simple if somewhat repetitious similes.

Not every congregation had its weekly or bi-weekly lesson made more pleasurable by the rhetorical skill of its minister or teacher. With commendable spirit, these less fortunate churches did not grieve over any lack of brilliancy revealed by their special leaders, but rejoiced in having "solid" and "useful" men. The diligent labors of many of these less talented preachers never found their way into print; only here and there in the published sermons are there preserved a few examples of the type of sermon to which many New Englanders must have had to listen.

Although Elder Robert Cushman preached at Plymouth in the strenuous year of 1621 and had the honor of delivering the first New England sermon to be printed, he was neither a university man nor an ordained minister, but a wool-carder by trade. Perhaps, therefore, it is not fair to compare his one surviving discourse,[73] composed at a time when the town was in great economic stress, with the more polished work of regularly trained clergymen. Cushman, lacking in elegance of speech but not in courageous determination to bring out his point as effectually as possible, makes an earnest plea for charity and

73 Cushman, *A Sermon Preached at Plimmoth in New-England December 9. 1621* (London, 1622).

for the sharing of whatever commodities were available in the poverty-stricken settlement—for co-operation in the fullest sense of the word. But he was not a man to be content with a gentle entreaty to the better nature of some men. The more selfish members of the community are attacked with scornful vehemence. There are, he bluntly declares with no mincing of words, two types of individuals in the town: the temperate good man and the "belly-God" who would "slop all into his own throat" and whose "griple gut shameth not to swallow all."[74] Not content with this graphic description of some of his fellow-townsmen, Cushman comes to the obvious conclusion about these unascetic human beings dwelling in the new town of Plymouth:

And what doth this shifting, progging, and fat feeding which some use, more resemble any thing than the fashion of hoggs?[75]

By the very forthrightness of his attack, Cushman was able to accomplish much. At least, the Pilgrims did not give up the struggle and reformed their ways enough to develop into a successful colony. There is a tale, too, that Cushman won his way back into the favor of the people by this timely discourse. Some preachers, equally plain in their manner, must have failed to excite their audiences by any such virulence. Also coming under this category of being a "solid and useful" preacher was the Reverend John Higginson, who served successively—for seventy-two years in all—the Saybrook, Guilford, and Salem pulpits. Born in 1616 and coming to America as a lad with his family, he antedated Harvard; consequently, he had to prepare himself to serve in the ministry. A self-taught man, he became known for his learning and especially for his knowledge of geography. While there is no doubt that Higginson knew much and had great zeal in imparting his wisdom to others, he unfortunately expressed himself in a dull and lifeless style, sadly lacking in interesting imagery. Brief excerpts from his sermons would hardly show the painful dullness of his work as a whole; as his elegist, the Reverend Nicholas Noyes, said with kindness and with at least partial truth:

Thousands of Sermons he did Preach
Not to Please Ears, but Hearts to Reach.[76]

74 *Ibid.*, 7.
75 *Ibid.*, 10.
76 In Increase Mather's *Nunc Dimittis* (Boston, 1709).

A painfully prosaic style was not the only weakness which occasionally was apparent in New England preaching. By the 1660's the Puritan pulpit style was changing. This difference in taste was to become very obvious in a few years with the pronounced mannerisms of Increase and Cotton Mather, but the pulpit oratory of the Reverend Leonard Hoare, preacher at Boston and later president of Harvard, is a forerunner of that ornate style which was soon to be the accepted fashion. Inevitably using two words where one would do, Hoare has sinners "fall and perish," events happen "suddenly without delay." With the same prolixity, Hoare bedecks his sermons with double metaphors, pleasantly rhythmic in tone, if a little anticlimactic:

The things of this life are like a boat to waft us over the water, which can doe us no further service when we come on shore, as our cloaths that we put on in the morning and off at night."

Or he passionately, not unimaginatively piles up the details of his allegorical conception of sinning man's last hour:

So it may be said of every inhabitant of this earth when he comes to dye, the weight of sin, the unsupportableness of Gods anger, the terrors of hell, the nearness of the danger, the difficulty of salvation will all appear nakedly to the naked soul. When God makes darkness and it is night, then the beasts of the forest creep forth: every frog will be croaking towards the evening, every puddle will send up a stinking vapor in a foggy night; all the several shadows of things will unite, every thing will concur to make up and compleat the misery of the poor sinner, but the Rulers of the darkness of this world and powers of darkness set in to doe the last and worst in this life."

And with this deliberately sensuous appeal to man's blind terror at the great change that is called death, we see the doom of New England's plain preaching with its dominant tone of everyday wisdom.

The natural variations in ability are, then, apparent in the preaching of New England's first pastors. All had the Biblical and theological culture peculiar to seventeenth-century Puritanism; but some were able to satisfy their intellectual curiosity within definite boundaries, while others had scholarly interests leading them to construe in its broadest sense the acknowledged

77 Hoare, *The Sting of Death and Death Unstung*, 9.
78 *Ibid.*, 10.

requisite of general information fundamental to an adequate understanding of the Bible. Some were clear-minded and spiritual in their reaching for faith through a reasoned interpretation of the Bible; others showed some tendency to be desultory and formalistic in their argument. Some preachers were passionate and alive in their pulpit style, others dull and plodding. Some were tactful and apt in their approach to their congregation's point of view; others seem crass, or a best, plain-spoken. But all these ministers were equally earnest in their effort to convince their listeners of the necessity for faith and to admonish the various sinners inevitably in any gathering, even of the elect. Simplicity of pulpit style was deliberately cultivated, but purposeful sincerity seems to have been instinctive with New England's first ministers, who managed—as few men have managed—to forget themselves in Christ's cause.

VIII

THE RECEPTION OF THE SERMONS

There is nothing more difficult to evaluate than any given sermon or even any given man's lifetime of preaching sermons. And a critical approach to Puritan preaching offers some strange paradoxes. What should be the criterion? Is one soul saved worthy compensation for any labor, any devotion? If a man is preaching the Bible, he has good Scripture sanction for thinking that one regained soul is very important in heaven. Or must every listener be influenced for the better by that hour or two of pulpit oratory? For the Puritan the problem was made more complicated by the fact that that first saving grace had to come from Christ and all could not expect the privilege of sharing the fellowship of the elect—although all should prepare for it. And how long must this state of overwhelming desire for salvation, this heart-turning to God, last? Can any man, however ardent, expect the effect of his preaching to be other than temporary? From the Puritan viewpoint, could the most fervent believer hope for every one to stay in a state of preparation for grace, grace which an apparently arbitrary divine decree had deprived him of? Either a man was chosen, of the elect, or he was lost. If the latter, why try to change him? According to the Puritan preacher's own dicta, many times repeated, the good works of the unsaved stank in the nostrils of God; the responsibility seems to be shifted from the preacher's shoulders to his Maker. Even with the damned in the audience ignored, there is still a difficulty. Once saved, a man may still sin. He should not, of course, but his evil nature is strong. If he sins, he must be urged to turn back to God and to repent his erring ways. But if he repents, this is a sign of God's mercy, for the impulse has come from God. Again the preacher is but an intermediary, a voice; the responsibility is hardly his.

There is one other looming difficulty in determining the value and success of any sermons, and especially of Puritan sermons. Who shall have the privilege of judging the preacher and his preaching? Those who believe as he does, those who believe themselves saved? Obviously they will be prejudiced in his favor. Those whose standards are different from his, those who must be content to be lost from the flock? Just as obviously, by the old human instinct of sour grapes, these transgressors will be prejudiced against him and what he stands for. Opinions about New England's first preachers might be expected to vary from an attitude that approaches adoration to one that had no words violent enough to express itself.

The ministers themselves showed no sign of conceit about their own preaching. Their attitude is one of dedication to a great purpose; their fear is that they will not be equal to the service of God and his elect. Their standards of what was good preaching were high in two senses: spiritually, they were the mouthpieces of a great truth; and, considering the matter more prosaically, they knew much of the technique of the pulpit. Not only had they studied sacred rhetoric, but they had also heard great preaching in England. Theirs was an age of pulpit oratory. Every "experienced" lay Christian knew what to expect when he went to hear a sermon or lecture and could judge accordingly, with highly developed critical acumen. Much more did the preacher know whether he had fulfilled his obligation to his God and to his congregation.

Because of their feeling of dedication and their augmented sense of the effectuality their preaching ought to possess, the ministers often became almost morbidly concerned with the possible weaknesses of their sermons. Shepard, for instance, had an artist's temperament. Sometimes humility about his unworthiness to express his complete faith in God overcame him. Sometimes a sureness of his ability to move his listeners encouraged him. The resulting agony of soul was the more pronounced because of the intensity of his religious belief. The record of his daily meditations shows the self-torture that he indulged in week after week:

November 25, 1640: "I found my Heart and Mouth straitned on the lecture-Day, and for want of Enlargement much troubled. Hence I essayed to humble my Soul before God. . . ."

January 12, 1641: "On Lecture-Day Morning, I began to feel my Heart slight and vilify what I was to deliver. But the Lord put it into my Mind, that tho' the Truth is a poor mean thing in itself, as every Ordinance also is; yet very glorious, as it is appointed and separated of God for his own Ends. . . ."

April 4, 1641: "On Sabbath-Morning I saw the Lord frowning on me in several Providences. . . ."

May 23, 1641: "On the Sabbath . . . I came to a serious consideration, What Sins were between God and me, that eclipsed his Love? . . ."

May 30, 1641: "On Sabbath-Day after Sermon, I saw that my Sin was, (1) To look on my Ministry's Faults, and be discouraged. (2) To look on their Good, and be puffed up. (3) If all was done well, then to look upon them, as they were, *Absalom*-like that from the Head to the Foot of them there was no Blemish. But I loathed myself for it, and prayed for everlasting Blessing on them."

June 6, 1641: "On the Sabbath I desired the Lord to bind my Hands, or rather cut them off, I mean *my vile Will and Affections*. . . ."

June 13, 1641: "On the *Sabbath,* being *weak in my Body and Spirits,* I asked, 'Can God make use of such a poor wretch to preach the Gospel by?' And I considered Paul. . . . So the Lord could do by me most weak."

August 1, 1641: "On *Sabbath Day,* when the Lord had given me some comfortable Enlargements, I search'd my heart to see my Sin. . . ."

August 15, 1641: "I saw on the Sabbath four Evils that attend me in my Ministry:
(1) The Devil either treads me down by Discouragement and Shame: . . .
(2) Or Carelessness possesseth me: arising (1) Because I have done well and been enlarged, and have been respected formerly, and hence 'tis no such Matter though I be not always alike. (2) A natural Dulness and Cloudiness of Spirit which doth often prevail. (3) Infirmities and Weakness: (1) Want of Light, (2) Want of Life, (3) Want of a Spirit of Power to deliver what I am affected with for Christ. . . . (4) Want of success when I have done my best."

August 28, 1641: "*When I came from Preaching,* I saw *my own Weakness.* . . ."

September 5, 1641: "I was on *Sabbath-Day Night* secretly swelling against God that he did not bless my Ministry. . . ."[1]

In other words, if Shepard felt that his preaching had been successful, he agonized over his sin of pride; if he felt that his skill had temporarily deserted him because of his sinful spirit, he worried that he might not be a fit instrument to declare God's wishes for his elect.

1 Shepard, *Meditations and Spiritual Experiences . . . from November 25, 1640 to December 27, 1641: transcribed out of his own Book, written with his own Hand; and left by him to his Son, Thomas Shepard . . .* (Boston, Printed: Edinburgh Reprinted, 1749), 17, 21, 28, 37, 38, 52, 53, 56, 57. There are other entries of much the same nature.

Nor was Shepard alone in this humble spirit about his pulpit duties. In comparison to Shepard, Mitchell was a simple soul, but his diary also shows an almost overwhelming modesty:

In Preaching I was not to seek of what I had prepared; but my Heart was Drie, Carnal and Unaffected, and methought I could not speak, with any Evidence, or Presence of the Spirit of God; so that when I had done, I was deeply ashamed within my self, and could not but Loath my self, to think how miserably I had behaved my self, in that High Employment, and how unsavoury, sottish, and foolish my Heart had been therein; I thought I, and all I did, well deserved to be Loathed by God and man.[2]

Here Mitchell was writing of one of his first publicly delivered sermons, but one that was so impressive and pleasing to the people of Hartford that they promptly invited him to settle among them. One other proof of how universally these ministers suffered this dejection about their preaching may be seen in the Reverend Thomas Thacher's comment to his son, about to begin his service in a neighboring New England town: "Son, I never preach a Sermon 'till I cannot preach at all!"[3]

In contrast to this attitude of acknowledging their own preaching difficulties, was the ministers' praise of each other. A very fulsome volume could be gathered together from the many commendatory statements in the introductions and prefatory epistles to published collections of sermons; on the death of each minister another laudatory chorus rang out. Such panegyrics might well be disregarded as being prescribed by custom or the taste of the time. On the other hand, the ministers were pledged to the truth by their very faith and life, they took some pains to analyze the particular abilities of the men they extolled, and there was absolutely no grain of self-profit or sycophancy in these encomiums. During one synod, Chauncy and Mitchell were at some variance of opinion. Nevertheless, Chauncy is quoted as saying:

I know no man in the world I could envy so much as worthy Mr. Mitchell, for the great boldness, learning, wisdom, and meekness and other qualities of an excellent spirit with which the Lord Jesus Christ hath endowed him.[4]

2 Quoted by Cotton Mather, *Magnalia*, Book IV, 170.
3 *Magnalia*, Book III, 150.
4 William Anderson Mitchell and Josiah Sherman Mitchell, with additions by Mrs. Natalie Mitchell Seth: *Matthew Mitchell of Yorkshire, England and some of his descendants* (White Plains, 1935), 12.

Another example of the affectionate appreciation in which one preacher held another may be seen in the case of the Reverend Thomas Parker and the Reverend James Noyes, who were co-workers in the town of Newbury. After Noyes' death, Parker had this to say about his late colleague:

He was of a reaching and ready Apprehension, a large Invention, a most profound Judgment, a rare and tenacious and comprehensive Memory, fixed and unmovable in his grounded Conceptions; sure in Words and Speech, without Rashness; gentle and mild in all Expressions, without all Passion or provoking language.[5]

This is only part of a much longer eulogy. With similar spirit, Increase Mather, who as a young man must have known Davenport in the days of the latter's maturity, quotes Cotton in praise of the New Haven pastor. The Mathers so revered Cotton that the highest compliment is consequently paid by implication.

Well did Mr. Cotton *give this Testimony concerning him* Davenport, *that He is a Man mighty in Judgement, and Learning, and singular Prudence. And we doubt not but those that love and honour him farre less than we do, yet will say, that He is one of a thousand.*[6]

But it was not only the colonial clergy that appreciated their fellow preachers. Just as the New England ministers knew and admired their English brethren and the latter's publications, so the English clergy are reported to have respected the Puritans who had chosen to migrate to New England. The high regard of the ministers in Old England for those in New England often expressed itself in commendatory prefaces to the books sent across the ocean to be published. For instance, when a volume of Shepard's sermons was printed in London in 1654, two ministers combined their talents to write a suitable preface; one of them was Samuel Mather, who, after studying under Shepard, had returned to England and was preaching in a Dublin pastorate; the other was William Greenhill, a well-known English Puritan. Their tribute to Shepard, who had been dead some five years, reads in part:

His manner of preaching was close and certain, and with abundance of affection and compassion to his hearers. . . . He affected Plainness Together with Power in preaching; not seeking abstrusities nor liking to hover and

5 Quoted in *Magnalia*, Book III, 148.
6 Increase Mather, Preface to Davenport's *Another Essay . . . 1663.*

soar aloft in dark expressions, and so shoot his arrows, as many preachers do, over the head of his listeners.[7]

Some years later, on the occasion of another posthumous publication, that of *The Parable of the Ten Virgins,* English ministers praising Shepard's work included Edmund Calamy of Smectymnuus fame, and Bishop Kennett, the chronicler.

The prosperous and conservative colonial lay leaders would naturally be expected to join in this admiration of the church leaders. Such comment is limited because so few men took time to express in any detail their opinions of their fellow citizens or of the Sunday services to which they regularly listened. Most of the diaries of the period simply record the texts of the sermons heard or the name of the preacher occupying the pulpit on a certain date; deaths of the ministers are often noted just as laconically, with no reaction given. Governor Winthrop has a little more to say, noting that each regular Puritan minister was a "godly" man, sometimes even a "godly man and a prime scholar"; the few clergymen who could not get along with their churches or who left Puritanism proper for some faction are called "passionate" or "wanting discretion and moderation." The good governor takes time to speak more at length of a few men:

Those of the lower part of the river Pascataquack invited Mr. James Parker of Weymouth, a godly man and a scholar, one who had been many a year a deputy for the public court, to be their minister. He, by advice of divers of the magistrates and elders, accepted the call, and went and taught among them this winter, and it pleased God to give great success to his labors, so as above forty of them, whereof the most had been profane, and some of them professed enemies to the way of our churches, wrote to the magistrates and elders, acknowledging the sinful course they had lived in, and bewailing the same, and blessing God for bringing them out of it, and earnestly desiring that Mr. Parker might be settled amongst them. Most of them fell back again in time, embracing this present world.[8]

Evidently Winthrop admired Parker, but not to the point of refusing to note the transiency of the latter's reforms. Winthrop's tone occasionally in recording the death of a preacher is also far more restrained than that of the ministers in mourning the other

7 Preface to *Subjection to Christ* (1654).
8 Winthrop, *Journal* (under date of December, 1642), II, 89-90.

"lights in God's golden candlestick." For example, under date of July 2, 1644, the *Journal* has this brief eulogy:

Mr. George Phillips was buried. He was the first pastor of the church of Watertown, a godly man, especially gifted, and very peaceful in his place, much lamented of his own people and others.[9]

Only once does Winthrop really display his grief at the death of a minister. After noting the epidemic of sickness that swept the colonies in June of 1647, he writes:

But that which made the stroke more sensible and grievous, both to them and to all the country, was the death of that faithful servant of the Lord, Mr. Thomas Hooker, pastor of the church in Hartford, who, for piety, prudence, wisdom, zeal, learning, and what else might make him serviceable in the place and time he lived in, might be compared with men of greatest note; and he shall need no other praise, the fruits of his labors in both Englands shall preserve an honorable and happy remembrance of him forever.[10]

Surely no finer tribute could be paid to a contemporary—paid by one altruistic man to another, after both had agreed to disagree on a number of matters of some importance.

Another layman of considerable prominence in his own day was Captain Roger Clap, who served Massachusetts in both civil and military offices. Coming as a young man of twenty-one in the year 1630, he has this to say about New England preaching:

The Lord Jesus Christ was so plainly held out in the Preaching of the Gospel unto poor lost Sinners, and the absolute Necessity of the *New Birth,* and God's holy Spirit in those Days was pleased to accompany the word with such Efficacy upon the Hearts of many; that our Hearts were taken off from *Old-England* and set upon *Heaven.* The Discourse, not only of the Aged, but of the Youth also, was not, *How shall we go to England?* (tho some few did not only so Discourse, but also went back again) but *How shall we go to Heaven? Have I true Grace wrought in my Heart? Have I Christ or no?*[11]

A little later in his brief autobiographic memoir, Clap tells that he found hope of salvation through John Cotton's preaching on *Revelation,*[12] and he also relates hearing John Wilson and George Phillips preach many a good sermon, "their Meeting-Place being abroad under a Tree"[13] in those first days of pioneering.

9 *Ibid.,* (under date of July 2, 1644), II, 178.
10 *Ibid.,* (under date of June, 1647), II, 326-327.
11 Clap, *Memoirs of* (Boston, 1844), 20.
12 *Ibid.,* 24.
13 *Ibid.,* 42.

Clap has a certain homely air of good sense about his writing. He realized that there was no greater compliment to be paid to the New England clergy than to say that they could turn the thoughts of homesick men, young and old, from the known comforts they had left behind them, to the hopes of a heaven which would be theirs only after the purgatory of an unknown land and way of life. A much less restrained writer was Edward Johnson, a prosperous freeman who served as town clerk of Woburn. His *Wonder - Working Providence of Zion's Saviour in New England* is filled with effusive tributes to the ministers and teachers of each town. Even the less well-known men have their generous share of adjectives: Thomas Allen is a "cheerfull, grave, and gracious Soldier of Christ"; John Allen is "reverend, humble, and heavenly-minded"; Thomas Carter is "a reverend, godly man, apt to teach the sound and wholesome truths of Christ"; Jonathan Burr is "a holy, heavenly-minded man, and able gifted to preach the word of God."[14] William Hooke, whom later critics have praised as a distinguished rhetorician, Johnson fittingly calls "a man who hath received of Christ many gracious gifts, fit for so high a calling, with a very amiable and gracious speech labouring in the Lord."[15] Johnson also caught some of Richard Mather's strength of mind in characterizing him as "indued by the Lord with many Heavenly gifts, of a plaine and upright spirit, apt to teach, full of gracious expressions, and bent to follow the truth, as it is in Jesus."[16] So, in one involved period after another, Johnson finds some points of superiority about them all; and in so doing, the Woburn clerk set the style for New England's next two historians.

A few years later, Nathaniel Morton, using much the same tone as had Johnson, faithfully notes in his *New-Englands Memoriall* the arrival of the ministers and then their deaths, accompanying nearly every entry with a commendatory phrase: Francis Higginson and Samuel Skelton were "holy" men; John Wilson was a "Reverend and Worthy man . . . eminent for Love and Zeal"; George Phillips was "a worthy Servant of Christ and Dispenser of his Word"; John Eliot was a "Reverend and Use-

14 Johnson, *Wonder-Working Providence* 1628-1651. Edited by J. Franklin Jameson (New York: Charles Scribner's Sons, 1910), 171, 179, 215, 192.
15 *Ibid.*, 193.
16 *Ibid.*, 105.

ful Instrument"; John Cotton, Thomas Hooker, and Samuel Stone were "Gospel-Preachers of excellent worth and use in their places"; Thomas Shepard was "a soul-searching Minister of the Gospel," who "preached the Gospel profitably and very successively"; John Cotton was "greatly enriched with gifts & abilities, being an able expounder, and faithful applier of the Word of God"; John Lathrop was "a man of an humble and broken heart and spirit, lively in dispensation of the Word of God";" and John Norton was "a burning and a Shining light" whose death was a blow to the whole land, for,

He was singularly endowed with the Tongue of the Learned, inabled to speak a word in due season, not onely to the wearied Soul, but also a word of Counsel to a people in necessity thereof, being not onely a wise Steward of the things of Jesus Christ, but also a wise Statesman; so that the whole land sustained a great loss of him.[18]

In addition to his own praises of these men, Morton occasionally included elegies by other hands. From these the reader learns that Hooker's preaching combined the thunder of Farel, the tenderness of Viret, and the lively oracular power of Calvin;[19] Cotton, too, was to be classed with Calvin and Melanchthon.[20]

The Reverend William Hubbard in his *General History of New England* again repeats the eulogizing phraseology of Johnson and Morton. The earlier ministers are always spoken of as men of eminent piety, great learning, sound judgment, and remarkable zeal, courage, wisdom, and worth. Unfortunately, most of his remarks on his fellow preachers are disappointingly general; concerning Hooker, for example, he is content with Ezekiel Rogers' epitaph, so adulatory that it is almost unintelligible, and with one brief paragraph taken almost word for word from Winthrop's tribute.[21] A dearth of definite comment on the ministers' pulpit services is understandable in a book of this nature, which professes to be a history. Rarely is there an interesting notice of a preacher's success, although

17 Morton, *New-Englands Memoriall* (Cambridge, 1669), 78, 83, 84, 85, 91, 131, 135, 141, 165.
18 *Ibid.*, 165.
19 *Ibid.*, 126.
20 *Ibid.*, 136.
21 Hubbard, *A General History of New England* (Cambridge, 1815), 541.

Hubbard does tell his readers that the Reverend Henry Whitfield was a gracious, faithful pastor who showed himself to be "an experimental soul searching preacher, and the course of his ministry aiming at heart and life, and conversion, not without good fruit by the blessing of Lord Jesus Christ." Twice, too, Hubbard remarks on the reputed power that Hooker and Cotton had over the people. Early in the *General History* there is this statement:

And such was the authority they (especially Mr. Cotton) had in the hearts of the people, that whatever he delivered in the pulpit was soon put into an order of court, if of a civil, or set up as a practice in the church, if of an ecclesiastical concernment.[22]

Near the end of the volume Hubbard returns briefly to this theme:

It hath been observed by some, that a great part of New England's prosperity came along with Mr. Hooker and Mr. Cotton; it may be truly said, that it remained there, in great part, by Mr. Wilson's means, who, by his faith and prayers, kept off the storm from New England all his own time, as some have said of Luther, concerning Germany, and of which this good man had some secret and strong persuasions, as he did intimate to some of his most confident friends, scil. that no publick judgment or calamity should come upon the country in his time; what hath fallen out since, is well known to the world.[23]

It is pleasant to think of the Reverend John Wilson as appreciating his own weight in turning God's wrath from New England's shores!

This firm conviction that the first ministers were exceptional men and superior preachers remained traditional for some generations, especially as it was diligently transmitted by the clergy. Cotton Mather, writing at the end of the century, composed page after page of steady praise for the first comers to the colonies. With the usual exception of the few trouble-makers, every preacher is extolled for his holy spirit and for his ability to impart it to others; and every minister, with the exception of poor John Brock (whose scholastic crimes remain unrecorded), is lauded for his remarkable learning. Cotton Mather's adulatory tone, which certainly loses force by its continuousness, may be judged by his criticism of Urian Oakes:

22 Hubbard, *A General History*, 182.
23 *Ibid.*, 604.

Consider'd as a *Preacher,* he was an Orpheus that would have drawn the very *Stones* to discipline; had *Austin* been here, he might have seen *Paul in the pulpit*: indeed, he was, as one said, *An uncomfortable Preacher*: Why? he drove us to *Despair,* namely, *Of seeing such another.*[24]

To each and every minister Mather paid his florid compliments. Oakes might be a combination of Orpheus and Paul, but Davenport was acknowledged, even by his greatest enemies, to be among "the best of preachers," with impressive abilities:

So rich a treasure of the best gifts as was our *Davenport,* was well worth coveting by the considerablest Church of the Land. He was an incomparable Preacher, and a Man of more than ordinary Accomplishments; a Prince of Preachers, and worthy to have been a Preacher to Princes: He had been acquainted with Great Men, and Great Things, and was Great himself, and had a Great Fame abroad in the World; yea, now he was grown old, like *Moses* his *force was not abated.*[25]

Undoubtedly the theory that New England once had enjoyed the services of almost superhuman preachers reached its meridian in Cotton Mather's pages of eulogy, with two large, double-columned pages for the less important ministers and teachers, ten to twenty (or even more) pages for the outstanding leaders. But the tradition of New England's first glory lasted for a few more generations, at least among the clergy. The Reverend Thomas Prince was so much interested in Massachusetts' early history that he read and carefully preserved many of the first publications of the early sermons. He also repeats a popular story that he had heard from various old timers. He was told that even gentry and children often walked thirty miles on a Thursday to hear Shepard or his successor in the Cambridge pulpit, Mitchell, preach. And Shepard, Prince also reports himself as hearing, scarce preached a sermon but someone in the audience would cry out in agony "What shall I do to be saved?"—for so low yet so searching was the first Cambridge minister's preaching that no hypocrite could easily bear it, and it seemed almost irresistible.[26] Jonathan Edwards was another early eighteenth-century theologian who made himself familiar with the writings of Massachusetts' Puritanism. He paid Shepard the compliment of quoting with great frequency from the latter's *The Sound Believer* and *The Parable of the*

24 Mather, *Magnalia,* Book IV, 187.
25 *Ibid.,* Book III, 56.
26 Thomas Prince, *Six Sermons* (Edinburgh, 1785), 60, 61.

Ten Virgins; in mentioning Shepard, this admirer terms him "that famous experimental divine, Mr. Shepard."[27]   As a later occupant of the Northampton pulpit, Edwards also had reason to note the accepted opinion of the Reverend Eleazer Mather's services:

He [Mather] was one whose heart was much in his work, abundant in labors for the good of precious souls; he had the high esteem and great love of his people, and was blessed with no small success.[28]

The volume of praise that the ministers and their efforts brought forth far outweighs the censure that managed to be recorded.   Nothing could be more natural.   Only the members of the community in accord with the dominant party could hope to have their views published in the colonies.   English publication and the re-introduction of any subversive material would have been a costly and dangerous process.   Only the avowed opponents of Puritanism, sectarians who had fled New England, could be at all outspoken in their comments.   A few Quaker accounts, published in England some years later, show the other side of the picture—how the New England preachers appeared to those they had persecuted.   Incidentally, the Friends were quick to see and make much of the point that the first ministers had acknowledged the elect and their church to be faulty and that later preachers had constantly reiterated New England's virtue to be steadily declining.   Of course, said the Friends, after a bad beginning and all these years of getting worse, New England must be a vile place—so foul, in fact, that the very "priests" admitted its sad condition.

Far from content with general criticism and doctrinal disputes, the Quakers also attacked individual ministers.   The Reverend John Reynor is ridiculed because the poor man reputedly could not prove the doctrine of the Trinity to the satisfaction of a persistent Quakeress.   Pathetic lost soul that he was, he fled the scene of the argument and locked himself in his house with a big key.[29]   Various other preachers are called "inveterate

27 Edwards, *A Treatise concerning Religious Affections* in *The Works of President Edwards*, I, 58 *et alii.*
28 Edwards, *A Narrative of Many Surprising Conversions*, in *The Works of President Edwards*, III, 10.
29 George Bishop, *New-England Judged, by the Spirit of the Lord* (London: T. Sowle, 1703), 362.

Enemies to Truth," who make the Friends wonder that there could be such a "heap of blockish Priests in the Country."[30] Wilson, a determined persecutor of the Quakers, is usually named as "your bloody High-Priest" or just as a "Murthering Priest";[31] John Higginson fares less well, being termed

a speaker Evil of Dignities, a presumptuous Person; a Well without Water; a Cloud without Rain, driven about with every Tempest; a bloody Persecutor, who hath had to do in the Blood and Sufferings of many of the Servants of the Lord, whose wickedness is well known to the Lord, before whom are all his Ways and Wickedness, who will render unto him according to his Deeds.[32]

John Norton, another minister who had been particularly violent in his anti-Quakerism, naturally has his preaching judged somewhat harshly. This is John Rows' account of his experience in Boston around 1658:

Humphrey Norton and I were moved to go into the great meeting-house at Boston upon one of their lecture days, where we found John Norton their teacher set up, who, like a babbling Pharisee, ran over a vain repetition near an hour long. When his glass was out he began his sermon, wherein, among many lifeless expressions, he spake much of the danger of those called Quakers, a flood of gall and vinegar instead of the cup of cold and refreshing water! How often hungry souls have been deceived by him I leave to that of God in their consciences to judge.[33]

The Friends left no stone unturned in their efforts to discredit the Puritans. The violence of feeling on both sides of the controversy necessarily invalidates such acrimonious accounts of the ministers and their preaching. More interesting would be adverse judgments by members of the churches or at least by regular listeners to the Sabbath services. But such comments are seldom to be found. How promptly all contemptuous criticism of the ministers was punished may be seen by an occasional court record. For instance, at the Quarterly Court held during August of 1644 this case appeared:

Wm. Hewes and John his sone, for deriding such as Sung in the Congregation, tearming them fooles; also William Hewes for saying Mr. Whiting preaches confusedly; also John Hewes for charging Mr. Cobbitt with falshood in his doctrine. Wm. Hewes and John his son, shall pay 50s. a peece for a fine, and that it be Injoyned they shall make an humble confession at

30 *Ibid.*, 387, 465.
31 *Ibid.*, 124 *et alii.*
32 *Ibid.*, 380.
33 Quoted by Rufus M. Jones in his *The Quakers in the American Colonies* (New York: Macmillan & Co., 1911), 71.

Lynn, at a publick meeting, which according to it the Court will consider their fines.[34]

Nor was this the only case of this type. Some years later Thomas Wheeler, a man of some property, a mill owner, and a freeman, had to pay a heavy fine of over twelve pounds plus the fees of the court if he was unwilling to make public acknowledgment that his speeches had been "evil, sinful, and offensive"; Mr. Wheeler, in an angry moment, had compared the Reverend Mr. Cobbett to Korah.[35] On still another occasion, Henry Walton of Lynn was brought before the Quarterly Court for saying that "he had as Leave to heare a dogg Barke as to heare Mr. Cobbett preach."[36] Mr. Walton, apparently a frank soul, was acquitted of the charge for lack of evidence.

Three deductions may be made from these cases. The elect were alert, very much on guard against censure. Those in power did not hesitate to punish any one who dared in any way to voice his dissent or to seek to undermine the authority of the church. And there were detractors of the clergy to be found among regularly settled townspeople, and even among church members. Here and there may be seen other evidence of this opposition. Occasionally some little praising anecdote, told in good faith about a minister, betrays that the latter had a critic who, unaided by the rosy glasses of complete faith, saw a few flaws in this particular servant of God. In order to show the humble spirit of the revered John Cotton and how well the Lord protected him, Cotton Mather tells this sad tale:

One would have thought the Ingenuity of such a Spirit would have broken the *Hearts of Men,* that had indeed the *Hearts of Men* in them; yea, that the hardest *Flints* would have been broken, as is usual, upon such a soft bag of *Cotton*! But alas! he found it otherwise, even among some who pretended unto *high Attainments* in Christianity. Once particularly, an humorous and imperious Brother, following Mr. *Cotton* home to his House, after his Publick Labours, instead of the grateful Respects with which those Holy Labours were to have been encouraged, rudely told him, That his Ministry was become generally, either dark, or flat: Whereto this meek man, very mildly and gravely, made only this Answer: *Both, Brother, it may be, both: Let me have your Prayers that it may be otherwise.* But it

34 Alonzo Lewis, *The History of Lynn* (Boston: Samuel N. Dickinson, 1844), 123-124.

35 James R. Newhall, *The History of Lynn* (Lynn, 1883), 121.

36 William Samuel Harris, "Rev. Thomas Cobbett," in *Granite Monthly*, XLIX, 12.

is remarkable, that the Man sick thus of wanton Singularities, afterwards died of those damnable Heresies, for which he was deservedly Excommunicated.[37]

Such was Cotton's after-church encounter with one who "pretended unto high attainments in Christianity."

The Reverend Samuel Whiting evidently had his troubles during the services. One dull Sabbath in June of 1646, a Mr. Tomlins too obviously fell asleep in his pew. A more awake listener reports that Whiting, too, was a meek man:

Mr. Whiting doth pleasantlie say yt from ye pulpitt hee doth seem to be preaching to stacks of straw with men sitting here and there among them.[38]

Whiting, whose sermons usually lasted for an hour and a half, followed by a half-hour of prayer, apparently found his audience frequently drifting away from him to the pleasanter lands of slumber. He is reported as on one occasion interrupting his sermon to reach for his hat; he then went to feed his fowls, after remarking that he would be back when his congregation had finished sleeping. And once, although this story is scarcely believable, no matter how hard pressed the poor man may have been, Whiting wished for the Episcopal service so that the frequent rising would keep his listeners somewhat awake.[39]

Such incidents are revealing, but the sermons themselves offer the best evidence that all was not rapt attention to and reverent acceptance of the rendering of the Bible being presented by the ministers. An interpretation of failure might well be given to the constant ministerial harping on the theme that the churches had had their best day and that neither in faith nor in behavior did the colonists equal their fathers. If these constant fears did not mean that New England's religious state was getting steadily worse, they certainly do suggest that the preachers were not meeting with a proper response to their efforts. Moreover, the sermons from the beginning offer more concrete testimony that there were those in every congregation who regarded the minister neither as a paragon of ability and virtue nor as a "murthering High-Priest"; in fact, the attitude

37 Mather, *Magnalia*, Book III, 26.
38 Obadiah Turner's journal quoted in William Whiting's *Memoir of Samuel Whiting*, 2nd Edition (Boston, 1873), 95.
39 Whiting, *Memoir*, 170.

that the ministers remonstrated against was one not of love nor of hate, but one of indifference, perhaps of growing contempt. Many of the preachers, including some of the most distinguished leaders, complain about the lack of appreciation their efforts met with. Shepard, preaching in the 1630's and 1640's, grumbles that large families often are late getting to church,[40] that young people come with merely marriage in mind,[41] and that the old-fashioned habit of taking notes of sermons was dying out.[42] Even more bitterly does he protest:

Oh how many men are there that become quite sermon-proof now - adays! Are not men blockish, dull, senseless, heavy under all means, they taste not, smell not, whereas elsewhere, O how lively and spirited are they![43]

Hooker, too, has complaints about the behavior of congregations. Many men, he observes, are reading or praying or conferring even while the minister is preaching to them.[44] Again, he finds it necessary to urge that children and servants should not be allowed to "play and sport, and talk, and runne about" the church. The head of the family should make every endeavor to bring these offenders "under the word."[45] Nor is this lack of attention on the part of some of his parishioners all of Hooker's tale of woe. Some men listen to the minister only to resent what they hear; "swellings and bublings" against the word are the result, and the offending preacher is wished out of the country.[46] Hooker attributed this resentment to the bad consciences of some listeners.

Richard Mather, too, is distressed about those who despise the clergy; he felt that the most certain sign of true faith is a "high prizing" of the word and of the ministers, its interpreters. Consequently, he wonders about New England's true state.[47] By the 1650's he is noting that the times are such that many foolish people think that no great abilities are requisite of a minister. With no false modesty, but with a calm spirit of worthy service,

40 Shepard, *Of Ineffectual Hearing the Word*, 101; *The Parable of the Ten Virgins*, Part. I, 159.
41 Shepard, *The Parable of the Ten Virgins*, Pt. II, 100.
42 *Ibid.*, Pt. II, 146.
43 *Ibid.*, II, 6; for another complaint, *cf. The Sincere Convert*, 69.
44 Hooker, *The Paterne of Perfection*, 278.
45 Hooker, *The Unbeleevers Preparing for Christ*, 111.
46 *Ibid.*, 99.
47 Mather, *The Summe of Certain Sermons*, 27-28.

Mather disproves this heresy by stating that not one man in a thousand is fit to serve God in this way.   Such scoffers should remember *Job* 33:23.[48]   Chauncy around the same time protests that many "coveteous earth-worms" will not acknowledge New England's great mercy, "a faithfull sound and able" ministry. Indeed, some of these ungrateful wretches go so far as to abuse and weary their good pastors by raising factions in the churches. Others count it a happiness to remove themselves from the blessing of having a church; hence they prefer to live "in the worst howling wilderness without any ministry, or schole, and means of education."[49]

By the late 1660's and early 1670's the discontent with the ministers had grown; or, perhaps, there had been a deepening of the air of gloom, of the feeling that nothing in the present equalled the glory of the past.   Danforth speaks of the good old days, when all were eager, attentive to the word, "painful" in recollecting and repeating and discoursing about what had been delivered from the pulpit.   Then the ministers had been held in proper esteem; then every listener had been diligent in studying Scripture; then everyone had been zealous against sectaries and heretics, even as all were devoted to the care of their sister churches; then all had shown their reverence for each council and its decisions; in fact, in that golden time, all had lived in faith, love, and charity, taking good care of the spiritual well-being of their children.   And what was to be seen in this later New England?   Nothing but a "careless, remiss, flat, dry, cold, dead frame of spirit."   If the colonists did not want more calamities and more deaths among the ministers, they must have faith and show it by listening to the ministers.[50]   This long tirade of Danforth's hardly proved more than that the preachers were still meeting adverse criticism from some elements in their audience.   Urian Oakes is more definite in his accusations, claiming that the ministers had to endure many hardships, among them disorderly behavior of listeners and prejudices upon the part of many; far too frequently reproaches, base nicknames, hard usage, and injurious dealing were the lot of God's mouthpieces.

48 Mather, *A Farewel-Exhortation*, 7-8.
49 Chauncy, *Gods Mercy*, 13-19.
50 Danforth, *A Brief Recognition of New Englands Errand*, 10-23.

In short, said Oakes sadly to all who might be heeding him at
an artillery election,

We live in times of great Degeneracy and in special of great Disaffection to
the Ministers of Christ.[51]

The admiration of the biased faithful for their ministers
can be interpreted as the natural feeling for each other that men
of similar views possess as a form of self-justification; or this
feeling on the part of their congregations can be given the meaning that the preachers must have been worthy, gifted leaders
in order to merit the respect of the other sincerely religious and
able men who settled New England.   The abuse that the equally
biased persecuted directed against their oppressors may be seen
as having an element of truth in its violence, for these ministers
were men who had a tendency to disregard all earthly values in
their bitter struggle to save the souls of some of their followers
and to keep God's wrath from New England.   But, according
to their own creed, Puritan pastors could not be otherwise than
intolerant, inasmuch as they owed their first duty to their concept of the revealed will of God and to their congregations, many
members of which had followed them across the Atlantic in
order to be protected and to have their children saved from error.

More important in one sense is the undeniable fact that,
judged by their own criteria, the preachers failed in their efforts.   The church prospered; many of the elect felt certain of
salvation; nevertheless, according to the testimony of their own
sermons, the ministers had felt this inefficacy from the beginning of their American careers.   The fault, they thought (and
had to think by their creed), was not theirs; no matter how
frequently and how fervently she was warned, New England
persisted in angering God.   Perhaps the preachers only imag-
ined that sin grew more rampant each succeeding year.   This
notion undoubtedly was part of their fixed opinion that the world
was steadily growing worse.   But there can be no doubt that
America changed in spite of the ministers and their sermons;
whether this development was for the better or the worse matters little, as change was failure in their eyes.   On the other

51 Oakes, *The Unconquerable, All-Conquering & more-then-Conquering Souldier*,
    33.

hand, considered in a larger sense, these preachers succeeded better than they knew. Not only did Hooker give his community a tradition of democracy; not only did Shepard offer future generations the solace of a mystic and all-abiding faith; the preachers, one and all, by each sermon contributed to New England's mental and moral philosophy. Lost causes have a way of living in men's minds. Who can deny that the Puritan concept of God and of man's duty and dignity as that God's creation and fellow-covenanter, has left its impress upon the New England character? And any loyal son of Massachusetts or Connecticut would promptly say that influencing New England was but the first step in molding the thought of the United States.

BIBLIOGRAPHY

Part One: The Sermons

I. *The First Ministers — Mostly Cambridge and Oxford Graduates*

JOHN ALLEN (1596-1671)

The Spouse of Christ coming out of Affliction, leaning upon her beloved: Or a sermon preached by Mr. John Allin the late reverend Pastor to the Church of Christ at Dedham, at the administration of the Lords Supper, August 6, 1671. . . . Cambridge: Printed by Samuel Green, 1672.

Second title: *The Lord Jesus his legacie of peace, to arm his disciples against trouble and fear: Or, a sermon preached by Mr. John Allin the late reverend pastor of the Church of Christ in Dedham, August 13, 1671. Being the last that he preached before his death, which was August 26, 1671.*

Both sermons are reprinted in *Dedham Pulpit: Or Sermons by the Pastors of the First Church in Dedham, in the XVIIth and XVIIIth centuries; . . .* Edited by E. Burgess. Boston: Perkins & Marvin, 1840. pp. 1-27.

EDWARD BULKELEY (c. 1614-1696)

A Thankefull Remembrance of Gods Mercy to several Persons at Quabaug or Brookfield: Partly in a Collection of Providences about them, and Gracious Appearances for them; And partly in a Sermon Preached By Mr. Edward Bulkley, Pastor of the Church of Christ at Concord, upon a day of Thanksgiving, kept by divers for their Wonderfull Deliverance there. Published by Captain Thomas Wheeler . . . Cambridge: Printed by Samuel Green, 1676.

The sermon has been reprinted, New Hampshire Historical Society *Collections*, II.

PETER BULKELEY (1582-1659)

The Gospel-Covenant: Or The Covenant of Grace Opened. Wherein are explained:

1. *The differences betwixt the Covenant of grace and the Covenant of workes.*
2. *The different administration of the Covenant before and since Christ.*
3. *The benefits and blessings of it.*
4. *The Condition.*
5. *The properties of it.*

Preached in Concord in New-England . . . Published according to Order. London: Printed by M.S. for Benjamin Allen, 1646.

Also London, 1651—"The Second Edition, much enlarged, and corrected by the Author. And the chiefe heads of Things (which was omitted in the former) distinguished into Chapters."

CHARLES CHAUNCY (1592-1672)

Gods Mercy, Shewed To His People in Giving Them a Faithful Ministry and Schooles of Learning for the Continual Supplyes Thereof. Delivered in a Sermon preached at Cambridg, the day after the Commencement, . . . Published with some additions thereunto, at the request of diverse Honourd, and much Respected friends, For publick benefit, as they judged. Cambridge in New-England: Printed by Samuel Green, 1655.

The Plain Doctrin of the Justification of a Sinner in the sight of God, . . . Explained and Applied in six and twenty Sermons, in a plain, Doctrinal and Familiar way, for the Capacity, and Understanding of the Weak and Ignorant. London: Printed by R. I. for Adoniram Byfield, 1659.

THOMAS COBBETT (1608-1685)

A Practical Discourse of Prayer. Wherein is handled, The Nature, the Duty, the Qualifications of Prayer; the several sorts of Prayer; viz: Ejaculatory, Publick, Private, and Secret Prayer. With the Necessity of, and Ingagements unto Prayer. . . . London: Printed by T. M. for Joseph Cranford, 1654.

A variant 1654 edition has "London: Printed by T. M. for Ralph Smith," but otherwise seems to be identical. Other editions: London, 1657; Boston, 1856.

JOHN COTTON (1585-1652)

A Briefe Exposition of the whole Book of Canticles: Or, Song of Solomon: Lively describing the Estate of the Church in all the Ages thereof, both Jewish and Christian, to this day: . . . London: Printed for Philip Nevil, 1642. Other editions: London, 1648, 1655.

A Briefe Exposition with practical observations . . . upon the whole book of Ecclesiastics . . . London, 1654. Another edition: London, 1657.

Christ the Fountaine of Life: Or, Sundry Choyce Sermons on part of the fift [sic] Chapter of the first Epistle of St. John. London: Printed by Robert Ibbetson, 1651.

The Churches Resurrection, or the Opening of the Fift and sixt verses of the 20th Chap. of the Revelation. London, 1642.

The Covenant of Gods free grace most sweetly unfolded . . . London, 1645. Another edition: London, 1655.
Reprinted as:
A Treatise of the Covenant of Grace. As it is dispensed to the Elect Seed, effectually unto Salvation. Being the substance of divers Sermons preached upon Act. 7.8. by that eminently holy and judicious man of God, Mr. John Cotton . . . The second Edition, by a Copy far larger than the former, and corrected also by the Author's own hand . . . London, 1659. Another edition: London, 1671.

A Discourse upon 1 Cor. 14.40. . . . Whether it be lawfull for Church-Governors to command indifferent decent things in the Administration of God's Worship. In *Some Treasure fetched out of Rubbish: or three Short but seasonable Treatises.* . . . London, 1660.

An Exposition Upon The Thirteenth Chapter of The Revelation. London: Printed by M. S. for Livewel Chapman, 1655. Another edition: London, 1656.

Gods Mercie Mixed With His Iustice: Or, His Peoples Deliverance in times of danger. Laid open in severall Sermons. London: Printed by G. M. for Edward Brewster and Henry Hord, 1641.
Reissued as:
The Saints Support and Comfort in the Time of Distress and Danger. With divers other Treatises. . . . London, 1657.

Gods Promise to His Plantation. 2 Sam. 7.10. . . . As it was delivered in a sermon. London: Printed by William Jones for John Bellamy, 1630. Other editions: London, 1634; Boston, 1686; also in Old South Leaflets, no. 53 and in *New England Historical and Genealogical Register*, II.

The New Covenant, Or, a Treatise, unfolding the order and manner of the giving and receiving of the Covenant of Grace to the Elect. As also: Showing the difference between the Legallist and the true Christian. Being the substance of sundry Sermons . . . . London, 1654.
Reprinted as the first part of:
The Covenant of Grace . . . London, 1655.

The Powring Out of The Seven Vials: Or An Exposition, Of The 16. Chapter of the Revelation, with an Application of it to our Times. Wherein is revealed Gods powring out the full Vials of his fierce wrath. 1. Upon the lowest and basest sort of Catholicks. 2. Their worship and Religion. 3. Their Priests and Ministers. 4. The House of Austria, and Popes Supremacy. 5. Episcopall Government. 6. Their Euphrates, or the streame of their supportments. 7. Their grosse Ignorance, and blind Superstitions. Very fit and necessary for this Present Age. Preached in Sundry Sermons at Boston in New-England: . . . London: Printed for R. S., 1642. Another edition: London, 1646.

A Practical Commentary, or An Exposition With Observations, Reasons, and Uses Upon The First Epistle Generall of John. . . . London: Printed by R. I. and E. C. for Thomas Parkhurst, 1656. Another edition: London, 1658.

A Sermon Preached by the Reverend, Mr. John Cotton, Teacher of the First Church in Boston in New-England. Deliver'd at Salem, 1636. To which is Prefixed, a Retraction of his former Opinion concerning Baptism, utter'd by him immediately Preceeding the Sermon here Emitted. . . . Boston, 1713.

The Way of Life, or God's Way and Course, in bringing the soule into . . . and carrying it on, in the wayes of life and peace. Laid downe in foure severall treatises on foure Texts of Scripture. . . . London, 1641.

ROBERT CUSHMAN (1580-1626)

A sermon preached at Plimmoth in New-England December 9, 1624. In an Assemblie of his Majesties faithfull Subjects there inhabiting. Wherein is shewed the danger of selfe-love and the sweetnesse of true Friendship. Together with a Preface, Shewing the state of the Country, and Condition of the Savages. Rom. 12.10. . . . Written in the year 1621. London: Printed by J. D. for John Bellamie, 1622.

Reprinted 1724:
The Sin and danger of self-love described in a sermon preached at Plimouth in New-England, 1621. Boston: Printed by S. Kneeland, 1724.

Reprinted, 1785:
The Sin and Danger of Self-Love described in a Sermon Preached in Plymouth, in New-England, 1621. By Robert Cushman. London: Printed; Plymouth (Massachusetts): Reprinted by Nathaniel Coverly, 1785. This edition has unsigned "Appendix" (by Hon. John Davis) giving brief account of Cushman and the circumstances in Plymouth at the time the sermon was delivered.

Reprinted 1788: Similar to 1785 edition except for date.

Reprinted 1815:
A Sermon Preached at Plymouth, (New England,) A.D. 1621. By one of the Pilgrims who landed in Plymouth in the Year sixteen hundred and twenty . . . England: Printed 1622; Boston, New England: Reprinted by T. G. Bangs, 1815.

Reprinted 1822:
A Sermon describing the Sin and Danger of Self-Love. Preached at Plymouth, in New England, 1621, By Robert Cushman. From an old edition. Stockbridge: Printed by Charles Webster, 1822. This edition has the biographical note and comment of 1785 edition.

Reprinted 1846:
The Sin and Danger of Self-Love Described in a Sermon . . . by Robert Cushman. With a Memoir of the Author. Boston: Published by Charles Ewer, Dec. 22, 1846. Has biographical sketch—as of 1785, 1788, 1822 editions—, but a changed comment. Signed by Hon. John Davis.

Reprinted 1846:
Boston: Published by Rebecca Wiswell, 1846.

Reprinted 1847:
Self-Love: By Robert Cushman. 1621. . . . New York: J. E. D. Comstock, 1847.

Reprinted 1855 in:
A Historical and Biographical Genealogy of the Cushmans: the descendants of Robert Cushman, the Puritan, from the year 1617 to 1855. By Henry W. Cushman. Boston: Little, Brown and Company, 1855.

Reprinted 1858: (similar to New York 1847 edition.)

Reprinted 1870:
A Sermon Preached at Plimoth in New-England December 9, 1621. By Robert Cushman. Supposed to be the earliest printed sermon delivered in the English Colonies in America. With an Historical and Bibliographical Preface (By Charles Deane). Boston: 1870. This is a lithographic facsimile of the 1622 edition.

Reprinted 1878:
A Sermon Preached at Plymouth, (New England) A.D. 1621, By One of the Pilgrims Who Landed in Plymouth . . . England: Printed 1622; Boston: Reprinted 1815; Hartford: Press of Clark and Smith, 1878.

JOHN DAVENPORT (1597-1670)

Gods Call to His People to Turn unto Him; Together with his Promise to turn unto them. Opened and Applied in II. Sermons, at two Publick Fasting-dayes. Cambridge: S.G. and M.F. for John Usher, 1669. Other editions: London, 1670; Cambridge, 1672.

The Knowledge of Christ Indispensably required of all men that would be saved; or Demonstrative proof from Scripture, that Crucified Jesus is The Christ. Wherein the Types, Prophesies, Genealogies, Miracles, Humiliation, Exaltation, and the Mediatorial Office of Christ are Opened and Applyed: In Sundry Sermons on Acts 2.36. London: Printed for L. Chapman, 1653.

A royall Edict for Military Exercises: Published in a sermon preached to the Captaines, and Gentlemen that exercised Armes in the Artillery Garden at their generall meeting. In Saint Andrews Undershaft, . . . London: Printed by Elizabeth Allde for Ralph Mab, . . . , 1629.

The Saints Anchor-hold, in all Storms and Tempests, Preached in sundry Sermons. And Published for the Support and Comfort of Gods People in all Times of Tryal. London: Printed by W.L. for Geo. Hurlock, 1661. Other editions: London, 1682, 1701.

A Sermon Preach'd at the Election of the Governour, at Boston in New-England, May 19th, 1669. Boston, 1670. A facsimile of this edition is in the *Publications* of the Colonial Society of Massachusetts, X (Dec., 1904); again reprinted Cambridge, 1906 with an introduction by Lindsay Swift.

WILLIAM HOOKE (1601-1678)

New Englands Sence, of Old-England and Irelands Sorrows. A Sermon Preached upon a day of general Humiliation in the Churches of New-England. In the behalfe of Old-England and Irelands Sad Condition. London: John Rothwell, 1645.

Reprinted in Samuel H. Emery's *The Ministry of Taunton* (Boston, 1853), I, 99 ff.

New Englands Teares, For Old Englands Feares. Preached in a Sermon on July 23, 1640 being a day of Publike Humiliation, appointed by the Churches in behalfe of our native Countrey in time of feared dangers. London: Printed by E.G. for John Rothwell and Henry Overton, 1641. (Three printings)

Reprinted in Samuel H. Emery's *The Ministry of Taunton* (Boston, 1853), I, 75 ff.

The Priviledge of the Saints on Earth, Beyond Those in Heaven, In respect of Gifts and Graces exercised, Duties and Services performed, sufferings and Tryals undergone by them, which the Glorified are not capable of. Being the Sum of a Discourse upon a part of Hezekiah's Song of Thanksgiving after his Recovery from Sickness. To which is added, a Short Discourse of the Nature and Extent of the Gospel-day, reaching from the destruction of the Old, to the Erection of the New Jerusalem, out of Zech. 14. 6, 7. London: Printed for John Wilkins, 1673.

THOMAS HOOKER (1586-1647)

"Abstracts of 2 sermons 1638-9." Connecticut Historical Society *Collections*, I, 1-21. Hartford, 1860.

The Application of Redemption, by the effectual Work of the Word, and Spirit of Christ, for the bringing home of lost Sinners to God. Printed from the Authour's Papers. . . . written with his own Hand. And attested to be such, in an Epistle, By Thomas Goodwin, and Philip Nye. London: Printed by Peter Cole, 1656. Another edition: London, 1659.

The Application of Redemption By the Effectual Work of the Word, and Spirit of Christ, for the bringing home of lost Sinners to God. The Ninth and Tenth Books . . . . Printed from the Author's Papers, written with his own hand. And attested to be such, . . . London: Peter Cole, 1656.

The Christians Two Chiefe Lessons, Viz. Selfe-Deniall, and Selfe-Tryall. As also, The Priviledge of Adoption and Triall thereof. In three Treatises on the Texts following: Viz. Matt. 16.24. 2 Cor. 13.5. John 1. 12.13. By T.H. London: T.B. for P. Stephens and C. Meredith, 1640.

A Comment upon Christ's Last Prayer In the Seventeenth of John. Wherein is opened, The Union Beleevers have with God and Christ, and the glorious Prviledges thereof. London: Peter Cole, 1656.

The Covenant of Grace opened: wherein These particulars are handled; viz. 1. What the Covenant of Grace is, 2. What the Seales of the Covenant are, 3. Who the parties and subjects fit to receive these Seales. From all which Particulars Infants Baptisme is fully proved and vindicated. Being severall Sermons preached at Hartford in New-England. London: Printed by C. Dawson, 1649.

The Danger of Desertion: Or a Farwell Sermon of Mr. Thomas Hooker, Sometimes Minister of Gods Word at Chainsford in Essex; but now of New England. Preached immediately before his departure out of old England. London: G.M. for Geo. Edwards, 1641. (Two editions)

The Equall Wayes of God: Tending to the Rectifying of the Crooked Wayes of Man. The Passages whereof are briefly and clearly drawne from the sacred Scriptures. By T.H. London: for John Clarke, 1632.

An Exposition of the Lords Prayer. By T.H. London, 1638.

The 1645 edition has the title: *A briefe Exposition of the Lords Prayer: Wherein the meaning of the words is laid open to the understanding of weake Christians, and what the carriage of their hearts ought to be in preferring each Petition.* London: Printed by Moses Bell for Benjamine Allen . . . , 1645. (The Bodleian Catalogue lists: *Heaven's Treasury opened, in a faithfull Exposition of the Lord's Prayer.* London, 1645.)

An Exposition of the Principles of Religion. London, 1645.

(Listed in J. Hammond Trumbull's bibliography appended to George Leon Walker's *Thomas Hooker—Preacher, Founder, Democrat* (1891), but not found.)

The Faithful Covenanter, A Sermon preached at the Lecture in Dedham in Essex. Very usefull in these times of Covenanting with God. London: Christopher Meredith, 1644.

Foure Learned and Godly Treatises: viz. The Carnall Hypocrite.   The Churches Deliverances.   The Deceitfulnesse of Sinne.   The Benefits of Afflictions.   By T. H.   London: Thomas Cotes for Andrew Crooke, 1638.

The Garments of Salvation first putt off by the Fall of our first Parents. Secondly, putt on again by the Grace of the Gospel.   By T.H.
(Trumbull states: "Entered, 6 May, 1639, to R. Young and Fulke Clifton (*Registers*, iv. 465).   Mr. Arber queries, '? by Thomas Hooker.'   Certainly intended to pass for his.   I have not been able to find a copy of it." Bibliography attached to Walker's *Thomas Hooker*, 189.)

¹*Heautonaparnumenos: Or a Treatise of Self-Denyall.   Intended for the Pulpit; but now committed to the Presse for the Publike Benefit.*   London: Printed by W. Wilson, for Richard Royston, 1646.

The Immortality of the soule: the Excellencie of Christ Jesus, treated on.   Wherein the faithfull people of God may find comfort for their Souls.   By T.H.   Published according to Order.   London, 1646.

The Paterne of Perfection: Exhibited in Gods Image on Adam: And Gods Covenant made with him.   Whereunto is added an Exhortation, to redeem the time for recovering our losses in the premises.   And also some Miscellanies, viz. I. The prayer of Faith. II. A Preparative to the Lords Supper. III. The Character of a sound Christian, in 17. markes.   By T.H. London: Printed for R. Y. and F. Clifton, . . . 1640.

The Poor Douting Christian drawne unto Christ.   London, 1629.   Other editions: London, 1641, 1652, 1659, 1684, 1700, *et alii;* Boston, 1743; Hartford, 1845.
Also issued as *The Poore Doubting Christian Drawne Unto Christ.   In One Sermon.   Wherein the main letts and hindrance which keepe men from coming to Christ are discovered and removed in a volume of sermons entitled The Saints Cordials.   As They were Delivered In Sundry Sermons upon special Occasions, in the Citie of London, and elsewhere.*   London: Printed for Robert Dawlman, n.d.

The Saints Dignitie and Dutie.   Together with the Danger of Ignorance and Hardnesse.   Delivered in severall Sermons: . . . London: G.D. for Francis Eglesfield, 1651.
This volume contains seven sermons, each with a separate title-page: *The Gift of Gifts: or, the End why Christ Gave Himself;* (2) *The Blessed Inhabitant: or, The Benefit of Christs Being in Beleevers;* (3) *Grace Magnified: or the Priviledges of those that are under Grace;* (4) *Wisdomes Attendants: or the Voice of Christ to be obeyed;* (5) *The Activitie of Faith: or, Abraham's Imitators;* (6) *Culpable Ignorance, or the Danger of Ignorance under Meanes;* (7) *Wilful Hardnesse: or the Means of Grace Abused.*

The Soules Effectvall Calling to Christ.   By T.H.   London: J.H. for A. Crooke, 1637.
Usually bound with *The Soules Ingraffing,* with which its paging is

---

1. Although this sermon is commonly ascribed to Hooker, the title page bears no author's name in print; some copies have Thomas Hooker's name written on the title-page in ink.   The discourse bears every evidence of not being by Hooker, as it is entirely different in style, type of allusion, and doctrine from his known work.   For example, in this sermon the unknown author is extremely doubtful about and says that he hesitates to comment on Christ's atonement on the cross for sinners, a fundamental point about which Hooker never expressed any question and about which he wrote repeatedly.

continuous, but also published separately with a second title prefixed: *The Soules Vocation, or Effectual Calling to Christ.* London: Printed by John Haviland, for Andrew Crooke. . . . , 1638.

The Soules Exaltation. A Treatise containing The Soules Union with Christ, on 1 Cor. 6. 17. The Soules Benefit from Union with Christ, on 1 Cor. 1. 30. The Soules Justification. on 2 Cor. 5. 21. By T. H. London: John Haviland for Andrew Crooke, 1638.

The Soules Humiliation. London: Printed by I.L. for Andrew Crooke, 1637. Other editions: Amsterdam, 1638; London, 1638, 1640.

The Soules Implantation. A Treatise containing The Broken Heart on Esay 57. 15, The Preparation of the Heart, on Luke 1. 17, The Soules Ingraffing into Christ on Mal. 3.1., Spiritual love and Joy on Gal. 5. 22. London: R. Young, sold by F. Clifton, 1637.
Reprinted as: *The Soules Implantation Into the Naturall Olive. By T.H. Carefully corrected and much enlarged. With a Table of the Contents prefixed.* . . . London: R. Young, sold by F. Clifton, 1640.

The Soules Ingraffing also appears separately as *The Soules Ingrafting into Christ.* By T. H. London: J. H. for A. Crooke, 1637.

The Soules Possession of Christ: Upon Romans 13 :4, Acts 16 :31, Psal. 51 :16, John 7 :37, 2 Kings 2 :12, 1 Peter 5 :5, Zeph. 2 :3. By T.H. 8vo, 1638.
So entered to (R.) Dawlman, 13 Nov. 1637. Bodleian Catalogue has: *The Soules Possession of Christ: whereunto is annexed a Funeral Sermon on 2 Kings ii. 12.* London, 1638. Also: *Spiritual Munition: a Funeral sermon on 2 Kings ii. 12.* London, 1638.

The Soules Preparation for Christ, Or, A Treatise of Contrition. Wherein is discovered How God breaks the Heart and wounds the Soule, in the Conversion of a Sinner to Himselfe. London: R. Dawlman, 1632. Other editions: London, 1635, 1638; Netherlands, 1638; London, 1643, 1648.

Three sermons: I. The Wrath of God against Sinners. II. Gods Eternitie and Mans Humanity. III. The Plantation of the Righteous. By T.H. London: Printed by M.P. for John Stafford, 1638.
Reprinted as: *The Saints Guide in three treatises on Gen. vi. 13, Rom. i. 18, and Ps. i. 3. London, 1645* (Title from Bodleian Catalogue).

The Unbeleevers Preparing for Christ. Luke 1. 17. By T.H. London: T. Cotes, for Andrew Crooke, 1638.

RICHARD MATHER (1596-1669)

A Farewel-Exhortation to the Church and People of Dorchester in New-England. But Not unusefull to any others, that shall heedfully Read and Improve the same. As Containing Christian and Serious Incitements, and persuasions to the Study and Practise of Seven principal Dutyes of great Importance for the Glory of God, and the Salvation of the Soul, And therefore needfull to be Seriously considered of all in these declining times. Cambridg: Printed by Samuel Green, 1657.

The summe of certain sermons upon Genes. 15.6. Wherein Not only the Docrine [sic] of Justification by Faith is Asserted and Cleared, and

Sundry Arguments for Justification before Faith, discussed and Answered, But Also The nature and meanes of Faith, with the Imputation of our sins to Christ, and of Christs Righteousness to us are briefly Explained and Confirmed. Preached at Dorchester in New-England . . . . Cambridg: Printed by Samuel Green, 1652.

JOHN NORTON (1606-1663)

Three choice and Profitable Sermons Upon Severall Texts of Scripture; . . . By that Reverend Servant of Christ, Mr. John Norton, Late Teacher of the Church of Christ at Boston in N.E. The first of them being the Last Sermon which he Preached at the Court of Election at Boston. The Second was the Last which he Preached on the Lord's-day. The third was the Last which he Preached on his Weekly-Lecture-day. Cambridge: Printed by S.G. and M.J. for Hezekizh Usher of Boston, 1664.

THOMAS SHEPARD (1605-1649)

The Doctrine of Conviction of Sin, and Righteousness, and judgment. Delivered in Divers Sermons upon John 16. 8, 9, 10, 11, and thence Summarily drawn into Quest: and Answers by the same Authour. (Second part of *A Short Catechism.*) Cambridge: Printed by Samuel Green, 1654.

The Parable of the Ten Virgins Opened & Applied: Being the Substance of divers Sermons on Matth. 25. 1,—13. London, 1660. Other editions: London, 1695; Glascow, 1796; Falkirk, 1797; Aberdeen, 1838; London, 1839 (in part); Boston, 1852; Aberdeen, 1853.

The Saints Iewell, showing how to apply the promise. In A Sermon . . . [London], 1642. Other editions: London, 1655, 1657, 1659, 1664, 1667, 1672, 1680, 1692; Boston, 1743; London, 1812.

The Soules Invitation unto Jesus Christ (Printed with *The Saints Jewel,* after 1st edition). London: Printed for John Sweeting, 1655. Other editions: London, 1657, 1659, 1672, 1680; Boston, 1743.

Subjection to Christ, in all his Ordinances and Appointments, The best means to preserve our Liberty. Together with a Treatise of ineffectual Hearing the Word; . . . London: Printed for J. Rothwell, 1652. Other editions: London, 1654, 1655, 1657; Boston, 1853.

Then sayd all the trees to the Bramble raine over us. Election sermon, 1638. *New England Historic-Genealogical Register,* XXIV, 361-9.

Theses Sabbaticae, Or, The Doctrine of the Sabbath: wherein the Sabbaths: I. Morality, II. Change, III. Beginning, IV. Sanctification are clearly discussed. London: Printed by T.R. and E.M. for J. Rothwell, 1649. Other editions: London, 1650, 1655; Boston, 1853.

Wine for Gospel Wantons: or, Cautions against Spirituall Drunkenness. Being the brief Notes of a Sermon Preached at Cambridge in New-England, upon a Day of Publick Fasting and Prayer throughout the Colony, June 25. 1645. in reference to the sad estate of the Lords People in England. Cambridge, Printed in the year 1668.

JOHN WHEELWRIGHT (1592-1679)

His Writings, including his Fast-Day Sermon, 1637, and his Mercurius Americanus, 1645; . . . . And a Memoir By Charles H. Bell, A.M. Boston: Printed for the Prince Society, 1876.

Other editions of the sermon, all made from the two surviving manuscript copies, are to be found in the Massachusetts Historical Society *Proceedings,* 2d series, VIII, 256-74; a reprint of this edition, published by John Wilson and Son, Cambridge, 1867; in the *Historical Magazine* of April, 1867; a reprint of this edition by Henry B. Dawson, published at Morrisania, N. Y., 1867.

SAMUEL WHITING (1597-1679)

Abraham's Humble Intercession for Sodom, and The Lord's Gracious Concessions in Answer thereunto : Containing sundry Meditations upon Gen. XVIII. from Ver. XXIII. to the end of the Chapter. Printed and Sold at Cambridge, 1666.

A Discourse of the Last Judgement : or Short Notes upon Mat. XXV. from Ver. 31. to the end of the Chapter. Concerning the Judgement to come, and our Preparation to stand before The Great Judge of Quick and Dead. Which are of sweetest Comfort to the Elect Sheep, and of most dreadful Amazement and Terrour to Reprobate Goats. Cambridge: Printed by S.G. and M.J., 1664.

JOHN WILSON (1588-1667)

A Seasonable Watch-Word unto Christians Against the Dreams & Dreamers Of this Generation: Delivered in a sermon November 16th. 1665. And being the last Lecture, which was Preached by that Reverend, Faithful and Eminent Man of God Mr. John Wilson. Cambridge: Printed by S. Green & S. Green, 1677.

II. *Men Who Came Over With Their Education Incomplete But Who Antedated Harvard College*

SAMUEL ARNOLD (1622-1693)

David serving his Generation, or A Discovery Wherein is shewed that the great Care and Endeavour of every Christian ought to be, that he may be Serviceable unto God and to the present generation. Delivered in a Sermon Preached to the General Court of the Colony of New-Plimouth in New-England on the 3d. Day of June 1674. Being the Day of Election there. Cambridge: Printed by Samuel Green, 1674.

JAMES FITCH (1628-1702)

Peace the End of the Perfect and Uprigh [sic], *Demonstrated and usefully Improved in a Sermon, Preached upon the Occasion of the Death and Decease of that Piously Affected, and Truly Religious Matron, Mrs. Anne Mason:* . . . Cambridge: Printed by Samuel Green, 1672.

An Holy Connexion, or a True Agreement between Jehovahs being a Wall of Fire to His people, and the Glory in the Midst thereof: . . . *As it was Delivered in a Sermon Preached at Hartford on Conecticut in N.E. May 14. 1674. Being the Day of Election there.* Cambridge: Printed by Samuel Green, 1674.

JOHN HIGGINSON (1616-1708)

The Cause of God and His People in New-England, as it was Stated and Discussed in A Sermon Preached before the Honourable General Court of the Massachusets Colony, on the 27 day of May 1663. Being the Day of election at Boston. . . . Cambridge: Printed by Samuel Green, 1663.
Reprinted in part in *Elijah's Mantle.* Boston, 1722. (Also 1774).

Our Dying Saviour's Legacy of Peace To His Disciples in a troublesome World, from John 14.27. . . . *Also a Discourse On the Two Witnesses: shewing that it is the Duty of all Christians to be Witnesses unto Christ, from Rev. 11.3.* . . . *Unto which is added, Some Help to Self-Examination.* Boston: Printed by Samuel Green, 1686.

THOMAS THACHER (1620-1678)

A Fast of God's chusing, Plainly opened, For the help of those poor in spirit, whose hearts are set to seek the Lord their God in New-England, in the solemn Ordinance of A Fast . . . Preached on a Fast called by publick Authority, On 26, 1.74. Boston: Printed by John Foster, 1678.

III. *The Ministers Who Came from England in the 1660's*

JOHN OXENBRIDGE (1609-1674)

New-England Freemen Warned and Warmed, to be Free indeed, having an Eye to God in their Elections: In a Sermon Preached before the Court of Election at Boston, on the last Day of May, 1671. By J. O. Pastour of the First Church in Boston. Published by Order of the General Court. Cambridge, 1673.

A Quickening Word for the hastening a Sluggish Soul to a seasonable Answer to The Divine Call. Published by a poor sinner that found it such to him. Being the last Sermon Preached in the First Church of Boston upon Isaiah 55.6. By the Pastor there, on the 24th of the fifth Month, 1670. Cambridge: Printed by S.G. and M.J., 1670.

THOMAS WALLEY (1618-1679)

Balm in Gilead To Heal Sions Wounds: Or, A Treatise wherein there is a clear Discovery of the most Prevailing Sickness of New-England, both in the Civill and Ecclesiasticall State; As also sutable Remedies for Cure of them: Collected out of that Spirituall Directory, The Word of God. Delivered in a Sermon Preached before the Generall Court of the Colony of New-Plimouth on the first day of June 1669. being the Day of Election There. Cambridge: Printed by S.G. and M.J., 1669. Another edition: Cambridge, 1670.

IV.   *Early Harvard Graduates*

SAMUEL DANFORTH (1626-1674)

A Brief Recognition of New-Englands Errand into the Wilderness; Made in the Audience of the General Assembly of the Massachusets Colony, at Boston in N.E. on the 11th of the third Moneth, 1670. being the Day of Election There. Cambridge: Printed by S.G. and M.J., 1671.

The Cry of Sodom Enquired Into: Upon Occasion of The Arraignment and Condemnation of Benjamin Goad, For his Prodigious Villany—together with a Solemn Exhortation to Tremble at Gods Judgements, and to Abandon Youthful Lusts. Cambridge: Printed by Marmaduke Johnson, 1674.

LEONARD HOARE (1633-1675)

The Sting of Death and Death Unstung Delivered In Two Sermons In which is shewed the Misery of the Death of those that dye in their Sins, & out of Christ, and the Blessedness of theirs that Dye in the Lord. Preached on the occasion of the Death of the truely noble and virtuous The Lady Mildmay. Boston: Printed by John Foster, 1680.

SAMUEL HOOKER (1635-1697)

Righteousness Rained from Heaven, Or A Serious and Seasonable Discourse Exciting all to an earnest enquiry after, and continued waiting for the effusions of the Spirit, unto a communication and increase of Righteousness: That Faith, Holiness and Obedience may yet abound among us, and the Wilderness become a fruitful field. As it was Delivered in a Sermon Preached at Harford on Connecticut in New-England, May 10, 1677. Being the Day of Election there. Cambridge: Printed by Samuel Green, 1677.

WILLIAM HUBBARD (1621-1704)

The Happiness of a People In the Wisdome of their Rulers Directing And in the Obedience of their Brethren Attending Unto what Israel ougho [sic] to do: Recommended in a Sermon Before the Honourable Governour and Council, and the Respected Deputies of the Mattachusets [sic] Colony in New-England. Preached at Boston, May 3d, 1676. being the day of Election there. Boston: John Foster, 1676.

This sermon is usually appended to the first edition of Hubbard's *A Narrative of the Troubles with the Indians in New-England* (Boston, 1677).

ELEAZAR MATHER (1637-1669)

A Serious Exhortation to the Present and Succeeding Generation in New-England; Earnestly calling upon all to endeavour that the Lords gracious presence may be continued with posterity. Being the substance of the last sermons preached .... Cambridge: Printed by S.G. and M.J., 1671. Also Boston, 1678.

JONATHAN MITCHELL (1624-1668)

A Discourse of the Glory to which God hath Called Believers by Jesus Christ. Delivered in some Sermons out of I Pet. V Chap. 10 Ver. Together with an annexed Letter. London: Printed for Nathaniel Ponder, 1677.

Reprinted Boston, 1721—with a Preface by Increase Mather.

Nehemiah on the Wall in Troublesom Times; Or, a Serious and Seasonable Improvement of that Great Example of Magistratical Piety and Prudence, Self-denial and Tenderness, Fearlessnass and Fidelity, unto Instruction and Encouragement of present and succeeding Rulers in our Israel. As it was Delivered in a Sermon Preached at Boston in N.E. May 15. 1667. being the Day of Elections there. Cambridge: Printed by S.G. and M.J., 1671.

SAMUEL NOWELL (1634-1688)

Abraham in Arms; Or, The first Religious General with his Army Engaging in A War For which he had wisely prepared, and by which, not only an eminent Victory Was obtained, but A Blessing gained also. Delivered in an Artillery-Election-Sermon, June 3, 1678. By S.N. Boston: Printed by John Foster, 1678.

URIAN OAKES (1631-1681)

New-England Pleaded with, And pressed to consider the things which concern her Peace, at least in this her Day: Or, A Seasonable and Serious Word of faithful Advice to the Churches and Peoples of God (primarily those) in the Massachusetts Colony; . . . Delivered in a Sermon Preached at Boston in New-England, May. 7. 1673. being the Day of Election there. Cambridge: Printed by Samuel Green, 1673.

A Seasonable Discourse wherein Sincerity & Delight in the Service of God is earnestly pressed upon Professors of Religion. Delivered on a Publick Fast, at Cambridge in New-England. Cambridge: Printed by Samuel Green, 1682.

The Sovereign Efficacy of Divine Providence; Over ruling and Omnipotently Disposing and Ordering all Humane Counsels and Affairs, . . . As Delivered in a Sermon Preached in Cambridge, on Sept. 10. 1677. Being the Day of Artillery Election there. Boston in N.E.: Printed for Samuel Sewall, 1682.

The Unconquerable, All-Conquering & More-then-Conquering Souldier: Or, The successful Warre which a Believer Wageth with the Enemies of his Soul: As also the Absolute and Unparalleld Victory that he obtains finally over them through the love of God in Jesus Christ. As it was Discoursed in a Sermon Preached at Boston in New-England, on the Day of the Artillery-Election there, June 3rd, 1672. Cambridge: Printed by Samuel Green, 1674.

JOSEPH ROWLANDSON (1631-1678)

The Possibility of Gods forsaking a people, That have been visibly near & dear to him Together With the Misery of a People thus forsaken, Set forth in a Sermon, Preached at Weathersfield, Nov. 21, 1678. Being a Day of Fast and Humiliation. . . .Being also his last sermon. Boston in New-England: Printed for John Ratcliffe, & John Griffin, 1682. Other editions: London, 1682; Cambridge, 1682; London, 1812 — Somers' Tracts VIII; Lancaster, Mass, 1902—in the volume *The Narrative of the Captivity and Restoration of Mrs. Mary Rowlandson,* edited by Henry Stedman Nourse and John Eliot Thayer.

THOMAS SHEPARD (1635-1677)

Eye-Salve, Or A Watch-Word From our Lord Iesus Christ unto his Churches: Especially those within the Colony of the Massachusets in New-England. To take heed of Apostacy: Or, A Treatise of Remembrance of what God hath been to us, as also what we ought, and what we ought not to be to him, as we desire the prolonging of our Prosperous Dayes in the Land which the Lord our God hath given us. By Thomas Shepard, Teacher of the Church of Christ in Charlestown: Who was appointed by the Magistrates, to Preach on the day of Election at Boston, May 15, 1672. . . . Cambridge: Printed by Samuel Green, 1673.

WILLIAM STOUGHTON (1632-1671)

New-Englands True Interest; Not to Lie: Or, A Treatise declaring from the Word of Truth the Terms on which we stand, and the Tenure by which we hold our hitherto-continued Precious and Pleasant Things. Shewing What the blessed God expecteth from his People, and what they may rationally look for from him. Delivered in a Sermon Preached in Boston in New-England, April 29, 1668, being the Day of Election there. Cambridge: Printed by S.G. and M.J., 1670. Two editions.

Part of this sermon was reprinted in *Elijah's Mantle*, Boston 1722 and 1774; passages from the sermon were reprinted in Thomas Prince's *The People of New-England put in mind of the Righteous Acts of the Lord to them.* . . . Boston, 1730.

SAMUEL TORREY (c. 1632-1707)

An Exhortation unto Reformation, Amplified, By a Discourse concerning the Parts and Progress of that Work, according to the Word of God. Delivered in a Sermon Preached in the Audience of the General Assembly of the Massachusets Colony, at Boston, in New-England, May 27. 1674. Being the Day of Election there. Cambridge: Printed by Marmaduke Johnson, 1674.

PART TWO: GENERAL BIBLIOGRAPHY

Adams, Charles Francis, *Antinomianism in the Colony of Massachusetts Bay, 1636-1638.* Boston: Published by the Prince Society, 1894.

——————, *Three Episodes of Massachusetts History.* Boston and New York: Houghton, Mifflin & Company, 1892. Two volumes.

Addison, Daniel Dulany, *The Clergy in American Life and Letters.* London: Macmillan & Co., Ltd., 1900.

Albro, John A., *Life of Thomas Shepard.* Boston, 1852.

Ames, William, *A Fresh Suit against Human Ceremonies in Gods Worship.* Rotterdam, 1633.

Andrews, Charles M., *The River Towns of Connecticut. A Study of Wethersfield, Hartford, and Windsor.* Johns Hopkins University Studies in History and Political Science. Baltimore, 1889.

Archibald, Warren S., *Thomas Hooker.* Tercentenary Commission of the State of Connecticut. Committee on Historical Publications. New Haven: Yale University Press, 1933,

Backus, Isaac, *A History of New England with Particular Reference to the Denomination of Christians called Baptists.* Newton, 1871.

Bacon, Leonard, *The Genesis of the New England Churches.* New York: Harper & Brothers, 1874.

——————, "Historical Discourse, delivered at Norwich, June 23, 1859, before the General Association of Connecticut, at the celebration of its one hundred and fiftieth anniversary," in *Contributions to the Ecclesiastical History of Connecticut.* New Haven: William L. Kingsley, 1861.

——————, *Thirteen Historical Discourses on the completion of Two Hundred Years, from the Beginning of the First Church in New Haven.* New Haven: Durrie & Peck; New York: Gould, Newman & Saxton, 1839.

Bacon, Leonard and Walker, George Leon, *Sermons preached in The First Church of Christ in Hartford, by Rev. Leonard Bacon, D.D., LL.D., and Rev. George Leon Walker, D.D., on the occasion of the Settlement of the latter in the ministry over that church. To which is appended Some Account of the Early Meeting-Houses of the First Church.* Hartford, Conn.: The Case, Lockwood & Brainard Co., 1879.

Barber, John Warner, *Connecticut Historical Collections.* New Haven: Durrie & Peck and J. W. Barber, 1838.

——————, *Historical Collections of Every Town in Massachusetts.* Worcester: Dorr, Howland & Co., 1841.

——————, *Historical Collections of the State of New York.* New York: Clark, Austin & Co., 1851.

——————, *History and Antiquities of New Haven, (Conn.).* New Haven: J. W. Barber, 1831.

Bishop, George, *New England Judged by the Spirit of the Lord.* London, 1703.

Bliss, William Root, *Colonial Times in Buzzard's Bay.* Boston and New York: Houghton, Mifflin & Co., 1900.

Bradford, William, *History of Plymouth Plantation 1620-47.* Edited by W. C. Ford. Boston: Published for the Massachusetts Historical Society by Houghton, Mifflin Co., 1912. Two volumes.

Bradstreet, Simon, "Diary 1664-1683," in *New England Historical and Genealogical Register, October,* 1854.

Briggs, Charles Augustus, *American Presbyterianism: its origin and early history.* New York: Scribner's Sons, 1855.

Brightman, Thomas, *A Revelation of the Revelation that is, The Revelation of St. John opened clearely with a logicall Resolution and Exposition.* Amsterdam, 1615.

Brown, John, *Puritan Preaching in England.* New York: Charles Scribner's Sons, 1900.

Bruce, James F., *Life and Opinion in Massachusetts from 1630 to 1649. A Study of Puritan Character.* New South Wales: The Teachers' College (Sidney), 1912.

Burrage, Champlin, *The Church Covenant Idea.* Philadelphia: American Baptist Publication Society, 1904.

——————, *The Early English Dissenters in the Light of Recent Research (1530-1641).* Cambridge: The University Press, 1912. Two volumes.

Burrage, Henry S., *The Beginnings of Colonial Maine 1602-58.* Printed for the State, 1914.

Byington, Ezra Hoyt, *The Puritan as a Colonist and Reformer.* Boston: Little, Brown and Company, 1899.

——————, *The Puritan in England and New England.* Boston: Roberts Brothers, 1897.

Calder, Isabel MacBeath, *The New Haven Colony.* New Haven: Yale University Press, 1934.

Campbell, Douglas, *The Puritan in Holland, England, and America.* New York: Harper & Bros., 1899,1902. Two volumes.

Chaplin, Jeremiah, *Life of Henry Dunster, First President of Harvard College.* Boston: James H. Osgood and Company, 1872.

"Churches and Ministers in New Hampshire." Massachusetts Historical Society *Collections,* 3d series, XI, 299-322.

Clark, Henry W., *History of English Nonconformity.* London: Chapman and Hall, 1911-1913. Two volumes.

Clarke, Samuel, *Collection of the Lives of Ten Eminent Divines.* London, 1662.

——————, *Golden Apples. . . . Collected out of the writings of the most Orthodox, and judicious Divines.* London, 1659.

A Collection of American Epitaphs and Inscriptions with Occasional Notes. By Rev. Timothy Alden, A.M. Second Edition. New York: S. Marks, Printer, 1814.

Cotton, John, *The Keyes of the Kingdom of Heaven, and Power thereof, according to the Word of God.* London, 1644.

——————, *Singing of Psalms A Gospel-Ordinance.* London, 1647.

——————, *Sixteene Questions of Serious and Necessary Consequence.* London, 1644.

——————, *A Treatise I. Of Faith. II. Twelve Fundamental Articles of Christian Religion. III. A Doctrinal Conclusion. IV. Questions and Answers upon Church-Government.* Boston, 1713.

——————, *The True Constitution of a Particular Visible Church.* London, 1642.

——————, *The Way of Congregational Churches Cleared.* London, 1648.

——————, *The Way of the Churches of Christ.* London, 1645.

Dargan, Edwin Charles, *The Art of Preaching in the Light of its History.* New York: George H. Doran, 1922.

Davenport, A. Benedict, *History and Genealogy of the Davenport Family.* 1857.

Davenport, John, *An Answer of the Elders of the Severall Churches.* London, 1643.

——————, *A Discourse about Civil Government in a New Plantation whose design is religion.* Cambridge, 1663.

——————, *The Power of Congregational Churches.* London, 1672.

——————, *Letters of.* Edited by Isabel MacBeath Calder. New Haven: Yale University Press, 1937.

Davenport, John and Hooke, William, *A Catechisme containing the chief Heads of Christian religion.* London, 1659.

Davis, Andrew McFarland, *Hints of Contemporary Life in the Writings of Thomas Shepard.* Cambridge: John Wilson and Son, 1908.

Dean, John Ward, *A Memoir of the Rev. Nathaniel Ward.* Albany: J. Munsell, 1868.

DeNormandie, James, "Some Early Religious Matters at the Piscataqua," in Massachusetts Historical Society *Proceedings,* May, 1902, p. 175 *et sqq.*

Dexter, F. B., "Early Private Libraries in New England," in American Antiquarian Society *Proceedings, New Series,* XVIII (1907), 135-147.

"Sketch of the Life and Writings of John Davenport," in New Haven Colony Historical Society *Papers,* II (1877), 205-238.

Dexter, Henry M., *The Congregationalism of the Last Three Hundred Years, As Seen in its Literature.* New York: Harper & Brothers, 1880.

——————, *Congregationalism: What it is: Whence it is: How it works.* Boston: Nichols & Noyes, 1865.

Disosway, Gabriel P., *The Earliest Churches of New York and its Vicinity.* New York: James G. Gregory, 1865.

Drake, Samuel G., *Annals of Witchcraft in New England, and Elsewhere in the United States.* Boston, 1869.

——————, *The Histories and Antiquities of Boston.* Boston: Luther Stevens, 1856.

Dunton, John, *John Dunton's Letters from New-England.* The Publications of the Prince Society. Boston: Printed for the Society, By T. R. Marvin & Son, 1867.

——————, *The Life and Errors of John Dunton, Citizen of London.* London: Printed by and for J. Nichols, Son, and Bentley, 1818. Two volumes.

Edwards, Jonathan, *A Treatise concerning Religious Affections. The Works of President Edwards, III.* New York: Leavitt, Trow & Co., 1844.

——————, *A Narrative of Many Surprising Conversions. The Works of President Edwards.* New York: Leavitt, Trow & Co., 1844.

Egglèston, Edward, *The Beginners of a Nation.* New York: D. Appleton & Co., 1900.

Eliot, Samuel Atkins, *A History of Cambridge, Massachusetts, 1630-1913.* Cambridge, 1913.

Ellis, Arthur B., *History of the First Church in Boston, 1630-1880.* Boston, 1881.

Ellis, George E., *The Puritan Age and Rule in the Colony of the Massachusetts Bay 1629-1685.* Boston and New York: Houghton, Mifflin and Company, 1888.

Evans, Charles, *American Bibliogrraphy, 1639-1820.* Chicago, 1903-34. Twelve volumes.

Felt, Joseph B., *The Ecclesiastical History of New England.* Boston: Congregational Board of Publication, 1855-62. Two volumes.

Fish, Henry C., *History and Repository of Pulpit Eloquence.* New York: Dodd, Mead & Co., 1856. Two volunes in one.

Fisk, Franklin W., *Manual of Preaching. Lectures on Homiletics.* New York: A. C. Armstrong and Son, 1884.

Fiske, John, *The Beginnings of New England.* Boston: Houghton, Mifflin & Co., 1889.

Forbes, Harriette M., *New England Diaries, 1602-1800.* Topsfield (Mass.), 1923.

Francis, Convers, *Life of John Eliot, the Apostle to the Indians.* New York: Harper & Brothers, 1841.

Fraser, James of Brea, *Memoirs of the Life of the Very Reverend Mr. James Fraser of Brea Minister of the Gospel at Culross.* Written by *Himself.* Edinburgh: Thomas Lumisden and John Robertson, 1738.

Gerish, W. B., "Charles Chauncy," East Herts. Archaeological Society *Transactions,* III (Hertford, 1908), 274-280.

Good News from New England (London, 1648), Reprinted Massachusetts Historical Society *Collections,* 4th Series, I (1852), 195-218.

Goodell, Abner C., Jr., "Beverly and the Settlement at Bass River," in Colonial Society of Massachusetts *Publications,* I, 77-84.

Goodwin, John A., *The Pilgrim Republic. An Historical Review of the Colony at New Plymouth.* Boston: Ticknor & Co., 1899.

Graves, Frank Pierrepont, *Peter Ramus and the Educational Reformation of the Sixteenth Century.* New York: Macmillan, 1912.

Hall, Thomas Cuming, *The Religious Background of American Culture.* Boston: Little, Brown & Co., 1930.

Haller, William, *The Rise of Puritanism.* New York, Columbia University Press, 1938.

Hanbury, Benjamin (ed.), *Historical Memorials relating to the Independents, or Congregationalists: from their Rise to the Restoration of the Monarch, A.D. MDCLX.* London: Printed for the Congregational Union of England and Wales; Fisher, Son & Co., and Jackson & Walford, 1839-44. Three volumes.

Heard, John, *John Wheelwright 1592-1679.* Boston: Houghton, Mifflin & Co., 1930.

Hill, Hamilton A., *History of the Old South Church (Third Church) Boston, 1669-1884.* Boston: Houghton, Mifflin & Co., 1890. Two volumes.

Historical Collections. Edited by Ebenezer Hazard. Philadelphia, 1794.

Holmes, Thomas J., *The Mather Literature.* Cleveland: Privately printed for William Gwinn Mather, 1927.

Hooker, Edward H., *The Life of Thomas Hooker.* Boston: Massachusetts Sabbath School Society, 1849.

——————, "The Origin and Ancestry of Thomas Hooker," in *New England Hist. and Gen. Register,* XLVII (1893).

Hooker, Margaret H., *The Descendants of Rev. Thomas Hooker, Hartford, Conn., 1586-1908.* Rochester, N. Y.: Printed for the Author, 1909.

Hooker, Thomas, *A Survey of the Summe of Church Discipline.* London: A. M. for John Bellamy, 1648.

Hubbard, William, *A General History of New England.* Published by the Massachusetts Historical Society. Cambridge: Hilliard and Metcalf, 1815.

Hutchinson, Thomas, *The History of the Colony of Massachusetts-Bay.* Edited by Lawrence S. Mayo. Cambridge, 1936. Three volumes.

Jenness, John Scribner, *The Isles of Shoals An Historical Sketch.* New York: Hurd and Houghton; Cambridge: The Riverside Press, 1873.

Jernegan, Marcus Wilson, *The American Colonies 1492-1750.* New York: Longmans, Green and Co., 1929.

Johnson, Edward, *Wonder-Working Providence of Sion's Saviour in New England.* Edited by William Frederick Poole. Andover: F. Draper, 1867.

Johnston, Alexander, *Connecticut A Study of a Commonwealth-Democracy.* Boston and New York: Houghton, Mifflin and Co., 1895.

Jones, Richard Foster, *Ancients and Moderns.* Washington University Studies—New Series—Language and Literature—No. 6. St. Louis, 1936.

Jones, Rufus Matthew, *The Quakers in the American Colonies.* New York: Macmillan, 1911.

Kennett, White, *A Register and Chronicle Ecclesiastical and Civil.* London: R. Williamson, 1728.

Ker, John, *Lectures on the History of Preaching.* New York: A. C. Armstrong & Son, 1889.

Kittredge, George L., *Witchcraft in Old and New England.* Cambridge: Harvard University Press, 1929.

Kittredge, Henry C., *Cape Cod. Its People and their History*. Boston and New York: Houghton, Mifflin Company, 1930.

Lechford, Thomas, *Plain Dealing or News from New England*. With an introduction and notes by J. Hammond Trumbull. Boston: J. K. Wiggin & Wm. Parsons Lunt, 1878.

Logan, Walter Seth, *Thomas Hooker The First American Democrat*. An address . . . delivered before The New York Society of the Order of the Founders of America. February 19, 1904.

Love, William DeLoss, *The Colonial History of Hartford Gathered from the Original Records*. Hartford, Conn.: Published by the Author, 1914.

——————, *The Fast and Thanksgiving Days of New England*. Boston: Houghton, Mifflin & Co., 1895.

Luther, Martin, *First Principles of the Reformation or The Ninety-five Theses and the Three Primary Works of Dr. Martin Luther Translated into English*. Edited with theological and historical introductions by Henry Wace, D.D., and C. A. Buchheim, Ph.D. London: John Murray, 1883.

Maclure, A. W., *Lives of the Chief Fathers of New England*. Boston, 1846.

"Massachusetts Election Sermons—Bibliographical Note," in *Bulletin* of Boston Public Library, January 1881.

Masson, David, *The Life of John Milton: Narrated in Connexion with the Political, Ecclesiastical, and Literary History of His Time*. London: Macmillan & Co., 1871-94. Seven volumes.

Mather, Cotton, *Johannes in Eremo*. Boston, 1695.

——————, *Magnalia Christi Americana: or, the Ecclesiastical History of New England, From its First Planting in the year 1620, unto the Year of our Lord, 1698*. London: Printed for Thomas Parkhurst, 1702.

——————, *Manuductio ad Ministerium Directions for a Candidate of the Ministry*. Reproduced from the Original Edition Boston, 1726 With a Bibliographical Note by Thomas J. Holmes and Kenneth B. Murdock. Published for The Facsimile Text Society. New York: Columbia University Press, 1938.

——————, *Nunc Dimittis, briefly descanted on. The Happy Dismission, of the Holy Believer, from the Work of Earth, to the Joy of Heaven: Considered in a Funeral Sermon, For . . . Mr. John Higginson.* Boston: Printed by B. Green, for Eleazar Phillips, 1709.

——————, *Piscator Evangelicus. Or, The Life of Mr. Thomas Hooker, The Renowned Pastor of Hartford-Church, and Pillar of Connecticut-Colony, in New-England.* Boston, 1695.

Mather, Increase, *The Life and Death of that Reverend Man of God, Mr. Richard Mather.* Cambridge: Printed by S. G. and M. J., 1670.

McKenzie, Alexander, *Lectures on the History of the First Church in Cambridge.* Boston: Congregational Publishing Society, 1873.

Mead, Edwin D., "John Cotton's Farewell Sermon to Winthrop's Company at Southampton," in Massachusetts Historical Society *Proceedings,* 3rd series, I (1907), 101-115.

——————, "Thomas Hooker's Farewell Sermon," in Massachusetts Historical Society *Proceedings,* XLVI (1913), 253-274.

Miller Perry, "The Marrow of Puritan Divinity," in Colonial Society of Massachusetts *Publications,* XXXII (1938), 247-300.

——————, *The New England Mind The Seventeenth Century.* New York: Macmillan Company, 1939.

——————, *Orthodoxy in Massachusetts, 1630-1650.* Cambridge: Harvard University Press, 1933.

——————, "Thomas Hooker and the Democracy of Early Connecticut," in *The New England Quarterly,* IV (1931), 663-712.

Mitchell, W. Fraser, *English Pulpit Oratory from Andrewes to Tillotson. A Study of its Literary Aspects*. London: Society for Promoting Christian Knowledge, 1932.

Morison, Samuel Eliot, *Builders of the Bay Colony*. London, Humphrey Milford, n.d. [1930].

——————, *The Founding of Harvard College*. Cambridge: Harvard University Press, 1935.

——————, *Harvard College in the Seventeenth Century*. Cambridge: Harvard University Press, 1936. Two volumes.

——————, *The New England Pronaos*. London: Oxford University Press, 1936.

——————, "A 'trial' Shepard bibliography," in the Colonial Society of Massachusetts *Transactions*, XXVIII (November, 1930), 321-400.

Morton, Nathaniel, *New-Englands Memoriall*. Boston: The Club of Odd Volumes, 1903.

Morton, Thomas, *New English Canaan*. Amsterdam, 1637. Reprinted Force Tracts, II, No. 5.

Mullinger, J. Bass, *History of University of Cambridge*. New York, 1888.

Murdock, Kenneth Ballard, *Increase Mather The Foremost American Puritan*. Cambridge: Harvard University Press, 1925.

Neal, Daniel, *The History of the Puritans ... from ... 1517 to 1688*. New York, 1843. Two volumes.

Norton, Arthur Orlo, "Harvard Text-Books and Reference Books of the Seventeenth Century," in Colonial Society of Massachusetts *Publications*, XXVIII (1935), 361-438.

Norton, John, *Abel being Dead yet speaketh; Or, The Life & Death of that deservedly Famous Man of God, Mr. John Cotton*. London, 1658.

——————, *A Brief Catechisme Containing the Doctrine of Godlines, or of Living unto God*. Cambridge: Printed by S.G. and M.J., 1660.

——————, *The heart of New-England rent at the Blasphemies of the present Generation.* Cambridge: Samuel Green, 1659.

——————, *The Orthodox Evangelist or a Treatise Wherein many Great Evangelical truths are briefly discussed, cleared, and confirmed.* London: Printed by John Nacock for Henry Cripps and Lodowick Lloyd, 1654.

Osgood, H. L., *The American Colonies in the Seventeenth Century.* New York: Macmillan, 1904-07. Three volumes.

Owst, G. R., *Literature and Pulpit in Medieval England.* Cambridge, 1933.

——————, *Preaching in Medieval England: An Introduction to Sermon Manuscripts of the Period c. 1350-1450.* Cambridge, 1926.

Palfrey, John Gorham, *A Compendious History of New England.* Boston: Little, Brown & Co., 1858-90. Five volumes.

Parrington, Vernon Louis, *The Colonial Mind 1620-1800.* New York: Harcourt, Brace and Company, 1927.

Peck, Epaphroditus, *Thomas Hooker and his Relation to American Constitutional History.* An address delivered . . . before the State Conference of Congregational Churches at New London, Conn. November 16, 1904. Bristol [Conn.], 1904.

Perkins, William, "The Arte of Prophecying. Or, A Treatise Concerning the Sacred and Onely True Manner and Method of Preaching. First written in Latine by Mr. William Perkins: and now faithfully translated into English . . . by Thomas Tuke," in *The Workes,* II, 643-673. London: John Legatt, 1613.

Peter, Hugh, *Gods Doings and Mans Duty.* London, 1646.

"Plymouth Church Records 1620-1859," in Colonial Society of Massachusetts *Publications,* XXII, XXIII. Boston, 1920.

Pool, David de Sola, "Hebrew Learning among the Puritans of New England Prior to 1700," in American Jewish Historical Society *Publications,* No. 20 (1911), 31-83.

Potter, Rockwell Harmon, *Hartford's First Church*. Hartford, Conn., October, 1932.

Prince, Thomas, *A Chronological History of New England, In the Form of Annals*. Boston, 1852. Two volumes.

——————, *Six Sermons*. Edited by John Erskine. Edinburgh: Printed by David Paterson for William Martin, 1785.

——————, *Some Account of those English Ministers who have successively presided over the Work of Gospelizing the Indians on Martha's Vineyard, and the adjacent Islands*. London, 1727.

Randolph, Edward, "The Present State of New England (1676)," in *Historical Collections relating to the American Colonial Church, III*. Edited by William Stevens Perry, D.D. Hartford, 1873.

Robinson, Charles F. and Robin, "Three Early Massachusetts Libraries," in Colonial Society of Massachusetts *Publications*, XXVIII (1935), 107-175.

Rose-Troup, Frances, *John White The Patriarch of Dorchester (Dorset) and the Founder of Massachusetts 1575-1648. With an account of The Early Settlements in Massachusets 1620-1630*. New York and London: G. P. Putnam's Sons, 1930.

Schneider, Herbert Wallace, *The Puritan Mind*. New York: Henry Holt & Co., 1930.

Scholes, Percy A., *The Puritans and Music in England and New England. A Contribution to the Cultural History of Two Nations*. London: Oxford University Press, 1934.

Shepard, Thomas, *The Autobiography of Thomas Shepard. . . . with additional Notices of his Life and Character*, by Nehemiah Adams. Boston: Pierce and Parker, 1832.

——————, *Certain Select Cases Resolved, . . . in a letter, to a precious Friend here*. London, 1648.

——————, *The Church Membership of Children, and their right to Baptisme.* Cambridg[e]: Printed by Samuel Green, 1663.

——————, *The Clear Sunshine of the Gospel Breaking Forth upon the Indians in New-England.* London: Printed by R. Cotes for Bellamy . . . , 1648.

——————, *A Defense of the Answer made unto the Nine Questions or Positions sent from New-England against the reply thereto by . . . John Ball,* by John Allen, Thomas Shepard. London, Printed by R. Cotes for Andrew Crooke, 1648. Reprinted as: *A Treatise of Liturgies, Power of the Keyes, . . . In Answer to the Reverend Servant of Christ, Mr. John Ball.* London: Printed by R. Cotes for Andrew Crooke, 1653.

——————, *The First Principles of the Oracles of God.* London, 1648.

——————, *Four Necessary Cases of Conscience. Of daily Use. Resolved in a letter.* London: Printed by F. L. for C. Meredith, 1651.

——————, *Meditations and Spiritual Experiences.* Edinburgh, 1749.

——————, *New England's Lamentation for Old Englands present errours.* London: Printed by George Miller, 1645.

——————, *A Short Catechism familiarly teaching the knowledg [sic] Of God, and of our Selves. First Composed and improved, for the private instruction of the younger sort in Cambridg [sic] in New England . . . Together with the Doctrine of Conviction of Sin, and Righteousness, and judgment.* Cambridg[e]. Printed by Samuel Green, 1654. (Facsimile edition, 1930.)

——————, *The Sincere Convert, Discovering the Paucity of True Beleevers; and the great difficulty of Saving Conversion.* London: Printed by Thomas Paine, for Matthew Symmons, 1640.

——————, *The Sound Beleever. Or, A Treatise of Evangelicall Conversion.* London: Printed for R. Dawlman, 1645.

————, *Two Questions, Viz. I. Whether an account of the Work of Grace is to be required* . . . . *II. Whether the whole Church is to be judge thereof.* Boston, Printed and sold by Bartholomew Green, and John Allen, 1697.

Sibley, John Langdon, *Biographical Sketches of Graduates of Harvard University.* Cambridge, 1873 - 1885. Three volumes.

Sprague, William B., *Annals of the American Pulpit.* New York: Robert Carter & Bros., 1857-1869. Nine volumes.

Stearns, Raymond P., *Congregationalism in the Dutch Netherlands; the Rise and Fall of the English Congregational Classis, 1621-1635.* Chicago: The American Society of Church History, 1940.

Sweet, William Warren, *Religion in Colonial America.* New York: Charles Scribner's Sons, 1942.

Swift, Lindsay, "The Massachusetts Election Sermons," in Colonial Society of Massachusetts *Publications,* I (1895), 388-451.

Trumbull, Benjamin, *A Complete History of Connecticut, Civil and Ecclesiastical, From the Emigration of its first planters from England, in the year, 1630, to the year 1764.* New Haven: Maltby, Goldsmith and Co. and Samuel Wadsworth, 1818. Two volumes.

Trumbull, J. Hammond, "Text and discussion of Hooker's Sermon before the General Court on May 31, 1638," in Connecticut Historical Society *Collections,* I, 19 *et sqq.*

Tuttle, Julius H., "The Mather Libraries," in American Antiquarian Society *Proceedings,* n.s., XX (1910), 269-356.

————, "Writings of Rev. John Cotton," in *Biographical Essays A Tribute to Wilberforce Eames.* Cambridge: Harvard University Press, 1924. Pp. 363-380.

Tyler, Moses Coit, *A History of American Literature.* New York: G. P. Putnam's Sons, 1878. Two volumes.

Vail, Robert W. G., "A Check List of New England Election Sermons," American Antiquarian Society *Proceedings,* XLV (1935), 233-266.

Venn, J. A. and John, *Alumni Cantabrigienses.* Cambridge, 1927. Four volumes.

Waddington, Charles, *Ramus (Pierre de la Ramee) Sa Vie, Ses Ecrits et Ses Opinions.* Paris, 1855.

Walker, George Leon, *Thomas Hooker — Preacher, Founder, Democrat.* New York: Dodd, Mead and Co., 1891.

——————, *Some Aspects of the Religious Life of New England, with special reference to Congregationalists.* New York: Silver, Burdett and Co., 1897.

Walker, Williston, *The Creeds and Platforms of Congregationalism.* New York: Scribner's, 1893.

——————, *A History of the Congregational Churches in the United States.* New York: The Christian Literature Co., 1894.

——————, *John Calvin, The Organizer of Reformed Protestantism 1509-1564.* New York: G. P. Putnam's Sons, 1906.

——————, *The Services of the Mathers in New England Religious Development.* [New York]: The Knickerbocker Press, 1893.

——————, *Ten New England Leaders.* New York: Silver, Burdett and Company, 1901.

Weeden, W. B., *Economic and Social History of New England 1620-1784.* Boston, 1890. Two volumes.

Wertenbaker, Thomas J., *The First Americans 1607-1690.* New York: Macmillan, 1927.

White, Andrew Dickson, *A History of the Warfare of Science with Theology in Christendom.* New York: D. Appleton and Co., 1897. Two volumes.

Whyte, Alexander, *Thomas Shepard Pilgrim Father and Founder of Harvard His Spiritual Experience and Experimental Preaching.* Edinburgh: Oliphant, Anderson, and Ferrier, n.d. [1912].

Willey, Basil, *The Seventeenth Century Background.* London: Chatto and Windus, 1934.

Winsor, Justin (ed.), *The Memorial History of Boston, 1630-1880.* Boston, 1880-81. Four volumes.

Winthrop, John, *History of New England.* Edited by James Kendall Hosmer. New York: Scribners, 1908. Two volumes.

Wisner, Benjamin B., *The History of the Old South Church in Boston.* Boston, 1830.

Wood, Anthony à, *Athenae Oxonienses.* Edited by Philip Bliss. London, 1813-20. Two volumes.

——————, *Fasti Oxonienses.* Edited by Philip Bliss. London, 1815-1820. Two volumes.

Wright, Thomas Goddard, *Literary Culture in Early New England 1620-1730.* New Haven: Yale University Press, 1920.

Young, Alexander (ed.), *Chronicles of the First Planters of the Colony of Massachusetts Bay, from 1623 to 1636.* Boston: Little & Brown, 1846.

——————, *Chronicles of the Pilgrim Fathers ... from 1602 to 1625.* Boston: Little & Brown, 1841, 1844.

INDEX

Adoption, as step toward salvation, 31.
Albigensian heresy, 144.
Albro, John, 145.
Alcuin, 117.
Alexander Cornelius, 18.
Allen, John, 6, 12, 164.
Allen, Thomas, 164.
Allusions, *see* Similitudes.
Alsted, Johann Heinrich, *Encyclopaedia*, 21, 71 n.
Ambrose, 20.
Ambrosius Catharinus, 20.
Ames, William, 22, 30 n, 63 n.
Anabaptism, 50.
Anabaptists, 117; on war, 78.
Ancren Riwle, 113.
Andrewes, Lancelot, 9.
Andrews, Charles M., 41 n.
Anecdotes, usage in sermons, 121-123.
Anselm, 36 n.
Anthropomorphism, 37-39.
Anthropopathism, 37-39.
Anti-Catholicism, 41, 51-54, 56, 87, 135, 142.
Antinomianism, 3, 22, 42 n, 50, 51 n, 52, 87.
Antipaedobaptism, 3.
Aquinas, Thomas, 20.
Architecture, for sermon tropes, 126-127.
Aretius, Benedictus, 22.
Arminianism, 3, 22, 51-52, 87.
Arnold, Samuel, sermons published, 7; on tolerance, 49; on magisterial powers, 66; on government, 69; preaching methods, 92-93.
Art, slight interest in, 126.
Artillery drills, Shepard's criticism of, 60.
Artillery-election sermons, 87-88, 115.
Athanasius, 19.
Augustine, 20, 25, 36 n, 43, 45, 65 n, 70 n, 107, 111, 128, 129.
Avery, Joseph, 12.

Ball, John, 22.
Ball, Thomas, 5.
Batchelor, Stephen, 12.
Baynes, Paul, 22, 23.
Bede, 117.
Bellarmine, Robert, 20.
Bernard, Richard, 23.
Bernard of Clairvaux, 20.
Berosus, 18.
Beza, Theodore de, 21, 33 n.

Bible, use of as authority, 13-14, 15-16, 17, 18, 60, 79, 143; usage of texts in sermons, 88-89, 93, 149; influence on pulpit style, 136-137; use of, for imagery, 139.
Bishop, George, 168 n.
Bolton, Robert, 36 n.
Brainerd, David, 144-145.
Brightman, Thomas, 53.
Brock, John, 166.
Brown, Edmund, 124.
Buchan, William, 71 n.
Bulkeley, Edward, 6, 125.
Bulkeley, Peter, sermons published, 6; English background and education, 10, 10 n, 11; main preaching theme, 27; comparison of two covenants, 30; alteration of sermons, 83; style, 151-152.
Bullinger, Heinrich, 117.
Burdett, George, 10 n.
Burr, Jonathan, 9, 10 n, 164.

Caeser, Julius, 118, 122.
Calamy, Edward, 162.
Calvin, John, praises Bernard, 20; general influence of, 21; on salvation of children, 33 n; on the importance of the pulpit, 82; authority for Scripture interpretation, 90; on Copernican theory, 100; use of Senecan quotations, 119; on music, 124; preaching ability, 165.
Cameron, John, 22.
Carnal sin, 43-47, 54.
Carter, Thomas, 12, 164.
Cartwright, Thomas, 22.
Catholicism, *see* Anti-Catholicism.
Cato, 118.
Caussin, Nicholas, 20, 126.
Chaderton, Lawrence, 22.
Chauncy, Charles, 31 n, 122, 125; scholarship, 4; position in New England, 6; on education, 14-16; preaching theories, 26, 90, 95, 136-137; on hell, 33; on cause of New England's troubles, 43; on long hair, 61; sermon texts, 88-89; adoption of Copernican theory, 100; on Elect, 113-114; parade of learning, 133-134; style, 150-151; praises Mitchell, 160-161; on declining times, 173.
Children, attitude towards, 111-114.
Christology, parts stressed, 27-29.
Chrysostom, John, 20, 128.

209